Helping Individuals with Disabilities and Their Families

Mexican and U.S. Perspectives

Address:
Bilingual Press
Hispanic Research Center
Arizona State University
P.O. Box 872702
Tempe, Arizona 85287-2702
(480) 965-3867

Helping Individuals with Disabilities and Their Families

Mexican and U.S. Perspectives

Edited by Todd V. Fletcher and Candace S. Bos

Bilingual Review/Press
Tempe, Arizona

ISBN 0-927534-84-3

Library of Congress Cataloging-in-Publication Data

Helping individuals with disabilities and their families : Mexican and U.S. perspectives / edited by Todd V. Fletcher and Candace S. Bos.
p. cm.
Includes bibliographical references.
ISBN 0-927534-84-3 (alk. paper)
1. Handicapped children—Education—Mexico. 2. Handicapped children—Education—United States. 3. Parents of handicapped children—Services for—Mexico. 4. Parents of handicapped children—Services for—United States. I. Fletcher, Todd V. II. Bos, Candace S., 1950-
LC4035.M6H45 1999 99-10362
371.91'07-dc21 CIP

PRINTED IN THE UNITED STATES OF AMERICA
Cover and interior design by John Wincek, Aerocraft Charter Services

Acknowledgments

The editors wish to thank the following organizations for permission to reprint material appearing in this volume:

Routledge, for the article "Special education and education reform in Mexico: Providing quality education to a diverse student population," by Eliseo Guajardo Ramos and Todd V. Fletcher. *European Journal of Special Needs Education* 13, no.1 (1998): 29-42.

The California Department of Education, for Appendix A of *The OLE Curriculum Guide.*

Partial funding provided by the National Institute for Disability Related Research through the Native American Research and Training Center and the Department of Special Education and Rehabilitation at the University of Arizona.

Contents

Foreword Judith E. Heumann xi
Assistant Secretary for Special Education, US Department of Education

Preface xiii

PART I FAMILIES AND EARLY CHILDHOOD

Chapter 1 The Social Integration of Individuals with Disabilities 3

Caré Fábila de Zaldo

UN Representative for Families and Disabilities, Mexico City

The family is the heart of social movements for individuals with disabilities. Highlighting the great changes taking place in Mexico, the author points out that the conditions of people with disabilities are not necessarily better in richer countries. This chapter provides historical perspectives on disability, integration, and human rights.

Chapter 2 Family-Centered Early Intervention 19

Berta Watkins

Director, Early Intervention Center, SEP, Mexico City

The time from birth to age three can be the most critical period for educational and therapeutic intervention designed to prevent developmental delays and promote optimal growth. The author presents a general panorama of early education and intervention in Mexico and discusses early intervention focused on the family.

Chapter 3 Early Language Assessment for Spanish-Speaking Children: Border Realities 35

Donna Jackson-Maldonado
University of Querétaro, Querétaro, Mexico

Early language assessment is a requisite for early language intervention. While a handful of tests and language development data exist to detect language problems in infancy for English-speaking children, the same is not true for Spanish-speaking children. This chapter addresses assessment by giving an overview of the instruments in Spanish currently available and their normative, validity, and reliability limitations. It then summarizes Spanish language development, particularly in children under three. Third, linguistic, cultural, and education realities of children living on both sides of the border are highlighted.

Chapter 4 Parents, Families, and Communities Ensuring Children's Rights: It's a Good "Idea" 53

Elba I. Reyes
University of Arizona

Parents, families, and communities have been the driving force in securing education and necessary services for children with disabilities. This chapter reviews how working together to advocate for children's rights results in change.

Chapter 5 Aiding Preschool Children with Communication Disorders from Mexican Backgrounds: Challenges and Solutions 63

Henriette W. Langdon
San Jose State University

Portraits of three children from bilingual homes illustrate some of the challenges that speech pathologists are called on to meet. Determining whether a Spanish-speaking child has a speech/language disorder, recognizing variations in children's family constellations, and offering suggestions for parent involvement are highlighted in this chapter, along with recommendations for strengthening collaboration with speech and language professionals across the border.

Chapter 6 Indigenous and Informal Systems of Support: Navajo Families Who Have Children with Disabilities 79

R. Cruz Begay

Northern Arizona University

Richard N. Roberts

Utah State University

Thomas S. Weisner and Catherine Matheson

University of California, Los Angeles

There are two complimentary systems that operate to fulfill needs of Navajo families who have children with disabilities. One is the indigenous adaptive system and the other is the bureaucratic system that has been instituted nationally in the United States. The authors describe the informal, indigenous system of family support.

Chapter 7 Overcoming Obstacles and Improving Outcomes: American Indian Children with Special Needs 95

Martha G. Gorospe

Director of EPICS Project, New Mexico

Community-based providers will undoubtedly work with Native American families with special-needs children. This chapter identifies some important issues that must be considered when providing services. These issues relate to cultural differences in communication, interaction style, concepts of personal relationships, and the level of the family's acculturation to non-Native American values.

PART II EDUCATION

Chapter 8 Bridge over Troubled Waters: Collaboration between the United States and Mexico on Behalf of Individuals with Disabilities 109

Sofíaleticia Morales

Advisor to the Secretary of Education, SEP, Mexico City

The provision of special-education services has a long history in Mexico. This chapter describes the current movement toward integration of students with disabilities into the mainstream of general education in Mexico, some of the obstacles encountered, and a number of potential avenues for collaboration between the United States and Mexico in special education.

Chapter 9 **Special Education and Education Reform in Mexico: Providing Quality Education to a Diverse Student Population** 121

Eliseo Guajardo Ramos
General Director of Special Education, SEP, Mexico City, Mexico

Todd V. Fletcher
University of Arizona

Mexico is a multiethnic, multicultural country. Extraordinary efforts in Mexico's educational system have recently begun to respond to this diversity. The author's examine educational reform in Mexico and the integration of students with disabilities in this context.

Chapter 10 **Educational Opportunities for Children with Disabilities in Mexico: Identification and Intervention** 135

Georgina Reich-Erdmann
University of the Americas, Mexico City

Low expectations that surround individuals with disabilities and the impact of these low expectations on social integration are examined in this chapter. Suggestions for promotion of higher expectations and for collaborative efforts between the United States and Mexico are presented.

Chapter 11 **Special Education for Latino Students in the United States: A Metaphor for What Is Wrong** 147

Richard A. Figueroa
University of California, Davis

The history of special education for Latino students in the United States demonstrates some of the pitfalls of applying reductionist philosophies to the educational challenges of underachieving students. The authors argue that, rather than a more of the same method, educators need to adopt an ethnomethodological approach to educational planning for all underachieving students, an approach that emphasizes the social construction of students' learning problems.

Chapter 12 Effective Literacy Instruction for Latino Students Receiving Special Education Services: A Review of Classroom Research 161

Nadeen T. Ruiz

California State University, Sacramento

This chapter examines and reviews current research on effective instructional environments for students from diverse backgrounds. It highlights the principles that embrace children's learning and integrate their cultural and linguistic heritage. The author also discusses the Optimal Learning Environment (OLE) model of instructional intervention.

Chapter 13 Many Ways Is the Way: Supporting the Languages and Literacies of Culturally, Linguistically, and Developmentally Diverse Children 175

Pamela J. Rossi

University of New Mexico

In this chapter, the reductionist paradigm of learning is challenged. As members of the larger human family, children have many ways of knowing, communicating, and being literate. In contexts that support their inquiries and imaginations, children will play according to their strengths, engage in transactions that interest them, recognize their interconnectedness with others, and construct deeper understandings of their possible worlds. This theme is illustrated with vivid portraits of bilingual first graders creating and producing an opera based on a Zuni story about a blue coyote.

Chapter 14 Native American Culture and Language: Considerations in Service Delivery 193

Sherry R. Allison and Christine Begay Vining

University of New Mexico

This chapter presents perspectives regarding American Indians with disabilities in view of culture, language, and traditions and examines how these affect their needs and concerns. Although education plays a significant part in addressing the needs of American Indians with disabilities, the family and community systems continue to play a role in their daily lives. Although the circumstances described in this chapter pertain to Native people in the United States, it is likely that indigenous people with disabilities in other nations have similar stories.

Chapter 15 Collaborative Endeavors: On Behalf of Children with Disabilities and Their Families in the United States and Mexico 207

Todd V. Fletcher, Candace S. Bos, and Lorri Johnson

University of Arizona

The editors summarize, highlight, and synthesize important themes and issues related to the social integration of individuals with disabilities in the United States and Mexico. A blend of U.S., Mexican, and Native American perspectives informs this discussion. The book concludes, as it began, with an agenda for collaboration between the various nations.

Acronyms 213

Foreword

The United States and Mexico have much more in common than just borders. We share languages, cultures, and history. We also share the conviction that persons with disabilities must be integrated into all aspects of community living.

Our countries have taken many steps to ensure that this belief becomes reality. We have taken these steps individually and in collaboration with each other. We want to achieve our common goal of creating better educational and employment outcomes for persons with disabilities.

We would like to create more exchanges between the two countries. We would like to continue to bring together parents, teachers, administrators, and researchers from Mexico and the United States and to create opportunities for them to learn more about each other's programs. We believe that true collaboration and understanding can take place through such efforts.

This book is an example of such collaboration. It came about because of a conference that took place in Tucson in April 1996. The conference was attended by teachers, parents, researchers, artists, and government representatives from the United States and Mexico. For several days, topics vital to both countries were covered: families and early childhood; education; business and employment; and the arts. The sessions were lively and engaging and provided the fuel necessary for further, more in-depth exploration of these areas.

The first topic of the conference, families and early childhood, which is discussed in the first section of this book, provides the foundation for those that follow. We improve outcomes for children with disabilities when families and parents are strong and knowledgeable advocates for their children. In the United States, the outcomes for disabled children have improved dramatically because of the active participation of their parents. Through different organizations, we continue to promote and encourage this participation. We also encourage educators and school administrators to reach out to parents, particularly those from diverse linguistic and cultural backgrounds. Collaboration must exist between schools and families; this sends the message to children that we are holding all of them to the highest possible standard.

The second topic, discussed in the second section of this book, focuses on education. Both Mexico and the United States are struggling to break down the barriers that keep children with disabilities from participating fully in their schools and their communities. In the United States, all children with disabilities are provided with an education. However, for some students this education takes place in segregated classrooms with a curriculum that is different from that of their nondisabled peers. Outcomes for both disabled and nondisabled students improve when they learn in integrated settings.

The conference also provided opportunities to discuss employment issues and the integration of the aids. In the United States, the unemployment rate for individuals with disabilities continues to remain around 70%, a rate that is simply unacceptable. Even as educational opportunities for individuals with disabilities improve, access to good jobs remains an elusive goal. In the United States, agencies established to improve employment options for disabled individuals are collaborating with other public and private agencies. In Mexico, people with disabilities are less likely than in the United States to rely on the federal government to assist them in finding employment. We have much to learn from each other in the different approaches we have taken in the employment of persons with disabilities.

In addition, many children and adults with disabilities have discovered artistic talents that have allowed them to succeed in school and at work. These talents are nurtured through strong programs in schools and communities that encourage people with disabilities to discover the joy of expressing themselves through art, music, dance, drama, and literature.

Through sharing our approaches to overcoming barriers to equal education and employment opportunities for all, we renew and refresh each other's commitment to progress and help each other find innovative paths to the goals we have set for ourselves.

¡Viva la colaboración entre México y los Estados Unidos!

JUDITH E. HEUMANN
Assistant Secretary for Special Education,
US Department of Education

Preface

This book is the result of a series of symposiums, conferences, and congresses held jointly by the United States and Mexico between 1994 and 1998 focusing on the special needs of individuals in both countries. These activities represent a unique historic event in which the two countries have actively engaged in collaboration and worked with each other to change policy and practice for individuals with disabilities.

This series of meetings, initiated by the Department of Special Education and Rehabilitation at the University of Arizona, brought together leading disabilities professionals and advocates in the United States and Mexico. They promoted collaborative efforts in the development of new policies and practices to integrate individuals with disabilities from Mexican, Mexican American, and indigenous communities more fully into society. The first event was the First Interamerican Symposium on Disability for the United States and Mexico held in Tucson, Arizona, in April 1994. This symposium, attended by approximately two-hundred leaders from both countries, set forth mechanisms for developing a sustained dialogue and communication between Mexico and the United States on behalf of individuals with disabilities and focused on four areas: (a) early-childhood education, (b) education, (c) the arts, and (d) business and employment. The theme, "Families and Communities in Action: Commitment for the Twenty-First Century," embraced the United Nations' 1994 declaration of the "International Year of the Family." This symposium was an initial opportunity for leaders in education, rehabilitation, business, government, parent organizations, and advocacy groups from Mexico and the United States to come together to share knowledge and strengthen partnerships for advocacy, awareness, empowerment, and inclusion of individuals with disabilities and their families.

One of the primary outcomes of this first working symposium was the commitment by our Mexican colleagues to hold an international congress on disability issues in Mexico City the following year. A second and major outcome was the development of collaborative action plans between Mexico and the United States in the areas of families and early childhood, education, the arts, and business and employment. To facilitate ongoing communication, each participant left this first symposium with an action plan for their focus area and a communication list with participant contact information.

The initial symposium resulted in the second major event, the "First International Congress on Disability: Disability in the Year 2000" held in Mexico City in May 1995. The purpose of this congress was to raise the awareness level of Mexicans regarding recognition of civil and human rights for individuals with disabilities and to continue the collaboration between the United States and Mexico. The three themes of the congress were: (a) legislation and human rights, (b) education, art, and recreation, and (c) job training and employment. One of the unique features of this congress was that for the first time disability organizations in Mexico worked together toward a common goal. The results were rewarding: there were more than twenty-five hundred attendees, and significant commitments for the rights of individuals with disabilities were made by both the Mexican and the U.S. government.

Judith Heumann, assistant secretary for the Office of Special Education and Rehabilitative Services (OSERS) in the U.S. Department of Education and President Clinton's representative at the conference, spoke about her experiences and struggle to attend school and obtain a teaching certificate after being physically disabled by polio at a very young age. The president of Mexico, Ernesto Zedillo, delivered the closing address and assured the participants of his commitment by announcing that disability rights and education would be a feature of his reform platform. His National Development Plan includes specific provisions for economic assistance, including medical care, rehabilitation, education, and employment training for individuals with disabilities.

At this congress, those who attended the first symposium in the United States the previous year met to update the collaborative action plans and report on the progress to date. Discussion centered on the number of goals that had been met and what still needed to be accomplished. It was suggested that an important next step would be to convene a small group of experts and consumers/practitioners to further delineate policy and practice and disseminate the information to disability groups throughout the United States and Mexico.

The third and fourth symposiums concentrated on bringing together a core group of leading experts and consumers/practitioners and was expanded to include indigenous peoples from both countries. The first of these events was a "think-tank" symposium held in Tucson in April 1996 sponsored by the University of Arizona and funded in part by the Office of Special Education and Rehabilitative Services, entitled "Blending the Mexican and Native American Cultures through Collaboration between the United States and Mexico for Individuals with Disabilities and Their Families." The outcomes of this meeting included: (1) the development of a consumer-oriented policy and practice resource book based on the symposium, (2) the development of this edited volume in which best practices are discussed in greater depth related to future collaboration between the two countries, and (3) the presentation and discussion of the outcomes generated from these collaborative conferences at the Second International Congress on Disability held 12–14 March 1997 in Mexico City.

The fourth symposium, sponsored by the Mexican Department of Education and held in Oaxaca, Mexico, in August 1996, was coordinated by Dr. Sofíaleticia Morales, special assistant to the Mexican secretary of public education. This symposium, entitled "The Indigenous Vision of Integrating Individuals with Disabilities," provided a forum for indigenous groups from Mexico and the United States to discuss successful model programs for native peoples. This event was historic because it was the first time that government leaders from Indigenous Education and Special Education in Mexico met in a joint forum to discuss specific issues of concern to native peoples in Mexico. Indigenous leaders from the state of Oaxaca and five other Mexican states collaborated with governmental officials from the federal district in Mexico City and leaders representing indigenous groups in the United States, including a representative from OSERS. Information at this symposium was shared and exchanged on: (1) ways to encourage parent/family involvement while incorporating cultural sensitivity, training methods, and materials that have worked well in Native American and indigenous communities in the United States and Mexico; and (2) the multiple benefits that result when parents and families are supported and encouraged to be actively involved in their children's education and health care planning. Other discussion points centered on the importance of advocacy organizations and the enormity of their task and the prevalence of discrimination in the job market and limited employment opportunities for individuals with disabilities.

These smaller symposium were followed by the "Second International Congress on Disability: Disability in the Year 2000" held in Mexico City in March 1997. This congress refocused on the three themes of the first international congress and emphasized the importance of developing closer partnerships between governmental programs and the private sector, particularly with regard to education and employment issues.

The most recent event in the series of collaborative activities took place in July 1998 in Pátzcuaro, Michoacán. The "Multilateral/Multinational Workshop on Inclusion" focused on improving instructional practices and programs for students with disabilities in general education settings. From Mexico, two representatives, one in general education and the other in special education, from each of the thirty-one state departments of education and the federal district in Mexico City attended. Representatives from the United States included leading scholars, practitioners, and policy makers with expertise in the area of inclusion. This was the first event ever held in Mexico in which representatives from general education and special education attended a conference designed to foster greater collaboration in providing for the special educational needs of all students in inclusive educational settings. Its goal was to provide in-depth training and instruction for participants on effective strategies and techniques for students with mild and severe disabilities in more inclusive educational settings. The delegates returned to their respective states to disseminate new strategies and practices to area supervisors, who would provide training to professionals under their supervision. International participants in the seminar included representatives from the departments of education in South Africa, Uruguay, Colombia, Chile, Argentina, and Nicaragua. These representatives focused on educational reform in their respective countries and outlined current developments resulting from newly implemented legislation to bring the education of students with disabilities closer to the mainstream educational environment.

This series of collaborative efforts exemplifies the possibilities of achieving change based on dialogue and interchange of common themes in educational policies and practices. In this book, U.S. and Mexican authors examine and discuss current practices, policies, and trends in the field of special education that underlie the significant changes taking place in the provision of services to individuals with disabilities in both countries, specifically in the areas of early childhood and education. The authors represented in this book—educators, parents of children with disabilities, policy makers, administrators, and individuals with disabilities—demonstrate the impact these collaborative efforts have had in the United States and Mexico. In the chapters they have contributed they address critical issues in early childhood and education and provide recommendations for educational reform and collaboration within and between their respective countries.

This book comprises two sections. The first, "Families and Early Childhood," provides multiple perspectives on the education of children with disabilities in the United States and Mexico, describes formal and informal support systems for families who have children with disabilities, and highlights legislation and family-centered approaches to intervention. Garé Fábila de Zaldo provides a historical perspective on disability, integration, and human rights by discussing United Nations initiatives and the progress that has been made toward the social integration of individuals with disabilities since its inception. She emphasizes the importance of the family as the heart of social movements for individuals with disabilities and highlights changes currently taking place in Mexico. Berta Watkins emphasizes that the period from birth to age three is the most critical one for educational and therapeutic intervention, which, if appropriately implemented, can prevent developmental delays and provide optimal growth. She outlines the general panorama and structure of early education and intervention in Mexico and discusses early-intervention strategies focused on the family. Donna Jackson-Maldonado discusses early language assessment as a prerequisite to early language intervention. She provides an overview of the instruments available in Spanish, summarizes Spanish-language development (particularly in children under three), and discusses the linguistic, cultural, and educational realities of children living on either side of the border. Elba Reyes provides an overview of the new Individual with Disabilities Education Act of 1997 (IDEA-97). She discusses new provisions with respect to the participation of children and their families in special education and describes some of the salient provisions of IDEA-97 that deal with parent participation, collaboration, minority issues, and empowerment opportunities that evolve from the new law. Henriette Langdon illustrates through portraits of three different children some of the challenges that speech and language specialists confront when determining whether a Spanish-speaking child has a speech/language disorder. She emphasizes the importance of recognizing variations of the children's family constellations and makes suggestions for parent involvement and for strengthening the collaboration between speech and language professionals across the border. Cruz Begay, Richard Roberts, Tom Weisner, and Catherine Matheson collaborate on a chapter that discusses two complementary systems that operate to fulfill the needs of Navajo families who have children with disabilities. One is the indigenous adaptive system and the other is the bureaucratic system that has been instituted nationally in the United States. The authors describe in detail the informal indigenous system of family support. Martha Gorospe complements the preceding chapter and identifies some important issues that must be considered when providing services to Native American families with special needs. These issues relate to cultural differences in communication, interaction styles, concepts of personal relationships, and the level of the family's acculturation to non-Native American values.

The second section of the book focuses on educational issues spanning educational reform, policy and legislative issues, and effective instructional practices for students with special needs. As in the other section, collaboration and the connections between Mexico and the United States are highlighted. Sofíaleticia Morales reviews the history of collaboration between the two countries and reaffirms the need for continued collaboration and cooperation. She describes the current movement toward integration of students with disabilities by highlighting legislation, policy, and programmatic changes. She briefly describes the current status of education in Mexico and concludes by discussing a number of potential avenues for collaboration between the United States and Mexico. Eliseo Guajardo and Todd Fletcher examine educational reform in Mexico and the ways in which special education is currently being restructured and transformed. Mexico is a multiethnic, multicultural country, and the authors discuss the extraordinary efforts being made to respond to and accommodate this diversity in Mexico's educational system. The chapter also describes newly designed service delivery models that are being implemented in Mexico City and initiated throughout Mexico. Georgina Erdmann discusses issues and challenges in Mexican education, particularly as they relate to special education in the context of educational reform. Low expectations, which impede individuals with disabilities, and the impact of these low expectations on social integration are also examined. Richard Figueroa highlights some of the pitfalls of special education for Latino students in the United States, particularly in the use of diagnostic/predictive assessments, and argues for a significant change in the modus operandi of our educational system. He suggests that there is a need for a renewed and critical dialogue between the United States, Mexico, and Latin America and challenges us to consider an emerging powerful pedagogy based upon research studies in Mexico that might initiate an important dialogue on special-education practices and policies in the United States. In the following chapter, Nadeen Ruiz examines the micro- and macrocontexts of education and their impact on widespread educational reform. She provides an overview of current research on effective instructional environments for Spanish-speaking students and highlights four principles of effective instruction that embrace children's learning and integrate their cultural and linguistic heritage. Building on effective instructional practices, Pam Rossi provides a rich example of how such practices can be integrated into the arts. She challenges the reductionist paradigm of learning and discusses how children have many ways of knowing, communicating, and being literate. This is illustrated with vivid portraits of bilingual first graders creating and producing an opera based on a Zuni story about a blue coyote. Sherry Allison and Chris Begay Vining present multiple perspectives regarding Native Americans with disabilities in view of their culture, language, and traditions and show how these affect their special needs and concerns. Although education plays a significant part in addressing the needs of Native Americans with disabilities, family and community systems continue to play a central role in their daily lives and can be considered a major service delivery provider. In the final chapter of the book, the editors summarize, highlight, and synthesize important themes and issues related to the social integration of individuals with disabilities in the United States and Mexico. A blend of U.S., Mexican, and Native American perspectives informs this discussion. The book concludes, as it began, with an agenda for collaboration between the two nations.

PART I

Families and Early Childhood

1 The Social Integration of Individuals with Disabilities

Garé Fábila de Zaldo

The World Health Organization calculated that in 1990 there were 500 million people with disabilities in the world, and that by the year 2000 the number would reach 600 million. According to these figures, 10 percent of the total world population suffers from some type of physical, mental, or sensory disability. This is a serious problem, especially in developing countries where the greatest number of individuals with disabilities are reported to live.

The seriousness of the problem, however, is even more critical than numbers alone reflect. The majority of these people live in deplorable conditions, struggling against physical, cultural, familial, or social obstacles that prevent them from full social integration. There are millions of children, young people, adults, and elderly people in the world who, with their families, live in marginal conditions and are excluded and deprived of their rights. This problem is not limited to poor countries. Social injustice and the violation of human rights of disabled people are found both in developing and in developed nations alike. All of the above lead us to analyze, reflect, dream, and decide to fight against these circumstances with a clear vision of what we want to accomplish for our children, brothers, friends, or students. After all, this is a human rights issue.

Regardless of age, any person with disabilities affects his/her family. By the year 2000, more than 2.4 billion inhabitants of the world will be confronted with this problem unless we develop strategies to prevent some disabilities and minimize discriminatory conditions, abuses, social injustice, and the marginalization suffered by people with disabilities. Support systems must be created within societies to improve the quality of life for individuals with disabilities and their families. Finding global solutions to this problem must be viewed as a priority, as well as individual solutions in the different countries and even in different regions of the same country.

In 1995, a Summit Conference on Social Development was held in Copenhagen and, for the first time, the United Nations, along with representatives of the member states, recognized that the greatest concerns were for improving the standard of living, social development, and the well-being of all people and eliminating discrimination on the basis of color, race, religion, sex, or disabling condition. A great variety of issues and the need to accomplish significant changes related to social problems were recognized. Problems such as poverty, unemployment, and social exclusion, which affect all countries and create insecurity and social injustice, prevent millions of individuals with disabilities from having a dignified life.

In the case of disabled people, there is a wide range of social problems associated with disadvantaged conditions. Disabled individuals are a vulnerable group that often suffers social injustice, marginality, and poverty and affects millions of people and their families. For this reason society must respond appropriately and assume responsibility for the material and the spiritual needs of individuals, their families, and their communities. Social development and justice that promotes a better quality of life for all can only be achieved within a frame of peace and security, respecting human rights and fundamental liberties within a realm of human interdependence that involves all members of society.

At this Summit Conference it was recognized that social and economic development should be a social goal for everyone. Clear social policies that provide solutions for every problem should not remain in written norms, declarations, agreements, and national plans. They should represent real commitments for governments and society to strengthen, develop, and confer power to all sectors of society, thereby maximizing their capacities, resources, and equal opportunities. These plans should match reality by proposing different strategies to be analyzed, planned, implemented, and periodically evaluated to know if they are providing a better quality of life for the social sector in question. In the case of people with disabilities, it is critical for them to play an active role in determining the effectiveness of the strategies employed. The Summit Conference also recognized the importance of international cooperation based on a friendship that underlines the rights, needs, and aspirations of individuals with disabilities, empowering them to make joint decisions as part of the globalization process.

This chapter discusses the history and current issues surrounding global social integration and makes recommendations for future work. It also highlights the importance that families play in social integration.

History of Social Integration

Throughout history, individuals with disabilities and their families have been stigmatized by society. In Greece children with congenital malformations were thrown from the heights of mountains. In some parts of France during the middle ages, fortified towns were built as a place for sightless people to live. During the Second World War, Hitler ordered that all people with mental disabilities be exterminated. Hundreds of them were gathered in chambers filled with carbon monoxide or were injected with lethal substances. Christianity brought a humane change and some attempts were made to provide a better life to individuals with disabilities. Supported by charity, large asylums were created for individuals with mental or emotional disabilities. Separated from society, these places provided care for the disabled and, in terms of life conditions, some progress was made. This is how the custodial model originated.

This century has witnessed important changes as a result of parents' efforts. At first, they tried to provide educational services for their children in an isolated fashion. Later, together with other parents, they united their efforts to create small schools and organizations to improve the children's quality of life. These phenomena have been observed in all parts of the world, at different points in time and to different degrees. Always, parents have promoted change. At first, the organizations did not defend individual rights but provided services for children with disabilities. Separate schools and services for people with disabilities were created to assume the burden that these people represented for the community. All individuals with disabilities were placed into specific categories, often based on intelligence quotients provided by professionals. At the beginning, even the name of an organization denoted the disability category. This is how organizations such as the National Association for Retarded Citizens of the United States, the Canadian Association for Retarded People, and the International League of Associations on Behalf of Mentally Retarded People were founded.

After the two world wars, the number of people with disabilities increased. Governments had to find solutions for the thousands of citizens that came home from the wars with different disabilities. This generated a need for improvement of rehabilitation techniques and an interest in a medical model of rehabilitation for individuals with disabilities.

Simultaneously, educational services for people with disabilities improved and became specialized, reaching the pinnacle of special education, particularly in rich countries where a true educational model was created. Nevertheless, people with disabilities still were often undervalued. As a result, they were kept outside the community and were not allowed to engage in activities with normal children of the same age.

With time, changes in the original goals set forth by parents were modified to focus on institutionalization. At first, professionals, based on their expertise, offered parents a seemingly more comfortable lifestyle for the disabled that was favored by institutions, arguing that it was much better for them and their families. Separated from home environments, far away from cities and towns, large institutions were created all over the world to house individuals with disabilities. On many occasions thousands of individuals with mental retardation were gathered in a single building in subhuman living conditions.

Then, based on these circumstances, a movement toward de-institutionalization began. Pilot programs were created to show that individuals with mental disabilities or emotional disturbances could live within the community. The concept of human rights began to be seriously considered and large, isolated institutions were no longer recommended because these institutions deprived people with disabilities from the right to live with other citizens. This is the human rights model.

All along, parent organizations have been very important in promoting change. Professionals joined parents and, little by little, government and society, including people with disabilities assuming positions of leadership, united in their efforts, realizing this was the only solution if significant advances were to be made. In many countries, thanks to the struggle of many people with disabilities, their families, friends, and professionals, changes were legally approved.

Schwartz (1995) invites us to review critically and analyze the history of special education. Where are we now? Where do we want to go next? Often, we ask ourselves why in the past parents were rebellious and opposed to prevalent situations, and why today many are reluctant to participate in the changes that need to be made.

What makes some families facing difficult circumstances with children or parents accomplish so much while others in similar situations fall apart or opt to institutionalize members of their family? What makes some families stronger than others? Can this strength be transmitted from one family to another in similar circumstances? Is the development of a country inversely proportional to the desire of families to care for people with major disabilities? Are individuals with disabilities closer to their families in poor countries than in rich ones?

At any given time, laws, social policies, or national programs reflect current perspectives. We must believe that all changes have initially been planned conscientiously in response to current needs with the insight and the passion of those who sought changes. However, there is no universal panacea that solves everything. It is important to bear in mind that programs deteriorate and fail, causing people with disabilities to be worse off than before. That is why programs should be constantly evaluated by governmental organizations, civilians, and individuals with disabilities and their families, who are the true experts. United, we will be able to implement strategies that ensure that our ideals, our struggle, and our vision will be shared with society in order to receive the necessary help that secures permanent changes.

Society and individuals with disabilities have faced different ways of relating to each other, from extermination to charity, using rehabilitating medical or educational models, even through movements in favor of human rights. If we analyze the world today, we will find within our own country and all over the globe that, despite improvements, a wide variety of models to treat people with disabilities exist. We must find better strategies to generate the necessary changes that are good for a given region or country. Moreover, we must be flexible enough to consider cultural and linguistic differences among people. We must consider how behavioral and communicational factors, life in large or small cities, and marginal or rural areas affect their lives. It is important to consider people's living conditions, including those in the isolated jungle and those who have migrated to other places. Despite the lack of a single solution to all the problems, we are unified by the common goal to achieve social integration of individuals with disabilities into the community. We cannot limit ourselves to a single, drastic solution. Some solutions are valid in environments that have limited resources and where families lead a simple life in the country or in the jungle. Regardless of poor living conditions, families will promote social integration with almost no outside support. However, in large cities another kind of help is required on top of social participation.

The United Nations, Human Rights, and Social Integration

The United Nations, since its origins, has fought for the rights of all human beings and it has focused directly on the rights of individuals with disabilities. The history of these efforts is reflected in activities of the United Nations. Some efforts are present in themes specifically related to disabilities, while others include different declarations or agreements related to disabilities within general articles. Here are some of the most important documents.

1948 Universal Declaration of Human Rights

This declaration states that "All human beings are born free and equal in dignity and rights. Everyone is entitled to all the rights and freedoms set forth in this Declaration, without distinction of any kind, such as race, color, sex, language, religion. All are equal before the law and are entitled to equal protection against any discrimination. Everyone has the right to a standard of living adequate for the health and well-being of him/herself and of his/her family, including food, clothing, housing and medical care and other necessary social services, and the right to security in the event of unemployment, sickness, disability, old age or other lack of livelihood in circumstances beyond his/her control." Since its foundation, the UN has fought for individuals with permanent disabilities.

1971 Declaration on the Rights of Mentally Retarded Persons

The mentally retarded person has the same rights as other human beings including proper medical care, education, economic security, training, rehabilitation, social security, and the right to live with his/her own family or with foster parents. This declaration also refers to the right to protection from exploitation and abuse.

1975 Declaration of the Rights of Disabled Persons

All human beings, without any exception, shall enjoy the same civil, political, and economic rights. This includes the right to receive equal treatment and services which will enable everyone to fully develop his or her capabilities and skills to the maximum and hasten the process of social integration or reintegration. It also covers the right to social security and to a decent standard of living, taking into consideration the treatment related to their special needs in all stages of economic and social planning. The right to have leisure time, to work, and to receive fair remuneration against all exploitation is also important. Finally, these individuals shall have the right to avail themselves of qualified legal aid.

1976 International Covenant on Economic, Social, and Cultural Rights

This covenant recognizes that society must create the necessary conditions for everyone to enjoy human rights. It emphasizes aspects such as discrimination, the right to fair wages, the condition of mothers with disabilities, the improvement of living standards for disabled persons and their families, and the right to enjoy physical and mental health, education, and participation in cultural life.

1976 Covenant on Civil and Political Rights

This series of articles discuss the human rights protection against torture, punishment, inhuman or degrading treatment, and medical or scientific experimentation. This is particularly important because, in some cases, disabilities result from experiments against which individuals with mental disabilities are unable to defend themselves. Sometimes these individuals are unaware of the reasons for their arrest, or they are confined to psychiatric institutions and subjected to the worst kind of punishment and inhumane living conditions. In many cases their human rights have been violated. For example, massive sterilization is performed without informed consent.

1981 International Year of Individuals with Disabilities

The objective was to achieve recognition of the equality of disabled persons and to promote their full participation in society. These instruments are important because only through the interdependence of civil, political, economic, social, and cultural rights in all that is related to disabilities can true advances be achieved. For this reason, it is necessary for us to prepare ourselves to defend our rights.

1983 International Convention on Labor

Great efforts were made to promote vocational rehabilitation at this convention. Also recognized was the importance of active participation of people with disabilities in the planning, implementation, and evaluation of policies and programs that affect their integration or reintegration into active employment. This convention also emphasized the importance of training and employment of disabled people in rural areas.

1989 Convention on the Rights of Children

This convention established that the member states shall recognize that children with mental or physical disabilities have the right to a decent and full life. This includes consideration for treatment related to their special needs to help assure their dignity, promote their development, and facilitate their active participation in the community. The member states recognized the right of children with disabilities to special care and were committed to assure them and encourage governments to provide the necessary resources. It recognizes special assistance, which may be free of charge depending on the parents' financial resources, to ensure effective access to educational services, training, health care services, rehabilitation, and other services including those needed for cultural and spiritual development.

The International Convention on the Protection of the Rights of All Migrant Workers and Members of Their Families

These series of articles are relevant if we are to protect individuals with disabilities against violence, physical harm, or intimidation. Medical care shall be provided to preserve life or to avoid irreversible consequences. In the case of those countries that experience migratory problems, these articles should be made known to eliminate violations of human rights as a matter of course.

1982-1992 World Program of Action for People with Disabilities

In this program, an international covenant was signed by many state members who agreed upon long-term goals and programs designed to benefit people with disabilities. It provided objectives for social policies and guidance for the implementation of programs at national, local, and international levels. Prevention, rehabilitation, reintegration in community life, and equal opportunities were considered as the key issues. The program recognized the direct participation of individuals with disabilities as essential to achieving effective laws, plans, and instrumentation of new programs and services. It was endorsed by many UN agencies, national and international organizations for disabled people, and by the UN Center for Social Development. Poor diffusion of the covenant in many countries, however, prevented the predicted outcomes from being accomplished during those ten years.

1993 The Standard Rules on the Equalization of Opportunities for Persons with Disabilities

As a result of the Decade of Disabled People, Member States agreed upon an international document to protect the rights and opportunities of people with disabilities. These Standard Rules of the United Nations set forth to protect the rights and opportunities of people with disabilities and embraced a new philosophy as an international instrument. These rules helped to translate a conceptual revolution into concrete and coherent actions that directly benefited people with disabilities. It consisted of a number of articles within the Standard Rules that paid special attention to the equal enjoyment of all human rights and fundamental freedom by disabled persons, including their active participation in all aspects of society. It also offered a framework to be used by governments in order to achieve these objectives. Key to the rules was the premise that people with disabilities and their families, as well as organizations, government, and society, are responsible for overcoming the obstacles that prevent people with disabilities from full participation in society. We need preconditions for this equal participation in awareness-raising, medical care, rehabilitation, and support services. Changes in the physical environment according to the nature of the disability are vital for these people if they are to participate in social activities and enjoy available information and services. In the field of education, the Rules provide guidance for educational policies that assure appropriate education and adequate support and access to regular schools, jobs, and social security for persons with disabilities whose needs cannot be met in open employment within the community. In the field of social environment, the Standard Rules provide guidance against any kind of discrimination for personal integrity and for the family life of people with disabilities, protecting their right to have a family of their own, a religion, and participation in leisure activities as other citizens do. The United Nations appointed a special reporter as a monitoring mechanism designed to support the implementation of the Standard Rules for the assurance of higher standards of living.

1994 International Year of the Family

Over a period of two years, the UN had a task force for the study of families with disabled people to identify problems and propose solutions. A greater understanding was gained of the role of the family in the lives of people with disabilities from birth to old age, as well as the importance of providing the assistance required for their welfare.

Based on the activities just described, it is clear that the way society treats disabled people measures its development. Generally, disabled people are at a disadvantage everywhere, and society does not take their special needs into consideration. In developing countries, disabled people are viewed from the standpoint of their disability, and few enjoy economic or personal security. Individuals with severe disabilities and greater needs are excluded from society. Most of the 225 million people with moderate or severe disabilities do not enjoy full participation and equality in human development programs. Along with their families, they often suffer social injustice, marginalization, and poverty.

It is an important goal to ensure that social development programs also apply to people with disabilities. Economic, social, cultural, and environmental factors should be considered. Responsibility for developing these programs should be taken not only by governments, but also by people with disabilities themselves, their families, their organizations, and their communities.

Social Integration and the Family

The family plays a key role in the social integration of individuals with disabilities. The family is a system integrated by each of its individual members. There are different kinds of families: big and small, multigeneration, foster, and double or single parent families. Families can live in small or large cities, or in marginal or rural areas. Heterogeneous as they are, they evolve at different stages and it is impossible to make generalizations. Today, the family is threatened by emerging problems and by the social and political changes of contemporary society.

As members of the family, we protect and influence each other. We provide physical, economic and affective support as well as participate in social activities. Nevertheless, within families there is also aggression, violence, abuse, and marginalization. The family is a culture of its own and the source of unique heritage and cultural diversity. Different value systems determine how each family achieves its dreams. Along with the strengths and weaknesses of each individual member, each family is conditioned by its educational, socioeconomic, and sociocultural levels. Together they constitute neighborhoods, communities, states, and nations.

Each time a child is born, parents dream about the different qualities the child will have, the color of the eyes, and the profession that he or she will choose later in life. They have nine months to create the perfect image of their child, along with a feeling of pride and deep love. Every time a child with a congenital defects or with a disability is born, parents' attitudes suddenly change, and the child is not welcomed as in normal circumstances.

The way families with children with disabilities are informed by professionals will influence their whole future. A generalized complaint in many parts of the world is related to the lack of skills and sensitivity doctors have in dealing with this kind of information. This worsens the initial emotional shock, prolonging the pain and creating situations in which parents either overprotect or reject the baby. What follows is denial, emotional confusion, or a mixture of feelings of denial, anguish, anger, shame, fear, and inability to deal with the problem. Therefore, it is especially important to inform the siblings of the new baby's disability, asking them to be understanding and to participate in the adjustments the family might have to go through.

The degree of special attention required by the family and the disabled will vary depending on the sex, physical appearance, age, parental adjustment, seriousness of the disability, expenses from health-related problems, level of anxiety of the parents, training, confidence, the child's general health condition, and community attitudes and support. Generally, fathers are more affected by the disability and find it very difficult to accept. It is a severe blow to their self-esteem due to sociocultural values related to machismo, independence, competition, and achievement. Especially in cultures in which the father is not involved with homemaking and child care, it will be difficult for him to accept the disabled child. Mothers cope with the problem better. After an initial difficult period, they unite in support groups with mothers familiar with early intervention or rehabilitation services. Usually, they are more positive and worry a lot about the emotional well-being of the family. By spending more time with the child, they learn to accept and love him or her. Nevertheless, depending on the demands of the child, sometimes they feel isolated, depressed, tired, under stress. Mothers have the responsibility, almost entirely, of *all* the changes their family has to go through.

Statistical data support the idea that families with disabled children are more fragile than other families. It is the case that most marital problems existed before the birth of the child. In general, more open, cohesive, and organized families without economic problems are in a stronger position to make decisions and less vulnerable to stress. As a result, relationships become stronger and couples get closer. Mothers feel secure in their relationship and find solution to the problems. Often, a child with disabilities is a positive factor in the development of the family in which siblings increase their humanitarian feelings.

Especially when societal attitudes towards children with disabilities are negative, the family, in response to the initial shock, may close the door to friends, thus reducing opportunities of social participation and different alternatives. The child is often overindulged or rejected by one or both of the parents. In the latter case, the parents might even follow the physician's recommendation to institutionalize. If the child remains in the family circle, daily care and support by parents or professionals help to reorganize and balance life. A deep love develops from the daily struggle. Improvement in the parents' self-esteem and confidence in their parenting abilities and participation in support groups facilitate the adjustment process.

Family stability may fluctuate with time, depending on different traumatic events that shape the emotional life of its members. The birth of another child; change of school; restructuring of family routines; financial problems; difficulties within the couple; illness of the mother, father or grandparents; unemployment; or aging of parents may bring back emotions that the family thought already had been overcome.

Families with disabled children have certain needs for which society should provide. Attitudes of neighbors and friends are important, particularly in small cities. These facilitate or inhibit social interaction and normal daily life of individuals with disabilities. These children learn about themselves and the society in which they live. They also learn to recognize what they like or dislike within their families. It is within their families that they develop the first social ties and learn to love other siblings. They also learn about their disabilities and whether they are accepted, rejected, or loved despite them. Parents serve as role models and, based on family reactions, a sibling will construct an image of the disabled brother or sister, causing feelings of jealousy, shame, or even envy because of the time the parents spend with the child due to the special attention required. Pathological and painful relationships may develop among siblings which affect the family as a whole.

From the very beginning it is extremely important for the family to know about different services available for children with disabilities. This is especially true for early intervention. From the moment of birth and during the first years of life the child should participate in rehabilitation services to overcome deficits, developmental problems, or any other kind of disability.

It is also important for professionals to carry out educational campaigns in reproductive health, including information on the role of environmental stimulation in the development of children with disabilities. This will help parents to be involved in early stimulation and prevent the disability from worsening, particularly when extreme poverty and illiteracy are involved.

Social Issues and the Integration of Families of Individuals with Disabilities

In recent years, an international movement in favor of the defense of the rights and social integration of individuals with disabilities has developed. It promotes the right of the disabled person to be part of a community, constitute a family of his or her own, and have a better quality of life. It also defends his or her right to health services, education, productive work, leisure time, and cultural and artistic enjoyment. The human rights movement fights against the negative consequences of labeling that have excluded disabled people from society, thereby reducing them to marginal living conditions. It seeks to restore their place in society.

Not long ago mental disabilities were established on the basis of IQ scores derived from a battery of psychological tests. These scores also determined whether disabled people should be institutionalized or confined to a bed. Education and employment opportunities and other services were dependent on the prognosis, and scientists divided children into "educable" or "custodial," a classification which determined, in many cases, their right to live with their families. The situation has changed. Today, classification is completed on an individual basis so as to assure the fullest participation of the disabled person in society. Years of struggle for the integration of individuals with disabilities have made organizations change their names to avoid negative labeling as much as possible. Such is the case of The Arc of the United States, and the Canadian Association for Community Life or International Inclusion.

We always refer to social and educational integration, productive work, cultural, recreational and sports-related activities within the community, but we consider the family last. We forget that it is the family that has the greatest influence on the destiny of a baby, a child, or an elderly person. It is true that programs of all types are established, but we do not do not promote integration in the family.

For a number of years, I have had the opportunity to visit regular schools in other countries where children with mental disabilities are mainstreamed. I am aware of what it requires to include children in regular classrooms with the support of principals, teachers, special education teachers, children without disabilities and their parents, neighborhood members, and the entire community. I have not seen, however, the same interest in promoting family integration. It is true that we do not have to label disabled people or their families. Nevertheless, it is important to recognize that they require special attention. Inclusive communities, educational systems, or societies are not enough. Painful emotional processes that endanger family relationships are experienced every day by hundreds of families after the violent and painful shock of having a disabled child born into the family. For the baby's well-being, this should be carefully considered.

Efforts by the United Nations to change society and parents' organized movements to defend the rights of disabled people that promote integration would be meaningless if emphasis were not given to support programs for parents with a newborn who has cerebral palsy, mental deficiency, or a congenital malformation.

At a recent congress for parents of individuals with mental disability, held in Alberta, Canada, Knoster presented key elements to assist us in understanding our expectations of families and all that is required to promote children's social integration (see appendix). While these elements are not an ideal recipe, they do provide basic guidelines for action.

How can society support families in their efforts toward social integration? This may vary from case to case, but in general parents should have:

- access to clear diagnoses presented to them by professionals in tactful ways
- the necessary training to handle their personal circumstances in the best possible way
- community support to improve child care

- financial and human resources
- tax reduction
- information and guidance on available services
- quality health and education services
- home adaptations
- informed neighbors who support the family
- emotional support from parents in similar circumstances
- team work with professionals and other parents
- opportunities to participate in organizations in favor of individuals with disabilities
- social support to prevent isolation and provide leisure time to parents and siblings

This kind of social support helps families sort out their problems in creative ways and allows them to solidify as a result of mutual collaboration. It also promotes a philosophy that protects the rights of the child and supports families as they strive for their social integration into the community. Consequently, members of a community should be interdependent and cooperative, share a sense of belonging, respect differences, share responsibilities and collaborate with each other, and promote environments that favor learning, preserve human dignity, provide family support, and share a common vision.

Consequently, this means that all members without exception should be respected and have opportunities to contribute and participate. They should show friendship, promote security, be useful, take risks, and be cooperative. On the other hand, to be excluded from the community means that people with disabilities feel rejection, discrimination, and indifference. Furthermore, some of them experience anguish toward the present and the future and are often victims of physical, psychological, and sexual abuse. Because they are viewed as different they are denied opportunities and excluded from services and activities, causing them to feel inferior, depressed, undervalued, and powerless to defend their rights.

Basic strategies to promote social integration of individuals with disabilities and a better quality of life involve the community in a number of endeavors. For example, the community must be active in the fight against poverty, which affects 1.3 billion people in developing countries. It is believed that one out of every six people that live in poverty suffers from serious or moderate disabilities. Reasons vary from prenatal malnutrition and poor prenatal health services to poor general environmental conditions both during pregnancy and after delivery, such as lack of nutrition necessary for the proper development of the nervous system. Another example is the lack of schooling, poor quality services, and neglect in general. During the first years of life, child achievement may be poor due to mental deficiencies, poor nourishment, or lack of stimulation. A great number of children do not attend school either because their families do not consider it to be a priority or because of poor grades. No program will be effective if the child is not actively participating.

Several factors contribute to the current status of individuals with disabilities and their families. Attitudes that reject people with disabilities or do not consider the necessary adaptations required for them to benefit from community resources contribute to disabilities. Also, other environmental factors such as self-medication, drugs, alcohol, and automobile or work-related accidents contribute as well. In addition, low-quality services or a total absence of services is a factor. Often people with disabilities are eligible for rehabilitation and educational programs, but there is almost a complete absence of programs that would provide emotional support or training for their families. Likewise, individuals with disabilities and their families are not considered capable of monitoring services and providing feedback regarding their improvement.

Here are some recommendations that could assist in moving the status quo to a more positive, respectful community for individuals with disabilities and their families.

- Technical cooperation among countries to learn from each other's experiences, achievements, and failures, always keeping in mind sociocultural and economic differences to better apply those measures suitable for each country's own reality.
- Special education that provides support for individuals with disabilities both in the government and private sectors. The achievements obtained in this area should not be forgotten even in regular schools.
- Inclusion of children with disabilities in regular schools combined with extensive teacher and administrative personnel training and the awareness of society. The best alternative is to use existing facilities in special education schools for some of the children as a transition until there is enough space, knowledge, and support in regular schools.
- Technical support, such as a public network of services. In developing countries, particularly in areas located away from the cities, these programs serve a critical function and are possible if policies and national programs are adequate and if relevant sectors of society such as health educators, social workers, and rehabilitation specialists participate.
- Adequate support for families to develop the necessary skills, knowledge, and commitment required to make future decisions on services and opportunities available in the community. Families should be informed of their rights and the training process should consider issues related to the defense of the rights of children and their families.
- Active participation of individuals with disabilities and their families in programs that fight poverty and devise economic plans with government support. This includes programs within the community such as psychosocial stimulation, motivation, and support, so that children with disabilities may benefit from recreational and cultural activities and sports.
- Use of low-cost, high-quality equipment for workshops with the adequate technological support to manufacture and distribute orthopedic equipment, wheelchairs, auditory devices or glasses, and books.
- Creation of small daycare centers within the community or availability of individual support at home by volunteers provided by local governments to support individuals with severe disabilities and their families. This is critical because in developing countries, the family and the community have cared for individuals with severe disabilities. However, attitudes have changed and this kind of sup-

port has gradually disappeared due to urbanization of rural areas and the increasing number of women who work outside their homes.

- Educational programs designed to raise awareness and teach society and disabled people and their families that people with disabilities have the right to be part of a society.
- Regular modes of communication to inform people with disabilities and their families of changes in the laws that directly affect them.
- Human rights campaigns that target the inhumane treatment that is still the case in some countries toward individuals with disabilities. For example, physical, psychological, and sexual abuse of individuals with disabilities is still a problem worldwide. Acts of violence such as tying up disabled people in houses or schools, food deprivation or sedation with tranquilizers, straitjackets, electroshock or other kinds of technology are common practice. Psychological abuse based on punishment that deprives them from high-quality food or confines them to dirty quarters, creates an atmosphere of insecurity that generates fear. They are also victims of heterosexual and/or homosexual sexual abuse, rape, incest, castration, and sterilization. In some cases people with disabilities are denied economic rights such as inheritances that are theirs by law. They are forced into prostitution or to work long hours for low wages. There is no one in charge of monitoring the services disabled people receive or defending their rights. That is why it is extremely important to help families and the community become active human rights promoters.
- Professionals working together with parents and individuals with disabilities in true partnerships to meet the goals of each individual person with disabilities and to provide services to support their programs.

A high-priority goal for the end of the century should be to defend the rights of disabled people and their families. The government and the private sector alike should consider this population of the utmost importance and create programs that benefit the lives of these individuals.

To conclude, it can be stated that society has been faced with important changes as the twenty-first century draws near. International organizations have written important documents highlighting and emphasizing the rights of every human being, including those with disabilities. Nevertheless, these changes and the right to be treated with dignity and equitable opportunities have not yet reached all individuals with disabilities. This is the goal that has to be accomplished in the years to come if individuals with disabilities are to become fully participating members in society.

Appendix

Elements Required by Families to Be Able to Promote Disabled Children's Social Integration

1. With the understanding that a disabled child's development could progress better than expected, parents, with the help of professionals, should have long-term, realistic, and energetic plans to meet the child's needs from birth on.

2. To handle special situations, families need the necessary training and information about services available for the disabled child. Often this information could be provided by other parents of children with disabilities or through data bases listing services available by city, region, and country.
3. The acceptance and love of the disabled child by parents could be a powerful motivating factor in itself. However, if they have not been able to cope with their circumstances, they may need psychological support or the support of other parents to overcome related emotional problems.
4. Families should receive communal, human, and financial support either through direct participation or attitudes of solidarity, especially in developing countries.
5. With the support of other parents in similar circumstances or from professionals, families need to have flexible plans from the very beginning.

References

Aguilar Cuevas, Magdalena. 1993. *Derechos humanos.* Mexico, DF: Comisión Nacional de Derechos Humanos.

Blatt, Burton, and Fred Kaplan. 1974. *Christmas in purgatory.* Syracuse, NY: Human Policy Press.

Cunningham, Cliff, and Hilton Davis. 1991. *Working with parents: Framework for collaboration.* Philadelphia: Open University Press.

DIF. 1995. Programa Nacional para el Bienestar y la Incorporación al Desarrollo de las Personas con Discapacidad. Mexico, DF.

Lachwitz, Klaus. 1994. *How can persons with a mental handicap benefit from international human rights instruments.* Belgium: Inclusion International.

Liga Internacional de Asociaciones en Favor de la Personas con Deficiencia Mental Ninth World Congress. 1986. *Deficiencia mental un desafío para todos ¡Juntos podemos!* Brussels.

McGee, John J. 1989. *Being with the others: Toward a psychology of interdependence.* Omaha, NE: Creighton University.

Mittler, Helle. 1995. *Families speak out: International perspectives on families' experiences of disability.* Cambridge, MA: Brookline Books.

Mittler, Peter. 1992. *Making the most of the United Nations International League of Societies for Persons with Mental Handicap.* Brussels: ILMSH.

Mittler, Peter, and Helle Mittler. 1994. *Familias y discapacidad.* Vienna: United Nations.

Robertson, Sally. 1993. *Disability rights handbook.* The Disability Alliance. London: Universal House.

United Nations. 1945. *Charter of the United Nations and Statue of the International Court of Justice.* New York: Philip C. Duschnes.

_____. General Assembly. 1948. *Declaración Universal de los Derechos Humanos.* December 10.

_____. 1983. *World program of action concerning disabled persons.* N.p.: Division of Economic and Social Information; Centre for Social Development and Humanitarian Affairs.

_____. General Assembly. 1989. Convention on the rights of the child. November 20.

_____. 1991. *International year of the family*. New York.

_____. 1992. *World program of action concerning disabled persons*. New York.

_____. 1993. *Human rights and disabled persons*. Prepared by I. Leandro Despouy. New York. Sales no. E.92.XIV.4.

_____. 1994. *Guide for a national action program on the international year of the family*. New York.

_____. 1994. *Standard rules on the equalization of opportunities for persons with disabilities*. New York.

_____. 1995. *Copenhagen declaration on social development and program of action of the world summit for social development*. New York.

_____. 1995. *Human rights: A compilation of international instruments*. New York. Sales no. E.88.XVI.I.

2 Family-Centered Early Intervention

Berta Watkins

General Overview of Early Education in Mexico

In the 1960s, international awareness of the diverse educational needs of children under four years of age who require special education began in the disciplines of psychology, pedagogy, and anthropology. During the last thirty years, early intervention, as part of a general trend in early education, has gained acceptance and promotion worldwide, growing from virtual nonexistence into a broad range of services addressing the diverse problems that exist in different geographic areas and at varying sociocultural levels. It has also been demonstrated that early attention enhances the educational achievement of students and prevents costly social and educational problems (Department of Public Education 1992).

Attention to infants, toddlers, and young children has become one of the most important trends in special education and related services. Professionals in special education have become aware that:

1. The first three years of life can be the most critical for educational and therapeutic intervention to prevent slow development and to reach maximum potential.
2. Frequently parents of newborn infants and young children with disabilities require information, guidance, emotional support, and adequate orientation to effectively manage their child from educational as well as emotional perspectives.
3. Unfortunately, most of these children have to wait months or even years before they receive some educational assessment (Bailey 1988).

Consequently, the traditional view of education for specific periods in life, provided only in school settings with the unique and essential function of reproducing and transmitting certain mental frameworks, knowledge, and traditions for the individuals' adjustment to society, needs to be abandoned (Caballero 1982). Caballero reconceptualized education as a process that should extend throughout the life span of human beings. He also viewed educational reality as being manifested within the family context as well as in school and society. Therefore, the endeavors of each person involved with young children need to be redefined, and the objectives and mechanisms to accomplish these endeavors restructured. The potential of the family as a nurturing nucleus must be recognized and requires renewal and strengthening. This necessitates planning for the education of all family members and not leaving the responsibility to societal institutions or other support systems outside the realm of the family unit.

According to Stevens and King (1987) early education is defined as educational attention provided to children under four years of age and oriented toward the child's integrated development. Throughout the world, early education has developed for different purposes and with diverse names. Internationally, there is lack of clarity and little agreement in relation to the terms commonly used. This results in confusion and ambiguity. Most confusion occurs with terms such as early intervention and early stimulation. At the beginning, different authors from different countries used these two terms indiscriminately, and many consider these two terms as being synonymous, even though in many publications the difference is implicit.

In Mexico, early education consists of three modalities: initial education, early intervention, and early stimulation.

Initial Education

In Mexico initial education is defined as a "service that offers children an integrated education supported by an active participation of adults and centered on the development of the person, of his or her relationship with others, and with the environment." It has been consolidated as a nationwide service with the explicit and unique purpose, as stated by the Mexican government, to contribute to the harmonic growth and even development of children from birth to four years of age (Department of Public Education 1992).

Not long ago initial education was offered in public and private institutions and schools almost exclusively to provide for the rights and needs of working mothers. Recently a different orientation began. While it does not exclude the previous orientation, it broadens the focus and is now offered through two models: (a) a school-based program, offered at Centers for Infant Development (CENDI), and (b) a non-school-based program that operates as a community working strategy through the use of "operating circuits" that do not require a physical space and operate in the community in general (Department of Public Education 1992).

School-Based Initial Education

In this program, children are placed in Centers of Infant Development facilities for different lengths of time and cared for by adults. These facilities provide educational services to children of working mothers during their working hours. Children are admitted from forty days to six years of age. It is a privilege provided by public organizations and in some cases by assisting organizations or as a private service. CENDIs exist throughout the country but are primarily located in urban areas.

Children are not only cared for at the CENDIs, but they are also provided meals. CENDIs have a formative function, as they attempt to demonstrate how the child's environment should be and how better to accomplish the integration of the child into the social environment and the family. They foster the development of physical, cognitive, affective, and social capabilities and an active participation in the educational process (Department of Public Education 1992).

The services provided at CENDI are organized around the children's needs and interests, depending upon the age of the child. Children are grouped by ages as follows:

a) Lactants:	forty-five days to eighteen months
b) Maternals:	eighteen months to forty-seven months
c) Preschoolers:	four to six years

Non-School-Based Initial Education

The main objective of this model is to provide children under four years of age, mostly in rural and marginalized urban areas, and indigenous populations with equal educational opportunities by using the official program of the Department of Public Education (SEP) to optimize their developmental potential. Other stated objectives include the stimulation of solidarity attitudes, identity values, and social belonging. This service is organized according to the needs of the communities; the goal is to promote development and long-term optimizing of academic performance through the first years of elementary education (Department of Public Education 1992).

Attention to children in this service is not only non-school-based, but there is no direct interaction of "community educators" or "service providers" with the children. Children ultimately benefit from this service in spite of the fact that they are not being observed or directly assisted by professionals during home visits. In each community determined to be at risk, the most recognized and influential members of the community are selected to become the promoters of the program. They are also the designated persons who will train parents in different aspects of health, hygiene, feeding, environmental conservation, and pedagogical activities.

As mentioned, there are three target groups of communities serviced by this project: rural and low-SES, marginalized urban communities, and indigenous populations. There is no methodological difference in the work performed in these three types of communities. Nor has there been any resistance from the communities to accept such programs since they were initiated. In some communities it is necessary that the identified community members be bilingual. From the government perspective, this second service delivery model, of all the existing initial education programs, has the highest potential for impact, since it is less formal and adapts better to the various living conditions of the different communities and most impoverished social groups.

The different initial education services do not provide for all the existing demand for services. With respect to children with disabilities, a limitation of this model is that when children with disabilities are identified, parents are only made aware of the need to adequately attend and rehabilitate these children through the Programa Nacional para el Bienestar y la Incorporación al Desarrollo de las Personas con Discapacidad (DIF) but are not given instructions as to how to do it. As recently as a year ago, in the school-based services these children were rejected; parents received from school officials the explanation that there were no curricular adaptations or other specific actions that could be provided for their children. Currently, access for children with disabilities to SEP CENDIs as well as to other public facilities is being promoted and the bonding with SEP special educational services to create curricular adaptations, accessibility, and, where necessary, reconditioning of the physical structure of the buildings providing these services is encouraged.

Early Intervention

Young children ages forty-five days to four years who have special needs receive attention in this early intervention model. The early intervention model is characterized by providing education designed to attain the desired integrated development of an at-risk child or a child with disabilities according to his or her age and potential. The goal is to promote the child's integration into family, school, and society.

In Mexico, there have been no official early intervention programs, so each institution uses the conceptual framework that it considers best for its purposes. Some proposals were taken from commercial publications, others were individually developed, based on the development of each child and on the framework preferred by the professionals working at the institution. Recently, in services offered by the government, the regular curriculum is being promoted as the base line for intervention. The purpose is to contribute to the harmonious and balanced development of children from birth to age four. Early intervention services are characterized by providing children with an integrated education that is supported by the active participation of an adult and is centered on the development of the individual and his or her relationship with others and the environment.

Currently, at the government level, the development of physical, affective, and social capabilities of children at high risk and their active participation in the educational process are being emphasized in order to better integrate them into the social environment in which they live (Department of Public Education 1992). Nevertheless, there is no unified government objective either at the intrasecretarial or intersecretarial level. Each institution within the diverse government agencies that is focused on these types of interventions has been established by independent initiative and is working in accordance with the conceptual framework that underlies it or the personnel working in it. One of the advantages of this service is that it permits timely prevention and detection of complications secondary to the original problem.

Early intervention is provided throughout the Mexican Republic in urban as well as rural areas. Public, private, and social institutions provide facilities that vary in quality and location in either school- or non-school-based settings. In both formal and nonformal school-based settings it is contemplated that services be provided to children in special-education schools as well as to homebound children. Attention to children with special needs is provided at variable, but preestablished, schedules in small groups that serve between five and twenty children. Generally these institutions, either public, social, or private, work with comprehensive programs that target all areas of development and use diverse strategies and methods, depending on the conceptual framework that underlies their work.

Parental participation is also determined by the framework of each institution. Parents may be informed of the activities performed during the child's stay at the institution, or they may be involved in specific tasks that are to be performed at home in order to strengthen specific aspects of the child's functioning. Some institutions—generally those that provide assistantships—require the attendance of the parents on the premises during the intervention session. Parents assist the person in charge of the group, or sometimes they take care of their own children.

In the informal, non-school-based model, children are seen at home; they do not attend an institution on a daily basis. Services are provided three times per week, either individually or in a group setting. The difference between the non-school-based early intervention model and the non-school-based initial education model is the degree to which the early intervention takes place directly with the children and to a larger or smaller extent with the parents. In the non-school-based model, another difference is that work is done in "children-centered programs" or "family-centered programs," depending upon the conceptual framework that underlies these services.

These children-centered programs also include the parents as service providers. Family-centered programs not only involve the parents as service providers but also consider the child part of a basic social system. This system is the main focus of attention, and therefore intervention strategies are directed to the social system and not solely to the children. The personnel at these institutions consists of professionals in different disciplines and specializations who work together as an interdisciplinary team on interrelated tasks. It is not an interdisciplinary team that meets to discuss educational options, but rather a mutually supportive team that works directly with parents and children. The service it provides is based on the needs and interests of the child as well as the characteristics and needs of each family system. Parents are the focus of intervention; they are prepared, oriented, and guided to become the main service providers for their child. These early intervention services provide attention to a wide range of children with problems at various levels of severity and with all kinds of socioeconomic and cultural backgrounds. They constitute a flexible alternative capable of adapting to the diversity of those they serve. Unfortunately, institutions and centers dedicated to the provision of these services are unable to meet the potential demand throughout Mexico.

Early Stimulation

Early stimulation consists of a group of actions or techniques designed to favor specific areas of sensorimotor or cognitive development. It is sometimes used to promote an acceleration in the child's development, depending on the problem, specialist, or institution where it is provided. Early stimulation is the third alternative of services provided within early education. It is important to clarify once more that the differences lie in the practical application of these methods. This service delivery model is sometimes included within early intervention programs or in those of initial education, but it can also become an independent service that is used with normal as well as high-risk and disabled children in both school-based and non-school-based settings. One example of the types of early-stimulation programs that exist in Mexico are those that exist within the health system, such as the health department and DIF. Another example is independent specialists in a variety of areas and gyms for babies that are offering early-stimulation programs. Some of these have even been set up under the auspices of the Department of Public Education.

There is a practical difference between early intervention and early stimulation based on the differences in their conceptual framework. There is a difference in their approach to individual development. Children can be perceived as isolated living beings who have to be stimulated to elicit responses or who have to be conditioned to give a series of responses. They can also be perceived as more than just sensorimotor beings and as belonging to a fundamental social system, the family. Therefore, both society and family have to be facilitators of processes in which families provide the child with the means to enhance development and acquisition of what their potential allows.

To provide early stimulation, no underlying conceptual framework is required. The only requirement is to apply a series of stimulating techniques to obtain specific responses, which unfortunately can be detached from the context of the biopsychosocial unit. With respect to bonding with parents, in early stimulation parents are generally trained in diverse stimulating techniques to enhance the development of certain skills in their children. The parent usually will depend on a professional person that will tell him or her what to do and when to do it. In other cases, the parent is simply informed of what was done with the child during a therapy session. Regarding personnel in this model, there are centers where paraprofessionals conduct activities with the children under the supervision of a professional with expertise in a different field of study.

Generally, the center is designed according to the characteristics of the personnel, specific interests, or other diverse factors. Children have to adjust to these circumstances. Programs for different problems or disabilities tend to be preestablished by age and other factors, although they are adapted on a case-by-case basis.

Importance of the Family during the First Years of Life

Thirty years ago neither parents of children with disabilities nor medical doctors, special education teachers, or psychologists were aware of the great benefit that early intervention provided for these children, especially during the first months of life. Nor was there an awareness of the important role that parents and family have in early education.

Until recently, in many western and Latin countries, parents of children who were born with disabilities were advised to institutionalize them as early as possible to avoid the possible negative effects on the everyday life of the family. Unfortunately, these practices still persist, although they are isolated. This is due to several factors; among them Bailey and Woley (1984) mention a change of interest demonstrated by the members of society toward individuals with disabilities as well as minority groups. Environmental influences upon children's development and the importance given to education are also contributing factors. From the perspective of systems theory and according to modern anthropological trends, today it is recognized that a child, far from being an isolated individual, is a social being, who belongs to a major family system, which in turn is part of a broader social system. As such, the child has an influence on his or her family and is influenced by it. Therefore, changes in the family affect the child, and changes in the child affect all family members.

When discussing research related to social development, Bell (1968) emphasizes the bilateral nature of these disruptions. He argues against traditional unidirectional interpretations of the effects of maternal behavior upon the infant. More recently, Bell has suggested that children can have an effect that is as powerful on the behavior of parents as the effect parents have on their children and that it is even more so with children who have special needs. Bronfenbrenner (1977) stresses the need to consider development from an ecological perspective. From this perspective the child is nurtured within a family; this family is nested in a neighborhood or community system, and so on. Therefore, the amount of positive effect of the family upon the disabled child and the willingness to promote his or her integration into the family will have a positive influence on the attitude of the community toward the child and the family. Acceptance of the child and the family in the community will lead to more comprehensive and positive development of the child.

When the word "family" is mentioned within this conceptual framework, it is taken for granted that everyone knows what it is; the family institution seems natural to human life and to the vital experience of almost every person. Nevertheless, this view is often mistaken when we are talking about a pluralistic reality that is rapidly changing in time and space. Also, there is some ambiguity as to the concept of family and the way in which each of us has experienced it. Family is an institution as old as humanity itself, yet it has been under constant transformation as a response to the process of evolution of our existence. Prevalent living conditions determine its form in each place and time. In the current scenario, the concept of family is changing at an accelerated pace, with no two families exactly alike. Families have different ideologies and world views depending on their orientations, whether they be of urban, rural, or indigenous background. Other background differences such as racial origin, religion, and political beliefs also have an influence on their organization and functioning. Families act differently within their own communities, where they have a series of support services and resources. In some cases, extreme conditions of acculturation due to political imposition (hierarchical structures), religion, culture (values, norms, etc.), and social factors (family structures) exist.

Craig states that families are much more than the sum of persons who live in one space (1992, 19). According to the *Dictionary of Special Education*, a family is a social unit formed by a group of individuals bonded by affinity (the couple) or by consanguinity (parents, children, and other relatives) who keep a close relationship. The consanguineous family is an artificial social creation, and its current crisis has had repercussions on the conjugal family. In the modern urban community, for example, pressure from the consanguineous group and community to preserve a marriage is practically nonexistent.

The development of contraception techniques and the changing role of women in society, which have resulted in paid alternative occupations outside the household, have had revolutionary effects. There is a progressively decreasing economic interdependence of couples, with women having access to meaningful relationships outside of the family and home. It is important to emphasize that social and economic factors are essential in keeping family members together even though the biological need to mate and survive is still intact. The family has a complex function. It plays an important role in the education of children and the satisfaction of their socioemotional needs during their long-term dependence. It organizes the home economy, satisfies biological, economic, affective, and security needs, and provides emotional support and care of children. The family also allows for identity development and transmission of cultural and moral values; it provides sexual-identity models and direction in sexual relationships, provides and enhances education and socializing, and assures group continuity and integration of family members into society in general.

Parres (quoted in Dallal, *Génesis*) considers that today's family has two main roles: (1) to insure physical survival and (2) to construct the human component of an individual. He considers that among other purposes, the family has the following responsibilities:

1. Provide food, shelter, and other material needs to assure life and protection from danger.
2. Give opportunities for the development of personal identity linked to family identity, which provides for psychic integrity and strength to cope with new experiences.
3. Provide culture of learning and support the development of creativity and initiative.
4. Provide a social context for the development of affective ties within the family as well as a context for affective development.

5. Prepare for social integration and acceptance of social responsibility.

Dallal (1982) maintains that no other institution currently has such a critical and important job as families. He also points out that family functions can best be performed within an atmosphere of social unity and cooperation, especially in those families that face a special situation because of their children.

Kornblit and Chomsky (1984) consider it difficult to try to solve the complex situation that emerges when a child with a disability is born into a family. They also consider it difficult to generalize and to establish the specific facts that such families will have to face, as their reactions will be determined by the characteristics of each family. These authors point out some issues that should be stressed:

1. Parental reactions will differ, depending on the birth order of their children. The birth of a child with a disability will make parents question in a larger or lesser degree their capacity to attend to and satisfy the special needs of the child.
2. There is a need to recognize and respect the fact that each family needs time to accept reality and that puting on pressure in the opposite direction can have an iatrogenic effect; the lack of consideration and respect for this need has the potential to generate problems for other family members.
3. Professionals should always take into consideration the entire family and not just the disabled child. They should help families in the reorganizing process of accomplishing an adequate level of efficiency and functionality in relation to the child's problem.
4. The attitude of the neonatologist and other specialists involved toward the newborn and the family is vital. This is true not only at the time of diagnosis; the entire family feels a need for empathy, support, and orientation during a process they are just beginning. Instead of reprimanding them or being too demanding, professionals need to be aware of this process and allow all family members to externalize their feelings and ask questions; they should employ a clear, simple, and cordial language, especially during the initial moments when the implications of the disability are explained.
5. The family will undergo a radical, sudden, and probably rough transition in its functioning as soon as family members learn of the problem. When pregnancy starts, great expectations are built up; they come crashing down as soon as the disability is detected, inflicting a profound emotional wound. The state of shock that follows can create psychological chaos. The child that is not as expected can become a strange and unknown being for the rest of the family.
6. Family members have to actively participate from the earliest stages in the creation of a collaborative context for stimulation tasks, which are needed to accomplish the highest level of maturation that the child's condition will allow.

Parents play an important role in the emotional development of their child from early childhood. At the beginning only the child's survival instinct is present: when the child cries and obtains satisfaction of basic needs, experiencing pleasure, the relationship with the mother is soon identified as the main source of satisfaction. Benedeck emphasizes that the mother's disposition to feed and care for the child influences the way in which his or her essential emotional needs are satisfied, producing a feeling of security that is transmitted for optimal physical and mental development. Without this, frustration and fear would result.

Winnicott (1987) states that the function of professionals during this stage is not to try to get mothers to understand what they have to do; mothers know the needs of their child better than professionals and how to adapt to them. He suggests that theoretical knowledge can be useful but is not indispensable to establish the bond, and professionals should be ready to help in different ways and at appropriate times when something goes awry. In disabled children, there is a high risk for this bonding process to be interrupted by various factors such as medical needs during the first days (intensive therapy, incubation, etc.), the grieving process that parents go through after their child's disability is discovered, and the fears parents have of being unable to cope with the special child's needs. These conditions interfere with intimacy and with the quantity and quality of parent-child interactions.

Bailey (1988) states that there are at least five basic reasons that justify working with parents:

1. To fulfill legal mandates that indicate the need to analyze the basic needs of each family.
2. To conceptualize the child as a part of the family system.
3. To identify the needs of the family and provide the required services.
4. To identify the family strengths that will promote adaptation.
5. To expand basic assessment services.

Bailey observed that direct personal interaction with families helps professionals to attain better knowledge of the specific needs and potential of each family. He also confirmed, as suggested by the systems theory, that there is no need to work with each and every family member to accomplish the intended outcomes.

Family-Centered Early-Intervention Center

Let us remember the difference between early intervention centered on the child and early intervention centered on the family. Programs centered on the child are those that focus their attention on children even though they take into consideration and eventually work with parents. When parents participate, they do so under the guidance of a specialist who suggests what, how, and when to participate in different activities. In this kind of program the role of the parents is merely to follow the specialist's recommendations. Programs centered on the families are those that conceptualize the child as part of a basic social system into which he or she has to be integrated. In this model it is the family who guides, directs, and supports the developmental process of the child as the child becomes an integral part of society.

It is as important to observe the developmental process of the child and his or her capabilities as it is to observe the possibilities of the family and how it favors or interferes with the child's developmental process. When the family takes part in accomplishing the child's integration, parents are trained by a specialist so that they can observe the changes that take place in their child and find out, understand, promote, and design diverse actions directed to their child. In this case, they do not merely act according to the specialist's instructions but develop a way of thinking that will allow them to adapt their actions to the circumstances and needs of the child. In other words, parents develop the ability to facilitate the developmental processes of their child.

The Family-Centered Early-Intervention Center described in this chapter is based on the following premises: Family members, especially parents, are considered:

1. The elements most emotionally significant during the first months of the child's life. Professionals only orient the parents and do not foster parent-child relationships, thereby not interrupting them. They ensure that the basic bonding moments and processes between mother and child and between father, mother, and child take place.
2. Members of a particular system who should know, understand, and use the needed elements to foster their child's development.
3. Individuals who should put to work a current concept of education in which the potential of the child is recognized and assumed as the basic formatting nucleus.
4. Those who should understand that teaching is a process that facilitates learning, which can be accomplished in a variety of ways: modeling adequate behaviors, directing instruction, reinforcing behaviors, etc., but above all, providing an adequate environment and fostering, through their actions, the educational process according to how the child progresses and looking out for the child's needs and new possibilities.
5. Those who should have the ability to observe their child's needs and select or develop adequate strategies for his or her growth.
6. Those who should provide an environment that will foster learning in a pleasant and appropriate way, considering the child's age and interests.

As mentioned before, a family-centered service emphasizes the presence of the parent as an executor, and not as a means to deliver a service. The intention is to focus attention on the family, of which the child is a part. In addition, the emphasis on the entire family will benefit all its members, not only the disabled child, as it will affect the parenting style. It will also provide a better and more rapid integration of the child into the family unit and, as a consequence, into society as a whole.

The focus on the family thus considers parents a vital and active part, starting with the diagnosis, as they are not only an unlimited source of information regarding the child's advancements, accomplishments, and so on but an indispensable factor in finding out about the child's needs as well. Parents will do the work at home, using their own initiative, and will bring to the center the questions and problems they encounter; these may also be detected by the specialist. The parent will have the opportunity to consult the specialist regarding the different issues as often as needed. From a Mexican perspective, this type of service should involve a diverse group of professionals, such as medical doctors, rehabilitation personnel, psychologists, and others. Since the focus is on direct intervention, so far this service comprises only professionals with a background in pedagogy, social work, and psychology, receiving support related to other areas at an intersecretarial level.

In Mexico, special education is divided into six categories, according to the type of disability. They are (1) mental retardation, (2) auditory and speech and language disorders, (3) learning disabilities, (4) neuromotor disorders, (5) blindness and impaired vision, and (6) infringers and the socially maladjusted. In this service delivery model, the emphasis is on the way in which teamwork is conceptualized and performed and relationships with parents are set up. In contrast to usual procedures, in this model the professional is conceived of as the one who will orient, accompany, teach, and guide parents to help them acquire and develop the necessary skills, which will help all members of the family in developing positive social interactions.

As far as psychological assistance is concerned, family members receive initial support to overcome their grief over the loss of the kind of child they were expecting so that they can build up more realistic expectations. Parents also receive orientation and emotional support to relieve the pressure related to constant caring. They are taught to identify support available within their own families and communities and are made aware of the particular strengths and weaknesses of each. They are also empowered to recover the organization and equilibrium they had prior to the arrival of their disabled child. By giving attention to the specific characteristics of each family and soliciting their participation, professionals help them to discover the capacity needed to accomplish their role successfully. Specialists should provide information and, if needed, coordinate parents and specialists available in other services, to give optimal attention to the child. Family-centered service does not avoid direct intervention with the child, nor does it avoid assessment and information sessions in which the child's progress is discussed. Parents are oriented with regard to their child's management and discipline in general. All aspects related directly to the child are considered during assessment and specialist intervention sessions. Family and social issues are brought up, and for those children who attend a Child Development Center it is considered a school issue.

This implies that a frame of reference that is different from that of other professionals is used. The child is viewed in a global, sociological perspective, as opposed to a perspective that employs techniques to have the child develop or acquire specific skills, which is in conflict with a holistic conceptual frame of reference. On the other hand, it is important to stress that the specialist in charge is not selected according to the child's disability and his or her professional expertise, but rather according to the needs and characteristics of the family, the specific needs of the child, and the characteristics of the specialist.

Only one specialist is in charge of each case (child and family), but an interdisciplinary group of specialists gives assistance and orients the specialist, sharing its knowledge and providing suggestions. It is the specialist, not the parents, who puts the information together.

What has been presented in this chapter is the result of twenty-two years of working experience with disabled children in Mexico City. In particular, it is the result of eighteen years of work in a center where an interdisciplinary team put into practice the concepts described. Of course, working methods have not remained constant since the work was initiated; they have been modified, adjusted, and have evolved from a basic theoretical and dynamic framework, from experiences with families and their contributions, and from experiences and insights of the personnel that have collaborated with me. To accomplish this type of methodology, a permanent dialogue between all involved individuals is required in order to clarify theoretical and philosophical bases, educational repercussions, and ways to put them into operation. Special attention has been given to the problems faced by parents and their manner of interaction to support each other. This has been a basic operating procedure, since what we hope to accomplish is that all participants share a conceptual frame of reference that is based on conviction and not imposition. This method is imparted to each individual member of the staff as soon as he or she begins to provide services and continues through technical meetings that are organized as encounters for interaction and circles of discussion. Here, concepts and strategies, experiences, and questions are exposed and clarified. A disadvantage of this methodology, from some individuals' perspectives, might be that performance is dependent on the parents. Nevertheless, to the degree that we do a good job of raising the consciousness of parents and provide a clear picture of the type of service they will get, parents become more interested and involved. One disadvantage for parents is the fact that they have to come from their homes to the center, which represents transportation costs and time. Such costs would be minimized if these services were available in different sectors (delegations) throughout the city. This would also allow for optimal use of professionals' time, as it is the only possible way of working as a team.

As regards school-based systems that deal with early intervention and extrafamily institutions such as day-care centers, we consider that the family is still the best means by which to provide care and social experiences for the child. Hispanic people in general prefer to receive assistance from close or distant relatives, if necessary, rather than using a day-care center.

Undoubtedly, more fathers are moving toward becoming the main care givers of children, and occasionally they play a more active role in taking care of the household. Nevertheless, in the early stages of a child's life, the mother-child relationship is critical. In the case of Hispanic mothers, this practice still prevails, in spite of the fact that more and more women are working outside the home. Cultural differences predominate. For example, a Hispanic mother is still expected to supervise homework, clean the house, and prepare meals when she gets home from her work. This is in contrast to Anglo households in which these activities tend to be shared by the husband and wife.

Conclusions

Traditionally early intervention has been justified on the basis of children's needs. Nevertheless, it has been shown that benefits within the family as a group can be greatly enhanced and that a change in the focus of management can have important repercussions. There has also been a change in the conceptualization of intellectual potential as a fixed entity resulting from genetic inheritance. Today the influence of environment and especially of family context is recognized as a powerful force that molds all aspects of development. Early-intervention services should be enhanced because they not only produce beneficial effects directly on the observable behavior of disabled children but also expose secondary problems, reduce costs of further education as these children are integrated into regular schools, and facilitate integration of these children into the family. This will result in a more rapid integration of the child and his or her family into society as a whole.

Another result of our delivery service modality is permanence of population. There is a very low transience rate due to moving to another home, unemployment, pregnancy, and so on.

As regards long-term effects due to lack of continuity in applying our working method and differences in the conceptual frame of reference in further schooling, no significant repercussions in school were observed, although they may exist within the home and the close family environment.

A service delivery model such as ours offers the following advantages:

1. Accommodation of a broad age range of abilities within the limits of early intervention
2. Respect for each child's developmental pace, since we do not work on the basis of a certain disability, but rather on the basis of normal child development
3. Several different types of client services: individual, group, and family support and internal and external support to CENDIs and to professionals and students
4. Individual response to the specific needs of each family nucleus
5. Stimulation without pressure and broader opportunities to socialize with other children and parents according to the timing and needs of each
6. Family orientation to avoid isolation
7. Response to the diverse special needs, not only those of a specific segment of the population or to a specific type of disability
8. Furnishing of teaching materials
9. Cross-categorical teaching

Our service has the potential to become a Resource Center for Early Intervention. We know that there is no single correct philosophy or theoretical base and that each one has advantages and disadvantages. Nevertheless, we must try to work within a context that is in accordance with our own conception of what constitutes appropriate service within the realm of our needs and possibilities.

Education in Mexico is in the process of changing as a result of the educational model adopted by the government in 1992. At our institution we are aware of these changes, and we have started to reorient our services according to the principles of the proposed model. We are sure that early intervention with parents is fundamental. It is through this work that the needed strengths are acquired and developed from the earliest beginnings of life. Focusing on the abilities and potentialities of students with disabilities in the context of their families is critical for their integration into school and ultimately into a society where they will lead productive lives.

References

Bailey, D., and R. Simeonsson. 1988. *Family assessment in early intervention.* U.S.: Merrill.

Bailey, D., and M. Wolery. 1984. *Teaching infants and preschoolers with handicaps.* New York: Macmillan.

Bell, R. Q. 1968. A reinterpretation of the direction of effects in studies of socialization. *Psychological Review* 75:91-95.

Booth, T., and J. Statham. 1988. *The nature of special education: People, places and change.* London: Routledge and Open University Press.

Bromfenbrenner, U. 1977. Toward an experimental ecology of human development. *American Psychology* 32:513-31.

Butler, A., and N. Quisenberry. 1975. *Early childhood programs.* U.S.: Merrill.

Caballero, R. 1982. *Educación tradicional vs. educación contemporánea.* Mexico, DF: APEINAC.

Cabrera, M., and C. Sánchez Palacios. 1980. *La estimulación precoz: un enfoque práctico.* Spain: Pablo del Río.

Cambrodí, A. 1974. *La escolarización del niño subnormal.* Mexico, DF: Editorial Científica Médica.

Connor, F., G. Williamson, and J. Siepp. 1978. *Program guide for infants and toddlers with neuromotor and other developmental dissabilities.* New York: Teachers College Press.

Craig, G. 1992. *Desarrollo psicológico.* Mexico, DF: Prentice Hall Hispanoamericana.

Dallal, E. 1982. *Génesis y estructura de la familia.* Mexico, DF: APEINAC.

Dallal y Castillo, E. 1982. *El niño y la familia.* Mexico, DF: Asociación Científica de Profesionales para el Estudio Integral del Niño.

Department of Public Education. 1992. *Programa de Educación Inicial.* Mexico, DF: SEP.

_____. 1996. *Programa de Desarrollo Educativo, 1995-2000.* Mexico, DF: SEP.

Evans, E. 1987. *Educación infantil temprana: tendencias actuales.* Mexico, DF: Editorial Trillas.

García Etchegoyen, E. 1977. *Estimulación temprana.* Uruguay: Instituto Interamericano del Niño.

Heese, G. 1986. *La estimulación temprana en el niño discapacitado.* Argentina: Editorial Panamericana.

Ibuka, M. 1977. *Kindergarten is too late.* New York: Simon and Schuster.

Kornblit, A., and B. Chomsky. 1984. *Somática familiar.* Barcelona: Gedisa.

Mahler, M. 1977. *El nacimiento psicológico del infante humano.* Buenos Aires: Marymar.

Mapes, M., and J. Mapes. 1988. *Education of children with disabilities from birth to three: A handbook for parents, teachers, and other care providers.* Illinois: Thomas.

Orelove, F., and D. Sobsey. 1987. *Educating children with multiple disabilities.* London: Brookes.

Programa Nacional para el Bienestar y la Incorporación al Desarrollo de las Personas con Discapacidad (DIF). 1995. Mexico, DF: DIF.

Ramos, V., and R. Fernández. 1982. *Psicología genética y la nueva educación.* Mexico, DF: Editorial Ramos.

Rascovsky, A., et al. 1985. *El niño y la familia.* Proceedings of the eleventh Congreso Mundial de la Federación Internacional para la Educación de los Padres. Mexico, DF: APEINAC.

_____. 1982. *Observaciones sobre la fundamentación afectiva de la familia.* Mexico, DF: APEINAC.

Salvador, J. 1989. *La estimulación precoz en la educación especial.* Spain: Ediciones Ceac.

Spitz, R. 1972. *El primer año de vida del niño.* Madrid: Editorial Aguilar.

Erickson, E. 1950. *Childhood and society*. New York: Norton.

Stevens, J., Jr., and E. King. 1987. *Administración de programas de educación temprana y preescolar*. Mexico, DF: Editorial Trillas.

Stow, L., and L. Selfe. 1989. *Understanding children with special needs*. London: Unwin Hyman.

White, B. 1990. *Educating the infant and toddler*. U.S.: Lexiton Books.

Winnicott, D. W. 1987. *Los bebés y sus madres*. Mexico, DF: Editorial Paidós.

3 Early Language Assessment for Spanish-Speaking Children

Border Realities

Donna Jackson-Maldonado

An essential element of successful language intervention is early detection. Current research has begun to show linguistic and cognitive domains that can be assessed at very early ages (Thal and Kaitch, in press; Rescorla 1984; Rescorla and Schwartz 1990; Fischel et al. 1989). Most of this information is available based on normal language development. Studies of English-speaking children have shown that the comprehension and production of vocabulary as well as the use of gestures in children as young as one year are predictors of later language development (Thal and Bates 1988; Thal, Tobias, and Morrison 1991; Thal and Kaitch, in press; Rescorla 1984). Spanish-speaking children not only use a different language to communicate, but live in a different cultural environment independently of whether they reside in their home country or in the United States. Therefore, assessing children from a distinct reality poses a challenge to educators on both sides of the Mexico-U.S. border. Knowledge is needed of how children acquire Spanish, and observational instruments are required that take into consideration the diversity of the language and culture. It is only with this information that generalizations about linguistic and cognitive precursors for Spanish-speaking children can be made.

Cultural Characteristics of the Spanish-Speaking Community

The cultural heritage, value system, language, beliefs, and attitudes of the Spanish-speaking community as a whole, both in Mexico and in the United States, are not shared by the majority of the Anglo community residing in the United States. Even the Hispanic community is not homogeneous. The Spanish-speaking population in the United States comes from a variety of countries and there is more than one reason for people to immigrate: they may be socioeconomic, political, or personal. There is a diversity of social strata, from severe poverty to extreme wealth, although the majority of those who live in the United States (except Miami) has lower incomes. Moreover, in Mexico alone, more than fifty indigenous languages are spoken, and a large percentage of the population is either monolingual, speaking a language other than Spanish, or it is bilingual, speaking Spanish and a non-European language.

Despite this diversity, certain characteristics stand out as compared to non-Hispanics. Foremost, the population that immigrates to the United States shares, as a whole, the Spanish language. This is significant not only on the grammatical level, but on the communicative level as well. Children acquire many more family and person terms at an early age than their English speaking peers because of strong family ties (Langdon 1992; Jackson-Maldonado et al. 1993). Mexican Spanish contains many politeness forms, such as *gracias*, "thank you," *sería usted tan amable de . . .* , "would you be so kind as to . . . ," and conversations begin by first asking about the family, friends, health,and other personal matters rather than getting to the point. During conversations Mexican children are taught to listen, not to speak out or interrupt, and they have more interaction with peers than do English-speaking children (Langdon 1992). Laosa (1982, 1984) has shown that Hispanic mothers are also more directive, whereas Anglo mothers are more descriptive and make more comments about actions.

Educationally there are also differences between Hispanics and non-Hispanics. Hispanic families want their children to be respectable, to learn a profession, to study, to listen to the teacher, to behave, to earn enough to be able to eat, to learn English, to work, to be happy, to do something useful. This is in opposition to U.S. standards, which tell children to do their best, to compete, to be successful, maybe even to be rich (Delgado-Gaitán 1987). Hispanic families do not foster self-realization as much as solidarity with family and friends. The educational system that both lower- and higher-income Hispanic children go through in their homeland is structurally different from the U.S. system. Teaching methodologies differ, mainly because teachers' strategies are different. Book reading is not a common practice and is practically nonexistent among lower-income families (Laosa 1982). Put in a cognitive-style dimension, Hispanic teachers stress field dependent strategies whereas, traditionally, U.S. teachers stress field independent strategies (Jackson and Espino 1983).

Culturally, the differences are also extensive. Mexicans' values of life and death, security and precaution, time, and family unity do not coincide with Anglo values.

The general belief system is deeply rooted in pre-Hispanic and Catholic traditions and customs, and there is a more outright festive and ironic nature to life in general. This contrasts with an Anglo culture, where values are placed on completing tasks and competing to be the best, where culture is as diverse as the many different people that have immigrated to this country, and where family values have deteriorated with a high divorce rate.

Hispanics growing up in the United States and those growing up in their native country may also not share living conditions. Many have immigrated to the United States to look for a better economic situation. A vast majority has changed its consumer status (that is, they now own a VCR and a car) and earn dollars rather than, say, pesos. Still, their living situation remains similar, as they may share a home with the extended family or several other families.

The Spanish-speaking population living in the United States for economic reasons uses the American educational and health care systems. Implied in this system is the ability to follow instructions, fill out forms and return papers on time, behaviors uncommon in their native countries. The illegal status of many places them at a disadvantage in their involvement at school and in receiving adequate medical attention.

As a whole, though, members of the Spanish-speaking community who have immigrated for economic, social, or political reasons share cultural and linguistic characteristics. Their access to information, education, and health services and the possibility of social development, however, vary depending on the background they come from. At the same time, the Spanish-speaking community across the border also shares cultural and linguistic characteristics. Their daily reality, though, is not the same. In their homeland they are usually living closer to family and tradition. On the social level they have legal access to educational and health facilities, not to say a right to use their social and political system.

School Achievement

As mentioned earlier, schooling in most Spanish-speaking countries is field dependent, whereas it is field independent in the United States. Hispanic mothers' language addressed to young children is more directive, and Anglo mothers use a more descriptive style (Laosa 1982, 1984). If these factors, along with less possibility of family involvement (because of language and culture barriers at school), a lower literacy level, and different attitudes toward language are summed up, they may affect the child's ability to succeed in school in the United States. In fact, the high-school dropout rate is very high, and reading level and school achievement are in general below those of English-speaking peers (Trueba 1987).

Taking into consideration this serious disadvantage, it is probable that the frequency of speech and language disorders is even higher than the estimated 10% of the population, due to malnutrition and the difficulty in accessing services because of language, attitude, and political barriers (Langdon 1992). Moreover, few adequate and fair tests are available, either in the United States or Mexico, to assess these children (Jackson-Maldonado 1988; Mattes and Omark 1991; Langdon 1992). It is also true that if developmental lags are detected at earlier ages, the predictions of educational success are higher.

This chapter addresses language and cognitive functions that should be a part of early assessment and thus early detection. First, an overview of domains that need to be observed in children under three are discussed. Second, the availability of information and instruments in Spanish and for Spanish is presented. Finally, a proposal for assessing children on both sides of the border is summarized to give an example of aspects that should be included in early assessment.

Prerequisites of Early Language Development

Most of the first systematic research in child language in the first years of life emphasized language production. Communicative intent and semantic functions based on natural language samples were analyzed (Brown 1973; Bloom 1970; Dore 1974, 1975; Bates 1976). Vocabulary studies looked at number of words produced, relations between word meanings, and generalizations (Nelson 1973; Clark 1973). These studies influenced the field of language disorders. Currently, children are described according to their developmental stage based on MLU (mean length of utterances), which is a measure of language production and word counts, along with communicative ability, often based on natural language samples of language production. New insight in the field, though, has shown that the predictors of language development are not in the realm of language production, but more like a function of language comprehension, gesture use and individual differences (Bates, Bretherton, and Snyder 1988; Thal, Tobias, and Morrison 1991; Thal and Bates 1988; Rescorla and Schwartz 1990; Acredolo and Goodwyn 1988).

These finding are partially based on research that compares normal and deviant language development. Several groups of researchers have taken up the task of analyzing language comprehension and production as well as nonverbal cognitive factors. They have found that word comprehension, and recognitory[2] and communicative[3] gestures are better predictors of early language development than word production (Thal 1991; Thal and Kaitch, in press). A study by Acredolo and Goodwyn (1988) looked at the relation between first words and symbolic gestures, based on maternal interviews. They found positive correlations between gestures depicting objects and vocabulary development. They also found that children who had smaller vocabularies used more gestures. Caselli (1990) showed that children use their first words at the same time as first gestures appear. Developmentally, though, when vocabulary increases, gesture use decreases. Shore (1986) and McCune-Nicolich (1981) found a positive correlation between early word combinations and gestural combinations in children twenty and twenty-four months of age.

Another perspective is seen in studies of children with specific language impairment. Rescorla (1984) showed that these children had fewer play schemas and structured gesture sequences than normal controls and that they seldom used substitute objects for gestures, as normally developing children would. Rescorla (1984, 97) also stated that word comprehension "is a better index of the child's competence in lexical development" than word production.

Research on late talkers carried out by a San Diego group has looked at the relation between language and gesture use as well (Thal and Bates 1988; Thal, Tobias, and Morrison 1991; Thal and Tobias 1992). In this case, late talkers were seen in a follow-up study to determine which aspects of communication could be predictors of language delay rather than disorder. Late talkers were compared to age and language controls. The children who remained delayed after a year were lower in their word comprehension and gesture production (as well as word production) at the first visit. The children who first were delayed, but caught up, used significantly more communicative gestures at the first visit. As Thal states, "based on these studies, comprehension and gesture production were proposed as potential reliable predictors of language outcome" (Thal and Katich 1996, 16).

This short summary of a large body of research shows that despite the fact that language production has typically been the indicator of language delay, language comprehension and gesture use may be better predictors of future language development. The implication is that emphasis be put on measures that assess comprehension as well as production. Because of strong test biases and limitations, natural language samples have come to be a frequent and invaluable source of information on language use. Unfortunately, they are not adequate for determining language comprehension levels, and most of these samples are not used to measure gesture use. Therefore, new measures that depict comprehension and gesture use, along with language production, are much needed for assessing communicative ability in young children, together with natural observations. Although instruments are beginning to appear for analyzing English, little is available for Spanish.

Assessment Instruments Available for Spanish-Speaking Children

Although the developmental tendencies exposed before are mostly based on English-speaking, middle-class children, many of the relations that have been established may be applicable to other languages and social groups. Research carried out in Italy has shown similar predictors and correlations between language and gesture (Volterra and Caselli 1985; Camaioni et al. 1990). A larger cross-linguistic study using parental report instruments also has shown that the relations between language comprehension, language production, and gesture use have the same developmental tendencies in English, Spanish, Italian, Japanese, and American sign language (Fenson et al., Parent report, 1993). More information about the development of Spanish-speaking children in different social contexts is necessary both to reinforce theoretical issues of language and cognition and to assess these children, based on criteria that are known to be language- and culture-specific.

Information from studies of language development has been the foundation of many current assessment instruments. Paradigms have changed and developmental processes have been used to determine language form, content, and use by age and stage (Lahey 1988) and observational techniques have evolved. This has been possible because of new data about how English is acquired. Unfortunately, studies in Spanish language development have not been favored by this ample store of knowledge. Assessment instruments for Spanish are seldom based on Spanish and Hispanic culture; they are more like translations (and sometimes adaptations) of tests developed for English. At the same time, most of them do not have adequate norming, reliability and validity data (Jackson-Maldonado 1993; Mattes and Omark

1991; Langdon 1992). Many times English norms are used for Spanish-speaking children. A brief description of several tests used for young children and an evaluation of their strengths and weaknesses will illustrate this phenomenon.

An extensive review of Spanish-language tests and their norming limitations was done by Merino and Spencer (1983), who carefully analyzed five bilingual tests: the Basic Inventory of Natural Language (BINL) (Herbert, 1980), the Bahia Oral Language Test (BOLT) (Cohen, Cruz, and Bravo, 1977), the Bilingual Syntax Measure I and II (BSM) (Burt, Dulay, and Hernández-Chavez, 1976), the Language Assessment Battery (LAB) (Board of Education of the City of New York 1976), and the Language Assessment Scales I and II (LAS) (DeAvila and Duncan 1986). They considered three types of validity: criterion, content, and construct; four types of reliability: test-retest, interscorer, internal consistency, and interexaminer; and the population on which the test had been normed. Based on these psychometric criteria, they analyzed the strength of each test. Of special interest was whether language and culture differences were considered in the creation of the test. This would be reflected mostly in the content validity measures and in the norming studies. The results of the Merino and Spencer study showed that content validity was not carefully monitored in the Spanish versions of the tests. The Spanish versions seemed to reproduce the English versions. The few cases that tried to obtain relevant vocabulary samples did not use strict procedures. With this initial validity error, norms were obtained that may not truly correspond to the Spanish-speaking child's potential. The test may only reflect how these children performed as compared to the English version of the test. Also, of the tests reviewed by Merino and Spencer, none gave adequate or appropriate norming information. Although none of these tests are applicable to children under three (the population targeted in this paper), their results are of interest as an example of the limitations of Spanish-language testing in general.

The issue of the effectiveness of language tests should not be limited to an analysis of the reliability, validity, and norming. Although the measure may be appropriate in those terms, it is still highly probable that tests contain irrelevant items, culturally inappropriate images or contexts, and, many times, even linguistic errors. A few examples illustrate this point: At the vocabulary level, for instance, the Del Río test (Toronto et al. 1975) uses the word *transportación*, "transportation," which is an Anglicism for *transporte*; and *calefacción*, "heating," to refer to a campfire; *vestuario*, "wardrobe," to refer to what should be *ropa*, "clothing"; and *protegiendo*, "protecting," to refer to a soldier. At the grammatical level, in the Del Río test, oral commands consist of structures such as *pones este libro*, "(you) put this book," *vas a la ventana*, "(you) go to the window," instead of using the correct forms of either the imperative or the subjunctive (for negative commands): *pon* and *no pongas* and *ve* and *no vayas*. Some tests (Carrow 1974; Toronto et al. 1975) use the gerund or infinitive forms for depicting actions as it is done in the English versions. In Spanish, though, these forms cannot be used in isolated contexts as in English (Jackson-Maldonado 1988). The Screening Test of Spanish Grammar (Toronto 1973), a grammatical measure per se, has several grammatical problems: the future is expressed with the canonical suffix *rá*: *comerá*, "will eat," whereas the most commonly used oral form is *ir* + *a* + infinitive verb, *va a comer*, "he will eat"; the form *detrás de* is infrequent in Latin America, especially in children, and *atrás de*, "behind," should be used as a substitute; these are among other errors.

It is evident that there is a bias in the proficiency tests because they base Spanish structures on English concepts and in most cases do not consider form/content or use of the Spanish language. Sometimes, when using translations, they do not even change the order of the items to take into consideration different rates of acquisition. This lack of adaptation may affect the way children relate to the tests and their performance and affect their scores of communicative ability (Labov 1972; Walker 1987; Jackson-Maldonado 1988).

Most of the tests cited above are for children K-6. Fewer measures are available for children under three years of age. Of these, some have been adapted more carefully, whereas others are direct translations of the English versions. The Test de Vocabulario en Imágenes Peabody (TVIP) (Dunn et al. 1986) is one of the few tests that has norms based on Mexican and Puerto Rican children, internal reliability, and content and criterion validity. Although the words it uses were extracted from the English version, the final Spanish version contains several new words. The Prueba de Desarrollo Inicial de Lenguaje (Hresko, Reid, and Hammill 1982) has available norms, based on a small population. It is, however, problematic in that parts of it are direct translations of the English version and more validity information is needed. Moreover, it contains, as well, some of the grammatical problems of previous tests: in the phrase *el carro pego* [sic] *a la bicicleta, pegó*, "hit," requires the dative pronoun *le* before it; the child is requested to repeat the phrase *él ha estado comiendo*, "he has been eating," where the subject *él* could be deleted. The Expressive One-Word Picture Vocabulary Test: Spanish Edition (EOWPVT) (Gardner 1980) is also applicable to children two years and older. Contrary to the other two instruments, this is a direct translation of the English form and contains no Spanish norms. Although the test allows flexibility in word use, which reduces vocabulary errors, the images contain heavy cultural biases. One of the images used is the Statue of Liberty, which obviously is not something Mexican children (in Mexico) may readily identify, and words on the objects depicted are not translated: thus a milk carton says "milk" and not *leche*.

There are two measures that are applicable to early childhood (before the age of two) and observe more communicative behaviors: the Sequenced Inventory of Communication Development (SICD) (Hedrick, Prather, and Tobin 1979) and the Preschool Language Scale-3: Spanish Edition (PLS) (Zimmerman, Steiner, and Pond 1993). The SICD is a direct Cuban-Spanish translation of the English version. The tests examine receptive and expressive language skills. Unfortunately, norms for Spanish are not available, and many Spanish language-specific items are not covered in this instrument (Mattes and Omark 1991). Its strength lies in that it is one of the few tests available for very young children that is applicable to language-disordered populations via parental report. The scale, though, seems to present problems, as validity and reliability criteria are low. The PLS-3 Spanish Edition has recently been revised (Zimmerman, Steiner, and Pond 1993). It is applicable to children from age one. The revision has corrected many grammatical and cultural errors of the earlier version and contains a reference chart for different Spanish dialects, information for interpreting scores, and now has Spanish norms. Although many of the previous errors have been corrected, the test still contains structures such as *tú tomas una cuchara*, "you take a spoon," whereas the imperative form should be *toma la cuchara* (with the subject being deleted, as mentioned before), and *dame una cuchara a mí*, "give me a spoon," where the sought structure is *a mí*, but it is redundant, not obligatory. Like the SICD test, it is a direct translation from English and thus misses many Spanish language- and culture-specific items and structures but contains many items that are relevant for young children, and its application includes a variety of tasks that make the test more interactive. The scale also includes as task analysis checklist that summarizes by age groups different language functions that should be present and an articulation screener that is Spanish specific. The test has a language sample checklist that summarizes language form, content, and use. Unfortunately these checklists (except for articulation) are taken directly from English and map onto English ages and profiles, whereas their occurrence in Spanish may be present at different rates and moments. In general, however, although some basics of Spanish language acquisition are missing, it does provide one of the few instruments that have a more ample perspective.

The tests analyzed above address some language components that are relevant for children under three, such as vocabulary comprehension and production and early structures. Many clinicians use spontaneous language samples rather than tests. As stated above, though, at this early age is seems that one of the best predictors of future language development, along with comprehension, is gesture use. None of the tests analyzes this component in a systematic way. Furthermore, most of the tests that have been reviewed here share basic methodological and theoretical problems:

1. Very few tests have been developed specifically for Spanish, most are translations with inappropriate adaptations;
2. little if any adequate content validity development exists;
3. very little norming information is available; usually English norms are used, because most Spanish items are translations of English tests;
4. the tests have not been adapted to be culturally and linguistically relevant;
5. most (except the last five mentioned) target the school age population; only two can be used in children under age three;
6. many contain errors in vocabulary and grammar.

Assessing young Spanish-speaking children, then, is a difficult task. New proposals with adequate norms are necessary. As current U.S. legislation mandates, family involvement is a must. If parents are involved in the evaluation process, it could be a clinical asset as well. Research in other languages has shown that maternal reports can be a good index of language development in preschool children. Both the maternal report developed by Rescorla (1989) and the MacArthur Communicative Development Inventory (CDI) (Fenson et al., *MacArthur*, 1993) have been shown to be efficient ways to determine developmental tendencies in children below three years of age. A Spanish version of the CDI, along with other assessment measures, has been the goal of a long-term project to obtain data about language development and propose means to assess children in infancy. The study integrates observation with parental involvement.

Language and Cognition Assessment for Spanish-Speaking Children

The Language and Cognition Battery for Spanish-speaking Infants and Toddlers (Jackson-Maldonado and Thal 1994) addresses the domains that are considered to be important in early language development: comprehension and production of language and gesture use. The measures developed are based on (but not translated from) a previous study done in English and Italian (Bates, Bretherton, and Snyder 1988; Camaioni et al. 1990). Linguistically and culturally, the instruments have been carefully adapted to Spanish. The immediate objectives are to determine developmental tendencies, correlations, and predictors rather than to create instruments that can be used in clinical settings. In the future, though, parts of the battery will be applicable to testing children, and others will be useful only in answering theoretical questions and for obtaining information about language and cognitive development in Spanish-speaking children.

The battery consists of eight instruments that analyze linguistic and cognitive phenomena: comprehension and production of words and sentences (both known and unknown) and recognitory and combinatorial gesture use. Information is obtained by different observational means: maternal reports, controlled experimental situations, and natural language samples. Because of the position sustained thus far, it is important to underline aspects of the instruments that had to be modified, substituted, created, or discarded because of language and culture differences. Tendencies that have been found thus far will be summarized to show which domains of language and nonverbal communication should be considered in the evaluation process.

The MacArthur Inventario del Desarrollo de Habilidades Comunicativas

The MacArthur Inventario del Desarrollo de Habilidades Comunicativas (IDHC) (Jackson-Maldonado, Thal, and Bates 1992) is based on the English and Italian versions of the MacArthur Communicative Development Inventory (Fenson et al., *MacArthur*, 1993). The Spanish version in an adaptation (not a translation) that takes into consideration language-specific and culturally relevant items (Jackson-Maldonado et al. 1993). It shares the format of the other versions in that it is a parental report, which assesses vocabulary comprehension, production, gesture use, and early structures through recognition, not memory.

The IDHC has two formats: "Primeras Palabras y Gestos" and "Palabras y Enunciados." It is applicable to normal children between eight and thirty months of age. The first form, for children between eight and eighteen months, has sections of vocabulary comprehension, production, and gesture use. The second form, for children between sixteen and thirty months, only reports on vocabulary production and includes early language structures, such as verb forms, mean length of three utterances, and phrase complexity. At present the data being collected are based on normally developing children, and therefore it cannot be predicted how these forms will be applicable to language disordered children. The English form, though, has been used for different types of populations.

The IDHC is divided into word categories that are based on the structure of the language. Following are a few examples that illustrate the adaptation process:

1. Pronouns and articles: Because Spanish is a language with gender and number markers in the pronominal and article systems, the pronoun and article sections are larger.
2. Food: The food section includes both foods common to Mexican children (this instrument is based on Mexican Spanish) and some items that apply to Spanish-speaking children in the United States.
3. People: There are more items in this section, including cousins, priests, and god-parents.
4. Gestures: Some culturally relevant gestures are included, such as crossing oneself.
5. First phrases: The section is based solely on Spanish language acquisition data.
6. M3L (mean length of three utterances): Mean length of utterance is based on word rather than morpheme count because morpheme count is not relevant to the type of analysis that is being done.
7. Words: The total number is greater and the words are not translations of the words used in the English version. Some words are the same, though, as they pertain to children in early infancy.
8. Contact system: Whereas in the English study forms are mailed out to families, in the Spanish study all contact is done personally.

Norms have now been calculated and will be available shortly (Thal, Jackson-Maldonado, and Fenson 1999). Currently preliminary norms are available (Swaine et al. 1996), and validity and reliability studies have shown that the IDHC shares most of the strengths of its English counterpart (Fenson et al., *MacArthur*, 1993; Parent report, 1993). Strong correlations were also shown between the IDHC and natural language samples (Jackson-Maldonado et al. 1993).

Family involvement is a prerequisite of maternal report. Because of this, the way in which families are contacted and asked to participate in the norming study is completely different from that of the English study. All contact is done through personal means, in a variety of settings. Of particular interest is the fact that many lower-income families are included in the study. Some of the parents in these families have low literacy rates or are illiterate. In this case, parents receive help in filling out the forms. It is possible, though, that illiteracy is not the only problem in filling out forms; it may be a cultural issue as well. In order to address this problem, specific contrastive research is currently being carried out to determine differences in the population based on the mother's and father's educational level.

Spontaneous Naming

In this task, the child is presented with ten objects and asked what they are and what they can be used for. The objective is to see if the child can name the objects or uses a recognitory gesture. The objects used in this measure are age appropriate items that are familiar in most occidental cultures.

Some of the objects used in the original English study were changed. A toothbrush, for instance, was substituted for a comb. This was done because even though brushing teeth is important, it is not as culturally relevant within the general Mexican population.

Single Gesture Production

This experimental measure uses the same objects as the previous instrument, but in this case gestures and vocabulary are elicited through imitation. The goal is to determine whether the child reacts similarly to recognitory gesture in four modalities: using a real or substitute object and accompanying the gesture with neutral or support language

The same object modifications as in the spontaneous-naming task were used in this task, and one gesture was changed in relation to babies.

Comprehension Books

Comprehension Books follow the traditional format of forced choice picture identification. Two words are presented in picture pairs, and the child is asked to point to one of them. There are two books: Book I is based on comprehension of nouns, and Book II on verbs and adjectives. All pictures are monitored to include only relevant information.

Words for both books were selected from a Spanish child language data base and from frequency lists of words comprehended in the preliminary norming study of the IDHC. Words were chosen to create pairs that belonged to similar semantic classes and had shown the same level of frequency of occurrence. This means that the words that are used in this test are based solely on Spanish language acquisition. Care was also taken to insure that the elicitation sentences used for Book II (verbs and adjectives) were grammatical and appropriate. Verbs were conjugated in tenses, shown to be those first acquired (González 1983; Beléndez Sotero 1980; López Ornat 1994; Peronard 1987; Hernández Pina 1984). The sentences used in the elicitation respected Spanish structures and each pair of words elicited contained the same structure. Both words were either transitive or intransitive, and both contained a clitic *(la, lo)* for direct objects or a reflexive *se*, if necessary (Bicaci 1995).

Novel Concepts

This experimental measure assesses the initial acquisition and delayed recall of novel nouns and verbs with novel objects and actions. Two objects were created, and a novel action was applied to them. The names and verbs also included invented Spanish words. In the task, the interviewer shows the child the object and demonstrates what it does. The child is then asked to manipulate the objects the same way the interviewer did. In a second session, the child is asked to recall (by comprehension alone) the objects' names and to repeat the actions that are applied to them.

The objects and actions of the original English study (Bates, Bretherton, and Snyder 1988) were used in the Spanish version. The names of the objects were selected so as to insure appropriate Spanish phonological and early word structure, such as consonant repetitions, and most frequent verbs (final *ar*).

Canonical Commands

This task analyzes the comprehension of canonical and noncanonical commands. The children are asked to carry out an action related to two objects that are presented equidistant to them. One action depicts what is normally done with the object, and the other is something not commonly done with the object.

All sentences for this measure were generated for Spanish, although the objects are similar to the English version. Therefore, while in English a command would say, "Give Mommy the book," in Spanish the clitic *le* and preposition *a* are used: *Dale el libro a mamá.*

Scripted Event Sequences

This is a complex task that measures the amount and sequence of gestures in a scripted event. The child is asked to repeat a sequence based on what a teddy bear does that the interviewer acts out. Each event has four actions. This measure follows the basic parameters of the English version (O'Connell and Gerard 1985; Bates, Bretherton, and Snyder 1988) with respect to the number of events, sequence of events, etc., and includes the same basic events: bathing, eating, and sleeping.

Several modifications were made of the English version. Teddy was not reading a book (this is not common in Hispanic culture), and he was rocked rather than kissed. The instructions were also modified. Whereas in English the child is "invited" (can you do it?) to participate, a more directive form is used in Spanish *ahora hazlo tú*, "now you do it," *ahora te toca a ti*, "now it's your turn."

Spontaneous Language Sample

This part of the battery uses natural interactions with the parent and/or researcher. The parent and interviewer interact naturally with the child in three different segments and with a variety of age-appropriate toys. All children are given the same toys, and they select which ones they will use.

Different toys had to be selected for children in the lower-income group. They only looked at colorful plastic toys, but would not play with them. Therefore, similar toys (play food, pots, etc., instead of commercial plastic ones) were brought in that were commonly found in Mexican markets. Of particular importance here was also the type of interaction. Although the mother was instructed not to be intrusive or directive, this is contrary to Hispanic mothers' interactions. Therefore, mothers tended to be more directive and controlling than Anglo mothers, and this was accepted.

The project using these instruments was conducted in three different sociocultural and linguistic environments: monolingual Spanish-speaking middle-class children in central Mexico, monolingual Spanish-speaking lower-income children in

Querétaro, Mexico, and "second-language-contact" Mexican lower-income children residing in San Diego, California. The first stage of the project included a total of two hundred children in San Diego and Mexico in five age groups (forty per group): ten, twelve, twenty, twenty-eight, and thirty-six months. The second stage extended the population to include lower-income children and had a total of fifty subjects in the same age groups.

A complete proposal based on the results will be available in the near future. Several paradigms are part of the analyses: individual differences, effects of distinct experimental measures, relations between language and gestures, predictors of language development, differences between populations, validity and reliability of the measures, and development of norms for the IDHC. In this paper several issues are presented; complete answers will be available in the forthcoming publication of the results.

Experimental Measures

The battery uses three observational techniques: experimental measures, parental reports, and natural language samples. The latter two answer questions about parental involvement and interaction. First of all, can parents be a reliable source of information about their children's language development? Secondly, can their interaction with their children yield data similar to experimental measures? In response to these questions, analyses of the data may produce interesting results.

Correlations between measures may show whether parents report on language in a way similar to how they interact with their children in a "natural situation." The analyses will contrast the IDHC with natural language samples based on number of words, composition of the vocabulary, and mean length of utterance. They will also contrast vocabulary across all other measures. Tendencies thus far show strong correlations between all measures (Jackson-Maldonado et al. 1993, 1994).

Population Similarities and Differences

One of the issues that these data may respond to is whether socioeconomic status (SES) and second-language contact have an effect on language comprehension, production, and gesture use. Initial results have shown differences across all populations in relation to different aspects of language and cognition. The complete analyses of all measures, taking into consideration the three groups of children, will yield important data about what domains are most affected.

The questions that the SES differences bring forth are whether lower-income and middle-class mothers have the same notion of what is being asked of them on parental reports. A reflection on what their child understands is a rather abstract concept that may cause misconceptions that lead to overreporting. Social and educational factors and data from research with lower-income families would indicate that lower-income mothers may have difficulties reporting on their children's language (Hart and Risley 1995; Fischel et al. 1989). Results from the IDHC will be most helpful in attesting to this fact or refuting it. Furthermore, the comprehension of nouns versus verbs and adjectives, as observed in the Comprehension Books, will show whether mothers' reporting and children's direct behavior are similar.

The results of gesture use will give another perspective of the effect that SES and second-language contact have on development. Gestures are observed in experimental settings in different modalities: maternal report of communicative and recognitory gestures, as well as simple and sequential gestures in an elicited situation. It is expected that this will be one of the least affected domains if language use is similar. If lower-SES children fall behind their peers in language use, though, previous research (Thal and Bates 1988; Thal, Tobias, and Morrison 1991; Thal and Tobias 1992) suggests that communicative and gesture use may also be different. The Spanish data will provide evidence to either support or refute previous findings as to the role gestures play in language development.

Another important aspect of language that can be observed through the language and cognition data is the way first grammatical structures are used. Most of the information obtained from this project in this realm is through parental report. Data from natural language samples are also beginning to be analyzed for grammatical structures. Different aspects of grammar and word combinations across the different populations will be an important source in ascertaining strategies that children use in early Spanish syntax.

Vocabulary and Gestures as Predictors of Language Development

In previous sections it was pointed out that vocabulary comprehension and gesture use were predictors of future language development. To address this issue, several measures may be compared through correlational analyses. As evidence is now available on how English-speaking children behave on these tasks and what the results mean, these data may be useful in analyzing the results of the language and cognition battery. Spanish data will show whether gestures and comprehension, along with word production, are good indexes of language development (Thal, Tobias, and Morrison 1991; Thal and Kaitch, in press; Rescorla 1984). It seems possible, based on a first look at the results, that in Spanish vocabulary comprehension and production and gestures are precursors of communication. It is not far fetched, then, to propose that word production alone should not be an indicator of communicative ability.

Conclusions

This chapter has shown that early language should be assessed from a variety of linguistic and cognitive domains using different observational techniques. The data obtained through parental report or direct interaction with the children on language inventories are important sources in the evaluation process. Family involvement was stressed as an integral part of any observation. The assessment of children from diverse socioeconomic groups and with a second language was seen as an important issue to further understanding of the Hispanic population living on both sides of the U.S.-Mexico border. A brief review of available Spanish language tests showed that they are limited in number and scope. To solve this problem, a set of measures was proposed that aids in understanding how language develops in Spanish. The Language and Cognition Battery presented in this chapter has been a guideline for obtaining information about Spanish-language acquisition. It has the advantage of assessing a variety of linguistic and cognitive domains that are important aspects of the communicative abilities of children under three. Results will soon be available to support the hypothesis proposed in this paper.

One of the basic tasks in assessing young children's language is to determine which domains should be analyzed. This chapter proposed that children under three should at least be assessed in comprehension and production of vocabulary and early sentence structures, as well as cognitive predictors such as recognitory gestures.

The role that parents play in the assessment process was also discussed. It was suggested that information obtained from parental report was as reliable as, if not more reliable than, "natural" observations. The question was raised whether lower income parents had the same ability to report on their children's language as their middle-class counterparts.

The Language and Cognition Battery provides a guideline for what should be included in assessing young children's communicative ability. One of its great advantages is that it requires parental involvement and child-mother and child-interviewer interaction to elicit information. The variety of data obtained from this battery will show how Spanish is acquired and indicates some of the domains that should be assessed. Parts of the battery will be available in the near future as assessment instruments that involve the clinician and the family.

Notes

[1]Parts of the research for this paper were supported by a grant given to Donna Thal and Donna Jackson-Maldonado by the John D. and Catherine T. MacArthur Foundation, Network in Early Childhood Transitions. Special thanks for the use of the data are given to Donna Thal.

[2]Such as using a comb, using a phone to pretend to talk, etc.

[3]Such as, saying bye-bye, pointing, requesting an object with an outstretched arm, etc.

References

Acredolo, L., and S. Goodwyn. 1988. Symbolic gesturing in normal infants. *Child Development* 59:450-66.

Bates, E. 1976. *Language and context.* New York: Academic Press.

Bates, E., I. Bretherton, and L. Snyder. 1988. *From first words to grammar.* Cambridge: Cambridge University Press.

Beléndez Sotero, P. 1980. Repetitions and the acquisition of the Spanish verb system. Master's thesis, Harvard School of Education.

Bloom, L. 1970. *One word at a time.* The Hague: Mouton.

Board of Education of the City of New York. 1976. *Language Assessment Battery.* Palo Alto: Houghton Mifflin.

Brown, R. 1973. *A first language.* Cambridge: Harvard University Press.

Burt, M., H. Dulay, and E. Hernández-Chávez. 1976. *Bilingual syntax measure*. San Francisco: Harcourt Brace Jovanovich.

Camaioni, L., M. C. Caselli, E. Longobardi, and V. Volterra. 1990. Construction and validation of a parent report instrument for assessing communicative and linguistic development in the second year of life. Paper presented at the Fifth International Congress for the Study of Child Language, Budapest, Hungary.

Carrow, E. 1974. *Test of auditory comprehension of language English/Spanish*. Allen, TX: Learning Concepts.

Caselli, M. C. 1990. Communicative gestures and first words. In *From gesture to language in hearing and deaf children*, ed. V. Volterra and C. J. Erting. New York: Springer.

Clark, E. V. 1973. What's in a word? On the child's acquisition of semantics in his first language. In *Cognitive development and the acquisition of language*, ed. T. E. Moore. New York: Academic Press.

Cohen, A. D., R. Cruz, R. Bravo. 1977. *Bahia Oral Language Test*. Berkeley, CA.

DeAvila, E., and S. Duncan. 1986. *Language Assessment Scales I and II*. San Rafael, CA: Linguametrics Group.

Delgado-Gaitán, C. 1987. Parent perceptions of school: Supportive environments for children. In *Success or failure?*, ed. H. T. Trueba. Cambridge, MA: Newbury House.

Dore, J. 1974. A pragmatic description of early language development. *Journal of Psycholinguistic Research* 4:343-50.

_____. 1975. Holophrases, speech acts and language universals. *Journal of Child Language* 2:21-40.

Dunn, Lloyd, D. Lugo, E. Padilla, and Leona Dunn. 1986. *Test de Vocabulario en Imágenes Peabody*. Circle Pines, MN: American Guidance Service.

Fenson, L., P. Dale, S. Reznick, D. Thal, E. Bates, J. Hartung, S. Pethick, and J. Reilly. 1993. *MacArthur Communicative Development Inventories: User's guide and technical manual*. San Diego, CA: Singular Press.

Fenson, L., P. Dale, S. Pethick, D. Jackson-Maldonado, D. Thal, V. Marchman, E. Bates, V. Gutiérrez Clellen, T. Ogura, Y. Yamashita, T. Murase, M. Caselli, P. Casadio, J. Reilly, and U. Bellugi. 1993. Parent report data on communicative development in five languages. Symposium presented at the Sixth International Congress for the Study of Child Language, Trieste, Italy.

Fischel, J. E., G. J. Whitehurst, M. B. Caulfied, and B. C. DeBaryshe. 1989. Language and growth in children with expressive language delay. *Pediatrics* 82:218-22.

Flores, M., D. Thal, D. Jackson-Maldonado. 1996. Language on the edge: Development of Spanish-speaking toddlers living in a border city. Poster presented at the Symposium on Research in Child Language Disorders. Madison, WI.

García Coll, C. 1990. Developmental outcome of minority infants: a process-oriented look into our beginnings. *Child development* 61:270-89.

Gardner, M. F. 1980. *Expressive one-word picture vocabulary test*. Novato, CA: Academic Therapy.

González, G. 1983. Expressing time through verb tenses and temporal expressions in Spanish: Age 2.0-4.6. *NABE* 6:69-82.

Hart, B., and T. R. Risley. 1995. *Meaningful differences in the everyday experience of young American children*. Baltimore: Paul Brookes.

Hedrick, D., E. Prather, and A. Tobin. 1979. *Sequenced inventory of communication development*. Seattle: University of Washington Press.

Herbert, C. 1980. *The basic inventory of natural language*. San Bernardino, CA: Checkpoint.

Hernández-Pina, F. 1984. *Teorías psico-sociolingüísticas y su aplicación a la adquisición del español com lengua materna*. Madrid: Siglo XXI.

Hresko, W., D. Reid, and D. Hammill. 1982. *Prueba del desarrrollo inicial del lenguaje*. Austin: Pro-Ed.

Jackson, S., and L. Espino. 1983. Cultural antecedents of cognitive style variables in Mexican-American children. In *Early childhood bilingual education*, ed. T. Escobedo. New York: Teachers College Press.

Jackson-Maldonado, D. 1988. Evaluación del lenguaje infantil: Enfoque transcultural. In *Lenguaje oral y escrito*, ed. A. Ardila and F. Ostrosky-Solis. Mexico, DF: Trillas.

_____. 1993. Mexico and the U.S.: A cross-cultural perspective on the education of deaf children. In *Multicultural issues in deafness*, ed. K. Christensen and G. Delgado. New York: Longman.

Jackson-Maldonado, D., V. Marchman, D. Thal, E. Bates, and V. Gutiérrez-Clellen. 1993. Early lexical acquisition in Spanish-speaking infants and toddlers. *Journal of Child Language* 20:523-50.

Jackson-Maldonado, D., and D. Thal. 1994. Lenguaje y cognición en los primeros años de vida: Resultados preliminares. *Psicología y Sociedad* 21:21-27.

Jackson-Maldonado, D., D. Thal, and E. Bates. 1992. *Fundación MacArthur, Inventario del Desarrollo de Habilidades Comunicativas*. San Diego, CA: Developmental Psychology Lab, San Diego State University.

Jackson-Maldonado, D., D. Thal, and K. Muzinek. 1998. Gestos, comprensión y producción de palabras: Predictores del desarrollo lingüístico. *Nueva Revista de Filología Hispánica*.

Jackson-Maldonado, D., D. Thal, K. Muzinek, and E. Bicaci. 1994. Language and cognition in Spanish-speaking children: Preliminary results. Miniseminar held at the American Speech-Language-Hearing Association Convention, New Orleans, LA.

Labov, W. 1972. The logic of nonstandard English. In *Language in the inner city*, ed. W. Labov. Philadelphia: University of Pennsylvania Press.

Lahey, M. 1988. *Language disorders and language development*. New York: Macmillan.

Langdon, H. 1992. Language communication and sociocultural patterns in Hispanic families. In *Hispanic children and adults with communication disorders*, ed. H. W. Langdon and L. L. Cheng. Gaithersburg, MD: Aspen Publication.

Laosa, L. M. 1982. School, occupation, culture and family: The impact of parental schooling on the parent-child relationship. *Journal of Educational Psychology* 74:791-827.

Laosa, L. M. 1984. Ethnic, socioeconomic, and home language influences upon early performance on measures of abilities. *Journal of Educational Psychology* 76:1178-98.

López-Ornat, S. 1994. *La adquisición de la lengua española*. Madrid: Siglo XXI.

Maez, L. 1983. The acquisition of noun and verb morphology in 18-24-month-old Spanish-speaking children. *NABE* 7:53-68.

Mattes, L., and D. Omark. 1991. *Speech and language assessment for the bilingual handicapped*. San Diego, CA: Academic Communication.

McCune-Nicolich, L. 1981. Toward symbolic functioning: Structure of early pretend games and potential parallels with language. *Child Development* 52:785-97.

Merino, B. J., and M. Spencer. 1983. The comparability of English and Spanish versions of oral language proficiency instruments. *NABE* 7:1-31.

Nelson, K. 1973. Structure and strategy in learning to talk. *Monographs of the Society for Research in Child Development* 38:1-137.

O'Connell, B., and A. Gerard. 1985. Scripts and scraps: The development of sequential understanding. *Child Development* 56:671-81.

Peronard, M. 1987. *El lenguaje, un enigma*. Santiago de Chile: Ediciones Don Quixote.

Rescorla, L. 1984. Individual differences in early language development and their predictive significance. *Acta Paedologica* 1:97-115.

_____. 1989. The language development survey. A screening tool for delayed language in toddlers. *Journal of Speech and Hearing Disorders* 54:587-99.

Rescorla, L., and E. Schwartz. 1990. Outcome of toddlers with specific expressive language delay. *Applied Psycholinguistics* 11:393-408.

Shore, C. 1986. Combinatorial play, conceptual development and early multi-word speech. *Developmental Psychology* 22:184-90.

Swaine, K., C. Renda, D. Jackson-Maldonado, D. Thal, and L. Fenson. 1996. Norms for the Spanish language version of the MacArthur Communicative Development Inventories. Poster presented at the International Conference of Infant Studies, Providence, RI.

Thal, D. 1991. Language and cognition in normal and late-talking toddlers. *Topics in Language Disorders* 11:33-42.

Thal, D., and E. Bates. 1988. Language and gesture in late talkers. *Journal of Speech and Hearing Research* 31:115-23.

Thal, D., D. Jackson-Maldonado, and D. Acosta. 1994. Language and gesture in Spanish-speaking toddlers. Poster presented at the International Conference on Infant Studies. Paris, France.

Thal, D., and J. Katich. 1996. Does the early bird always catch the worm? Predicaments in early identification of specific language impairment. In *The measurement of communication and language*, Vol. 6, *Assessment*, ed. K. P. Cole, P. Dale., and D. Thal. Baltimore: Brookes.

Thal, D., and S. Tobias. 1992. Communicative gestures in children with delayed onset of oral expressive vocabulary. *Journal of Speech and Hearing Research* 35:1281-89.

_____. 1994. Relationships between language and gestures in normal developing and late-talking toddlers. *Journal of Speech and Hearing Research* 37:157-70.

Thal, D., S. Tobias, and D. Morrison. 1991. Language and gesture in late talkers: A one year follow-up. *Journal of Speech and Hearing Research* 34:604-12.

Toronto, A. 1973. *Screening test of Spanish grammar*. Evanston, IL: Northwestern Univ. Press.

Toronto, A., D. Leverman, L. Hanna, P. Rosenzweig, and A. Maldonado. 1975. *Del Río Language Screening Test*. Austin, TX: National Education Laboratory.

Trueba, H. T. 1987. *Success or failure?* Cambridge, MA: Newbury House.

Walker, C. 1987. Hispanic achievement: Old views and new perspectives. In *Success or Failure?*, ed. H. T. Trueba. Cambridge, MA: Newbury House.

Volterra, V., and C. Caselli. 1985. From gestures and vocalizations to signs and words. In *Sign language research '83*, ed.W. Stokoe and V. Volterra. Silver Springs, MD: Linstok.

Zimmerman, I., V. Steiner, and R. Pond. 1993. *Preschool language scale-Spanish*. San Antonio, TX: The Psychological Corp.

Parents, Families, and Communities Ensuring Children's Rights

It's a Good "IDEA"

Elba I. Reyes

Parents Impacting Change

History demonstrates that laws and legislation aimed at providing services to children with disabilities were preceded by civil action and landmark court cases that aroused national public concern. During the 1950s and 1960s, parents learned from the models of social activism how to organize into interest groups. They learned how to inform the community and the general public of needed reforms in the public educational system regarding education for children with special needs. Meeting in community agency buildings, churches, and even their own homes, parents organized and conducted classes to teach other parents (and anyone who was interested) about their rights, their children's rights, and how to assure that public policy would safeguard those rights (Turnbull and Turnbull 1997). Parent-to-parent training went beyond issues of how to take care of their children. They also learned about the need for laws to protect other basic human rights. Some of these initial informal groups became formal, well-respected organizations. For example, in 1950 parents from across the country established the National Association of Parents and Friends of Mentally Retarded Children, now known as The ARC, one of this country's most powerful advocacy groups. Parents' united efforts have resulted in landmark court cases that have helped shape the intent and focus of legislation regarding children's and parents' rights (e.g., *Hobson v Hansen* 1967; *Larry P. v Riles* 1974; *Mills v D.C. Board of Ed* 1972; *PARC v Commonwealth of Pennsylvania* 1971).

Families soon learned that parent and community advocacy is the most effective way to impact change among policy makers regarding an individual's rights. Perhaps the best examples of the efficacy of this type of advocacy was that (a) the decisions made in the courts became the hallmark of the original law, the *Education of All Handicapped Children Act* (P. L. 94-142, 1975), which is now known as the *Individuals with Disabilities Act of 1997* (Office of Special Education and Rehabilitation Services 1997), and (b) that the intent of the law has been maintained for over twenty years. The long-term result has been a change in the political and philosophical attitude in this country toward public education (Morse, Paul, and Roselli-Kostoryz 1997).

Foundations For Public Law

The *Individuals with Disabilities Education Act of 1997* (IDEA-97) has its history in the civil rights movement of the 1960s. During that time, individual human rights and equity in education were strongly debated issues around which laws and legislation were subsequently enacted during the 1970s. The legislation that stemmed from that era and that changed the educational experiences of children with disabilities was the *Education of All Handicapped Children Act*, known as Public Law 94-142.

Prior to the passage of P.L. 94-142 in 1975, over one million children were denied public education, and parents were blamed as the cause of their children's disability (Bettelheim 1967; Marcus 1977; Oliver, Cole, and Hollingsworth 1991). The parent-as-cause attitude permeated medical, social, and educational services. Parents were made to feel guilty and powerless, and many of children with disabilities were institutionalized or simply kept at home. The passage of P.L. 94-142 was an important turning point because it shifted part of the responsibility of the education of children with disabilities to the government sector. It was designed to fund public education in order to provide both direct and indirect services and support for children with disabilities. The law also initiated the change from a parent-as-cause attitude to a parent-as-partner philosophy. As a result, today more than 5.8 million children with disabilities are in classrooms receiving services that will help prepare many of them for their future roles in our society (Schulte, Osborne, and Erchul 1998).

The important components in P.L. 94-142 that were shaped by advocacy groups include the following:

> All public schools must ensure a free and public education to all children with disabilities at no cost to the parents, a provision referred to as FAPE.

> To the extent possible, the free and public education for all children should occur in an educational environment with their peers without disabilities. This concept of least restrictive environment provides for an array of education models, from services in the students' regular, general education classroom to education at home, or in institutional or private settings.
>
> Parents' and children's rights are safeguarded through due process. This means that public school agencies must ensure that parents are fully informed and understand all information regarding the evaluation of their child for special services. Furthermore, anytime parents are contacted and consent for evaluation must be obtained, all pertinent information must be made available to the parents in their primary language. In addition, if parents do not agree with the identification, evaluation, and educational placement of their child or if they feel that the provisions of FAPE have been violated, they have the right to request a hearing.
>
> The parents of children with disabilities have the right to inspect and review all education records with respect to the identification, evaluation, and educational placement of their child and to ensure that the provision of FAPE has been applied to their child.
>
> Parents must be allowed to be active participants in developing an Individualized Education Program (IEP) for their child. The IEP is a written statement that (a) defines the child's needs and current level of educational performance, (b) sets goals and objectives, (c) details the related services that are needed to help the child meet those goals and, (d) identifies the appropriate setting for the child as well as the start date and duration of those services.

Clearly, the rights of parents and their children were addressed in that legislation.

Vigilance Continued

Although the right to an education for all children was legislated in 1975, parents and community leaders continued to be vigilant. They challenged schools, school districts, and the courts to assure that the law was applied in appropriate ways. Often, courts interpreted the law in ways that favored parents' perceptions of the education and educational services their children should have. However, decisions have also been made based on the intent of the law that have not favored children's services. The following will provide some examples of both instances.

Defining the Law: Least Restrictive Environment and Minimum Standards of Education

Two areas that have become points of conflict between school districts and parents are the level of education that schools are expected to provide under the law and the child's educational placement. For example, in the case of *Board of Education, Sacramento City Unified School District v Holling* (786, F. Sup. 874, E.D.Cal.1992), the courts decided in favor of the parents' petition regarding least restrictive environment. In this case, the parents of a child with moderate mental retardation wanted their child to receive her education in the regular classroom. This was an important decision for two reasons: first, it established the application of the four factor criteria to determine the least restrictive environment and, second, it addressed not only the issue of academic progress, but also that of the nonacademic benefits of education.

The four-factor criteria to be considered in determining least restrictive environment are:

- The educational benefits of the placement
- The nonacademic benefits to the student
- The effects of the child's placement on the teacher and the other students in the class, and
- The cost of the placement

In this case, the parents of the young girl demonstrated that the regular classroom was educationally beneficial: their daughter was meeting her IEP goals and had increased her motivation to learn. They demonstrated that there were also nonacademic gains: she had developed friendships in the class, was excited about learning, and had improved her self-confidence. The parents were able to prove that the child did not disrupt the class and that she did not present any discipline problems for the teacher. Finally, it was decided that the cost of placing the child in a regular classroom would not increase beyond the cost of having her in a special education classroom. As a result, their daughter was placed in the regular education classroom with her friends and with the support services she needed to meet her objectives.

In contrast, in the case of *Board of Education v Rowley* (1982) the court decided that schools needed to provide only a minimum standard of educational opportunity. The case concerned an eight-year-old girl with profound hearing loss. The district had provided a tutor and a hearing aid, and the student was performing better than average in her class. However, the parents contended that the child was not reaching her maximum level of potential as was evident in the discrepancy between her potential and her actual achievement scores. They requested a sign language interpreter to enhance her educational experience. The Supreme Court maintained that it was not the role of public schools to assist students to reach their maximum levels of learning potential (McEllistrem, Roth, and Cox 1998). Rather, it was enough for the child to "receive passing grades and to pass from grade to grade" (458 U.S. 176, 102S.Ct. 3034, 1982).

Defining the Law: Private Schools as Placement Alternatives and Medical Support Services

In *Florence County School District Four v Carter* (1993), the parents felt that the public school was not providing an appropriate education as required in their child's IEP, and that the school district was not providing an appropriate alternative. They decided to place their son in a private school at the expense of the school district. The school district argued that the private school was not an approved setting and, therefore, the parents should pay for the tuition. However, the Supreme Court decided that when the present educational setting is not appropriate, the school district must provide an alternative setting. In this case the Court ruled that the tuition for the private school was to be paid by the school district because the district had not provided an appropriate alternative.

A controversial and milestone case that involved medical interventions in the classroom was *Irving Independent School District v Tatro* (1984). This was an important case because many children with disabilities require health services in order to benefit from education. An eight-year-old girl with spina bifida needed intermittent catherization during the school day. The school district argued that catherization is a medical procedure that the school staff was neither trained nor required to perform. However, the Supreme Court agreed with the parents by determining that procedures that did not need to be carried out by a physician could be carried out either by the school nurse or another person in the school with proper training. This case set a precedent for many other families whose children required health services that the schools had not been willing to perform, thereby preventing the children from attending school and benefiting from the social and educational benefits that other children were enjoying. Today, these children are in schools where they are making friends and learning.

By empowering themselves through group advocacy, parents and families have been able to impact educational policy and practice. Parents are no longer viewed as the cause of their children's disabilities, but rather as partners in designing appropriate service programs that have helped their children gain access to a better quality of life. However, advocacy is an on-going process and we must remain vigilant that the laws are not only enforced, but improved when necessary. The law today is an example of that vigilance as it represents the work of parents, families, and interested community groups across the country.

The Law Today: The Individuals with Disabilities Act of 1997

In 1996 there was great concern that the rights gained during the previous decades for the education of all children were being threatened. The new policy makers in the nation's capital were not informed and did not understand the need for public laws to protect children's rights in education. The collaborative efforts of parents and families, of interested local and national groups, and of persons with disabilities who had benefited from the previous laws were a major force in helping lawmakers to understand that the federal government still had a responsibility to guarantee a free and appropriate public education to all children.

IDEA-97 incorporated the components found in P. L. 94-142 and also clarified and expanded the law. Furthermore, the new law highlights the role of parents by mandating that they be included as active participants in developing and implementing their children's educational programs. Table 1 demonstrates a comparison of some of the provisions under the previous law with the provisions under the new law. A more comprehensive comparison list is available through the House of Representatives, and can be viewed from the Internet web site, http://www.house.gov/eeo/ideasumchart.htm.

We have seen that parents have won the right to be involved and actively included in group decisions about their children's eligibility and placement. This is an improvement over previous practices when parents were merely informed of the decisions of others and when parents, while they had the right to be included in education program planning meetings (the IEP meetings), were usually not active partners in the IEP program development. Now parents must be included in every stage of the decision-making process and are being trained to be active, participating members of those groups. Clearly, parents have been successful in assuring that their rights and that their children's rights are enforced and safeguarded.

TABLE 1 *Comparison of IDEA with IDEA-97*

IDEA	IDEA-97
Determination of eligibility	
Did not specifically address determination of eligibility. Again, subsequent regulations and policy directives were developed to guide education agencies in determining the eligibility of a student for special services.	Addresses requirements for qualification and ensures that the child's parent(s) is part of the team making the decision. They also assure that the parent will be given a copy of the evaluation report and documentation.
The education program: the IEP content	
Former law required a statement of the child's present levels of educational performance, a statement of annual goals, which in all cases must include short-term instructional objectives.	The IEP must include how the child's disability affects the progress of the child in the general curriculum. The new provisions also links the child's education program to the general curriculum.
Participation in state, and/or local assessment	
There was no provision in the former law.	An IEP include a statement if and what modifications need to be made in order for the child to participate in the same assessments as the students in general education, or if and how the child is to participate in alternative assessments.
Reporting the child's progress	
There was no provision in the former law detailing how progress was to be reported to the parents.	IDEA-97 now requires that a child's education program must include a statement of how the parents will be regularly informed of their child's progress in school. The law states that the parents of children with disabilities must receive the report at least as often as parents of nondisabled children receive a school report.

(continued)

TABLE 1 *Comparison of IDEA with IDEA-97*

IDEA	IDEA-97
Who is part of the IEP Team	
Included administrator, the teacher, the parents, and when appropriate the child as"participants" of a team to develop the IEP. However, parents did not have to be part of the team that decided the child's placement.	Parents must be part of any team deciding placement even if that group is different than the IEP team The law also adds to the team the regular education teachers to the extent appropriate as well as someone who can interpret evaluation test results.

Forming Alliances and Empowering Parents, Families, and Community

Families must insist on and monitor their child's progress throughout the child's education. This is accomplished when parents, families, and communities work together to define the necessary support and services that will lead to an enriched, responsive educational environment. But how can this be done? How can families who may feel uninformed, who do not have legal training, or who may be feeling overwhelmed with their situation make change happen? In fact, there are many effective strategies:

By Forming Small Support Groups

Often, informal groups of three or four families become strong sources of emotional, spiritual, and informational support. Sharing their knowledge and concerns and encouraging each other to become stronger advocates has an empowering effect. One way families can form such a group is by letting their children's doctors know that they can be contacted by other families who also have children with disabilities, and that the purpose of the contact is for supporting each other and sharing information. Another way families have formed small support groups is through their religious organizations.

Families can agree to meet only as often as their lifestyle permits. Some groups meet once a week while others meet once a month. These informal meetings should not become a burden, but rather an event that family members look forward to because it provides them with the support they need.

By Contacting Organizations That Assist Parents and Families and That Advocate for Children with Disabilities

Fiesta Educativa is an organization that was started by Latino families and professionals to educate and assist families in obtaining services and in caring for their children with special needs. These parents and families provide assistance, training, and advocacy to other Spanish-speaking families. Fiesta Educativa is located throughout the United States and Mexico. The national office can be reached by writing to Dr. Alfonso B. Pérez, Executive Director, Fiesta Educativa, 3839 Selig Place, Los Angeles, CA 90031, or through their web site at http://latino.sscnet.ucla.edu/community/fiesta2.html.

MUMS (Mothers United for Moral Support) is another parent-to-parent networking support group and was started by the parent of a child with cerebral palsy. Beginning with a couple of parents (moms and dads), this small group has now become an international organization for parents in over 42 countries. MUM's mission is to help parents who have a child with a rare diagnosis make connections with other parents in similar situations, providing free parent-to-parent matchings for those who speak the same language. Families can find out more about MUMS by writing c/o Julie Gordon, 150 Custer Court, Green Bay, Wisconsin 54301-1243 or through their Internet site at http://www.waisman.wisc.edu/~rowley/mums/index.html.

Our Kids is an organization that offers contacts through the Internet to over eight hundred people who represent the interests of children of varying diagnosis. This includes such diagnoses as indefinite developmental delays, sensory integration problems, cerebral palsy, and rare genetic disorders. Over 35 countries are represented on their list of families. The founder is a parent who formed this list on behalf of her son. This is a parent to parent, family to family method of networking and getting information, and is located at http://rdz.acor.org/lists/our-kids.

The Beach Center on Families and Disabilities is a group made up of professionals and parents that combines parent and family empowerment with research. This group has as its philosophy that people with disabilities and their families should be encouraged to envision a better life and provided with the rights and resources to make those dreams reality. Their staff develops journal, magazine, and newsletter articles, book chapters, books, training manuals, video/audio tapes, resource directories, workshops and presentations, anthologies, and other informational materials. They are located at 3111 Haworth, University of Kansas, Lawrence, KS 66045, and on the Internet at http://www.lsi.ukans.edu/beach/beachhp.htm.

The National Parent Network on Disabilities (NPND) is a parent advocacy organization that started in the United States and since has expanded to include several other countries. NPND sponsors an international parent conference every two years that has become one of the largest conferences for parents and families of children with disabilities. For the past several years parents, families, and interested individuals from as far away as Russia, India, South Africa, Afghanistan, Norway, New Zealand, and Japan have met to share their experiences and learn from each other. The organization has as its mission to serve as a unified voice for families and parent organizations advocating for children and adults with special needs as well as supporting the empowerment and training of parents to influence policy and effect change at all levels. This group can be contacted at National Parent Network on Disabilities, 1130-17th Street, NW, Suite 400, Washington, DC 20036, and on the Internet at http://www.npnd.org.

By forming such alliances, parents, families, and community members can better understand the issues surrounding the education of their children and can start to design ways to have those issues addressed.

Summary

In this chapter we have explored how parents, families, and interested community groups are able to make changes in the education that their children with disabilities receive. Experience has shown that the most effective way to bring about such change is through advocacy groups. History has also demonstrated that the most effective advocates have been parents and families who have become empowered through their participation with other families and interested people.

The capacity of such groups to bring about change is exemplified by such laws as the *Individuals with Disabilities Education Act of 1997* (IDEA-97). This law, which expanded the landmark *Education of All Handicapped Children Act* in the United States (P.L. 94-142), has helped define the concept of appropriate education for all children, and has also stipulated that parents and other caregivers are to be respected and included as participating partners in determining and planning the education of their children with disabilities.

Throughout the world, parents have observed the lessons learned by families in the United States and are developing similar models of parent and family education, empowerment, and advocacy. For example, organizations such as Fiesta Educativa, MUMS, and the National Parent Network on Disabilities are now available to families in Mexico. Working together, parents, families, and communities in Mexico can become informed and empowered on how to take action to obtain and guarantee the education their children need. We have seen that it takes determination and work and that it takes time and commitment from those concerned. However, the friendships that the children with disabilities are forming with their classmates, the education that they are now experiencing, and the life opportunities that are being made available to them clearly demonstrates that the work is worth the effort and that helping all children gain access to education is a good idea.

References

Beach Center on Families and Disabilities. 1998. Families and disabilities newsletter 9, no. 1. Lawrence: University of Kansas Press.

Bettelheim, B. 1967. *The empty fortress: Infantile autism and the birth of the self.* London: Collier-Macmillan.

Board of Education, *Sacramento City Unified School District v Holling,* 786, F. Sup. 874, (E. D. Cal. 1992).

Board of Education v Rowley, 458 U.S. 176, 102 S. Ct. 1982.

Hobson v Hansen, 44, F. R. D. 18, 299-30 N 10 D.C. 1967.

House Committee on Education and the Workforce. 1997. *IDEA Comparison Chart.* United States House of Representatives, Washington, D.C. [Online] Available: http://www.house.gov/eeo/ideasumchart.htm.

Irving Independent School District v Tatro, 468 U.S. 883, 104 S. Ct. 3371, 82L.Ed. 2d 664 1984.

Larry P. v Riles, 495 F. Supp. 926 (N.D.Cal. 1979).

Marcus, L. M. 1977. Patterns of coping in families of psychotic children. *American Journal of Orthopsychiatry* 47, no. 3:388-99.

McEllistrem, R., and C. McEllistrem. 1998. *Students with disabilities and special education*. Birmingham, AL: Oakstone Legal and Business Publishing.

Mills v Board of Education, 348 F. Supp. 866 (1972). [Online] Available: http://www.tourolaw.edu/Patch/Mills/index.html.

Morse, W. C., J. L. Paul, and H. Roselli-Kostoryz. 1997. The role of basic knowledge and the future of special education. In *Foundations of special education: Basic knowledge informing research and practice in special education*, ed. J. L. Paul et al. Pacific Grove, CA: Brooks/Cole Publishing.

National Parent Information Network. [Online] Available: http://npin.org.

Office of Special Education and Rehabilitation Services. 1997. The *Individuals with Disabilities Education Act: Amendments of 1997.* United States Department of Education, Washington, D.C. [Online] Available: http://www.ed.gov/offices/OSERS/IDEA/index.html.

Oliver, J. M., N. H. Cole, and H. Hollingsworth. 1991. Learning disabilities as functions of familial learning problems and developmental problems. *Exceptional Children* 57:427-40.

Pennsylvania Association for Retarded Children et al. v Commonwealth of Pennsylvania, E.D.Pa., C.A. No. 71-42, (PA 1971). [Online] Available http://www.tourolaw.edu/Patch/Parc/.

Schulte, A. C.; S. S. Osborne, and W. P. Erchul. 1998. Effective special education: A United States dilemma. *School Psychology Review* 27, no. 1:71-77.

Turnbull, A. P., and H. R. Turnbull III. 1997. *Families, professionals, and exceptionality: A special partnership*. Upper Saddle River, NJ: Prentice-Hall.

5

Aiding Preschool Children with Communication Disorders from Mexican Backgrounds

Challenges and Solutions

Henriette W. Langdon

Introduction

There is no question that the population of the United States is increasingly culturally and linguistically diverse. This presents a challenge to educators, other professionals, and families alike, especially when there is a language barrier between the client and the service provider. The problems are accentuated when the client, a child or student, has greater difficulty in acquiring English than others who have similar linguistic and experiential backgrounds. In those instances, it is necessary to determine if the delay is due to a language difference or reflects a language disorder.

In this study, I will describe the challenges in working with preschool children from Mexican backgrounds who are experiencing difficulties in acquiring English. Very often their parents or main caretakers report that these children have difficulties in communicating in Spanish as well. Although the issues discussed relate to a specific segment of the Hispanic population currently living in the United States, they are applicable to other Hispanic and language-minority groups. The various challenges will be illustrated with three case studies. The fact that I am bilingual and familiar with the culture facilitates my task because I can communicate with the children and their families directly. However, the challenges are greater when the teacher or the clinician does not share the language of the child. In that case, collaborating with an interpreter is necessary. In my daily work I encounter similar problems when my client speaks one of the numerous languages presently spoken in California. Following this discussion, I will comment on how parents and families of these young children need to be more proactive in providing assistance for their children's needs. Suggestions for teachers will be offered as well. Finally, I will outline some propositions on how the United States and Mexico can collaborate in facilitating this process.

Challenges

Three main sets of challenges in assessment and intervention for speech/language disorders as they relate to Spanish-speaking preschoolers can be identified. The first set includes the limited number of available formal assessment instruments in Spanish, the lack of methods for recognizing that a child truly has a speech/language problem, and limited access to trained bilingual clinicians or clinicians knowledgeable about second-language development and its disorders. The second set relates to a decision-making process regarding identification of a speech/language disorder, that is, determining the degree of influence of variables such as the structure of the children's families, their parents' and families' level of formal education and proficiency in English, their knowledge of community resources, and their acceptance that their child might have a speech/language disorder. The third set relates to intervention issues such as devising an optimal learning environment for these children in view of the limited number of bilingual programs and trained personnel to work with students who are acquiring English. A common belief is that second-language acquisition will proceed more rapidly if the child is exposed to more English. However, when this occurs it is often at the expense of the child's native language (Wong Fillmore 1991).

The challenges outlined above are not new and have been discussed extensively in the literature of the last decade and longer (Cummins 1984; Erickson and Omark 1981; Hamayan and Damico 1991; Figueroa, Fradd, and Correa 1989; Kayser 1989, 1995; Langdon and Cheng 1992a; Ortiz and Ramirez 1988). However, the issues are revisited in this paper with one of the youngest segments of the population who are the next generation of leaders, professionals, and workers of this country.

Who Are These Children?

According to the 1990 census, three- to five-year-olds represent 7.7% of the non-Hispanic population, compared to 10.1% for the Hispanic population in the United States. As of 1993, 35.9% of eligible three- to five-year-old children attended Head Start Programs, and President Clinton pledged to fund the Head Start Programs fully by 1999. During 1992 and 1993, 33% of the children enrolled in Head Start were whites and 23% were Hispanic. The percentage of Hispanic children in those programs is significant, considering their proportion in the overall population (22 million, or approximately 8%). Also, Head Start accepted 13.4% of children with various handicaps that included mental retardation, health impairments, speech and language impairments, and many other disabilities (Department of Health and Human Services 1993). This percentage is larger than that of handicapped children typically seen in public schools (about 10%). Although many of these children have received services while attending Head Start, there are many who remain unserved until they reach regular school age. Some reasons include the parents' and families' lack of awareness that a problem exists and that it can be addressed, lack of local resources, and reliance on professionals who say that "the child will outgrow the problem." Being a knowledgeable consumer is one of the major challenges facing linguistic- and cultural-minority groups (Harry 1992).

Portraits of Three Children

The following three cases illustrate some of the challenges previously outlined, namely, those that are related to the family structure, the parents' level of formal education, and languages used at home.

Carlos

Carlos is a four-year-old whose day-care center teachers are concerned about his limited expressive language skills in both Spanish and English. When he was three years old, Carlos's physician told his parents that his speech delay was due to simultaneous exposure to two languages. A hearing screening revealed normal hearing status at that time. Carlos's parents were aware that there was a difference between his language development and that of his two older siblings. Within a year's time, Carlos finally began putting sentences together, but both his parents and teachers continued to observe a delay in his overall communication skills compared to those of other children growing up bilingually. Although Carlos was exposed to Spanish at home, he has been using more English, which is the main language of interaction in his day-care center. Some of his teachers are bilingual, but they were encouraged by their supervisors to speak English "to accelerate" the children's second-language development. Unfortunately, parents are also told to learn English so that they can enhance their child's learning the language (Goodz 1994). Also, because parents feel that English is very important, they may no longer communicate in the native language and children lose their ability to speak it (Wong Fillmore 1991).

Carlos's parents are originally from Mexico. Mrs. D. is from Durango and Mr. D. is from Sonora. The couple emigrated to the United States more than fifteen years ago. The family visits relatives in Mexico once a year for about two weeks at a time. Mrs. D. can interact with coworkers, physicians, and teachers in English. She is currently employed in the housekeeping department of a large local hotel. In Mexico she had completed a course to be a secretary. Mr. D.'s formal education is limited to three grades of elementary school. When he was a young boy, he had to take a job to support his family. Mr. D. taught himself to read in Spanish, but his English oral proficiency and reading ability are very limited. He had been working as a painter in a body shop, but was recently laid off.

Carlos has attended day care ever since he was an infant. When he plays with bilingual children, he prefers to respond in English even when they speak Spanish to him. He does the same at home, although his mother reports that he tries to speak Spanish to his father. Carlos seems to be able to understand both languages, but he expresses himself with short sentences in both languages. When he is unable to verbalize his thoughts, he throws temper tantrums, and occasionally he hits other children instead of resolving conflicts by using words. Carlos was born in the United States. His birth and health history are normal. He likes to play with toy cars, and recently he began to enjoy listening to stories. His mother tries to tell him or read to him stories in Spanish.

Arturo

Arturo is another four-year-old child who is difficult to understand in either Spanish or English. A speech and language evaluation was requested by his grandmother, who is his legal guardian. No one in the family is able to understand him unless the context of the conversation is known. Arturo has been enrolled in a Head Start Program for almost a year. His teachers do not speak Spanish. There are a few Spanish-speaking children in his class, and when he interacts with them, he uses short sentences that often include words from both languages.

Arturo has been under the care of his grandparents since he was two years old. His father is serving a second jail sentence for drug dealing because he violated his parole. Arturo's mother lives in the area, but she abandoned him when he was only a few months old. Arturo lives with his grandparents and two young uncles, who are attending the local high school. Spanish is the main language spoken in the home, but Arturo's uncles prefer speaking English to him. Several relatives visit his home; the adults speak primarily Spanish and the children use more English. Arturo's father was only six years old when Mr. and Mrs. V. came to the United States from Michoacán, Mexico. Although Mr. and Mrs. V. have been living in the United States for seventeen years, their English is very limited. Neither of them received any formal education in Mexico. Very limited information was available about Arturo's mother, who was only sixteen years old at the time of his birth.

Arturo was born in the United States. His mother was reported to be on drugs throughout her pregnancy. He was born prematurely, at seven months of gestation, and was delivered by caesarean section. He needed to remain in intensive care and was discharged from the hospital after one month. He had to be readmitted for a hernia operation when he was still an infant. Arturo had a few ear infections when he was a toddler. At home, he spends a great deal of time watching TV. He also enjoys playing with toys, and bike riding is his favorite pastime. He has limited opportunity to play with other children his age except on the weekends when relatives visit his family. Arturo has never traveled to Mexico or any other Spanish-speaking country.

Cecilia

Cecilia is a five-year-old, predominantly Spanish-speaking child whose speech is difficult to understand. She likes to interact verbally and uses complete sentences for the most part, but other children tease her because she cannot pronounce certain sounds correctly. This is Cecilia's first time in school, and she has adjusted quite well. She is enrolled in a state preschool program, which is staffed by a bilingual teacher and teaching assistant. Her teacher uses the alternate-day approach, instructing her students one day in English and one day in Spanish. This is the ideal teaching approach for her students, as they are primarily monolingual English- or Spanish-speaking children. Cecilia plays well with other children, and she enjoys the school activities. Yet, she has learned very little English compared to other children who came to the program at the same time.

Cecilia lives with her parents and a six-year-old sister. Several other relatives share the same rented house, including a cousin who is two years old. Her parents are originally from Nayarit, Mexico, and have been in the United States since Cecilia was an infant. Mr. M. completed high school in Mexico, and he can communicate in English fairly well. He is an assembler for a computer company.

Mrs. M. completed junior high school and works as a waitress in a Mexican restaurant. She does not yet communicate very well in English. Spanish is the language spoken in the home, and all adult and young visitors of the family use Spanish, including her older sister. Cecilia has never gone back to Mexico for a visit. Her sister had a similar, but apparently more serious, speech problem and has made significant progress in the last year after receiving speech therapy. Cecilia enjoys playing school and other imaginary games at home. Her sister is her main playmate. Her family can understand her, but at times she is asked to repeat what she says because it is difficult to understand her.

Cecilia was born in Nayarit, Mexico, following a normal pregnancy and delivery. She learned to walk at fourteen months, but did not form sentences until she was three years old. Her parents report that the clarity of her speech has improved since she has been attending preschool. No hearing or vision difficulties were reported, and the screenings that were conducted prior to the referral were normal.

Discussion

The previous descriptions of preschoolers illustrate some typical cases of children that I am asked to evaluate. If they have a speech and language problem that merits intervention, I work very closely with them, their teachers, and their parents and family. Even when their problems reflect a language difference rather than a disorder, I spend time providing suggestions to their families and teachers.

Carlos's, Arturo's, and Cecilia's cases have some common characteristics. All three children come from homes where Spanish is the main language, and their families came from Mexico, but each family has resided in the United States for a different number of years. Carlos and Arturo were born in the United States and interact in both Spanish and English with children at school or those who visit them at home. Cecilia was born in Mexico and, at this time, speaks only Spanish. The latter appears to be the result of her limited contact with English outside of school. All three children are enrolled in preschool programs; in Cecilia's case only, the teachers speak and use Spanish as one of the languages for instruction. In all three cases the parents and families are interested and supportive in finding out whether their child has a speech or language disorder. However, there are instances where parents fear a diagnosis, especially when the children otherwise seem to develop normally (Langdon 1992a). All three children were referred because they have expressive language problems and, in Arturo's case, receptive and comprehension problems are noted as well. All of them have the advantage of being enrolled in programs where specialized staff can assess and work with them if necessary.

In each of the three cases, the family structure is different but is characteristic of that of many other families in the population at large. Carlos and Cecilia live in intact families, whereas Arturo is being raised by his grandparents. Carlos lives with his parents and siblings in a more traditional setting. Arturo's and Cecilia's homes are also shared by other adults and younger relatives. Arturo has a health history that very likely has had an impact on his speech/language development: Arturo's mother had been a drug user during her pregnancy. The other two children's health and developmental history have been unremarkable.

Taking a Closer Look

The major challenges in identifying a language disorder in children growing up in a dual-language environment are bound to the still limited available description of how each language develops, and further research is needed to "pinpoint the reasons for the different rates of acquisition in each language" (Goodz 1994, 69). The process is further complicated by the limited number of language assessment instruments that are adequately normed on monolingual/bilingual Spanish-speaking children and that also capture all major aspects of language, that is, form, content, and use. Thus, the assessment of children exposed to two languages presents challenges to monolingual and bilingual speech and language clinicians alike. It is a particularly difficult task when the clinician does not share the child's language. In this case the clinician needs to work with an interpreter, which requires training and time. Langdon et al. (1994) provide some guidelines on effective strategies to collaborate with an interpreter.

We do have some information on how children acquire two languages, and we can make assumptions about which environments are most likely to enhance the development of two languages. However, most of the data are based on single case studies where the two languages are highly valued by the child's community. For example, studies indicate that a child can grow up speaking two or more languages with no problem. In those situations each language is used by either the parent or in specific situations in which the child is involved. Children are aware from a very young age that they are growing up in an environment where two or more languages are spoken. Children exposed to two languages seem to have greater metalinguistic awareness compared to their monolingual counterparts, and other cognitive advantages have been identified as well. For a more complete review of the literature on early bilingual language development the reader is referred to Langdon and Merino (1992). The case studies discussed include children who used each language with specific persons and in specific situations. Recent research indicates, however, that language borrowing is inevitable in a dual-language environment but does not appear to interfere with language development (Goodz 1994). This research mirrors previous findings by Bergman (1976), Lindholm and Padilla (1978), and

Huerta (1977). Nevertheless, we do not have longitudinal studies data on how language and communication skills of bilingual language-disordered children progress over time and how each language can be used to facilitate a parallel development of the two languages.

Becoming bilingual or multilingual is a natural process if and when the environment encourages the learning and use of more than the mainstream language. For example, I grew up in Mexico City speaking two languages until age five. I spoke Polish to my parents, grandparents, and family friends and Spanish to my brother and peers. When I was five years old, I was enrolled in a French school, which followed an immersion program model. By age six, I was able to communicate in three languages with equal ease. Over the years, I have maintained my skills in all these languages, and I also acquired English as my fourth language. I was first introduced to English in junior high school, and I was able to improve my language skills through classes and private lessons through college, at which time I began my graduate studies in the United States. Each language was connected to specific persons or situations, but was also supported by the community. Cases such as mine are extremely common; it would be fair to state that there are more bilingual or multilingual persons in the world than monolinguals (Grosjean 1982). Yet, it does not mean that I am equally proficient in each language in different oral or written contexts. For example, I can easily lecture in English or in Spanish, and I can work with language-disordered children in either Spanish, English, or French, but not as easily in Polish. I can only read and write simple material in Polish because I never had formal instruction in Polish. When the primary language of the child is not valued by the community and bilingualism is not supported, it can have devastating consequences for successful communication between parents and children. Thus, it is equally important to consider the attitude of the community toward other languages and the family's attitude toward acquiring the majority language (Langdon 1996).

The limited number of language assessment instruments available in Spanish or any language other than English renders the task of determining a language disorder more difficult. This problem is directly related to the limited information available on Spanish-language development and simultaneous Spanish-English-language development (Merino 1992). Although Spanish adaptations of English language tests are currently available, only a few of those tests have been normed on Spanish-speaking or bilingual Spanish-English-speaking children. For a review the reader is referred to Langdon (1992b). Therefore, the results of such tests or of any tests need to be interpreted with great care.

In addition to the challenges mentioned above it is necessary to ascertain that the child has had experience in responding to specific questions presented in a testing situation. For example, the child may be able to point to a bicycle or a car but may not be able to point to the one that is slower or faster. Also, the child may not have had the opportunity to be engaged in tasks in which there was need to demonstrate his or her knowledge. Also, once a possible language disorder has been identified, it may be difficult for the family to accept that a problem exists even when the family was supportive in allowing the child to be assessed. Langdon (1992a) discusses how families may accept more readily that a problem exists when there is an identified medical basis for the problem, such as a cleft palate or a hearing loss. Many parents have more difficulty accepting that their child has a language disorder when the child's development is adequate in all other areas and there are no obvious medical reasons for the problem. Some Hispanic families in particular may equate the problem with the child being *enfermito* "sick" or being confused because of the simultaneous exposure to the two languages (Harry 1992; Langdon 1992a). This attitude is also prevalent among other linguistic groups (Cheng 1991).

I encounter the challenges mentioned above in my daily work. To illustrate the points that I made, I will describe the steps I follow in determining if a preschool monolingual or bilingual Spanish-speaking child indeed has a speech or language disorder. Because of the scope of this paper, only Carlos's case will be described in greater detail, and a summary will be provided for Arturo's and Cecilia's cases.

Carlos was assessed over two sessions. The first session was conducted using primarily Spanish, and the second one was conducted primarily in English. Carlos's mother was present during one of the sessions. Throughout the two sessions Carlos appeared very shy, and his verbalizations were minimal. He rarely initiated any of the interactions. When asked to make a comment or to respond to a question, he said, "No, I don't know," in about 20% of instances. Otherwise, he was silent or communicated using three to four words at a time, with minimal expansion. This was observed in both languages, but he was somewhat more fluent in Spanish. Carlos was otherwise cooperative. He followed directions well when he was asked to perform two- or three-step commands or when he was asked to place objects in specific places.

During play with his friends Carlos used English, but his comments were generally brief, mostly to request their attention. Overall, his language output was more reduced than that of his peers, but he seemed to be able to communicate basic needs and feelings in both languages. He responded in Spanish when spoken to in Spanish and in English when spoken to in English. To assess his ability to understand and respond verbally to specific questions, I used several adapted or translated tests currently available in Spanish, which included the Expressive One-Word Picture Vocabulary Test (EOWPVT) (Gardner 1990), the Preschool Language Scale-3 (PLS-3) (Zimmerman, Steiner, and Pond 1992), and the Structured Photographic Elicitation Language Test (SPELT) (Werner and Kresheck 1989). To supplement the information, I collected a language sample while we played together and while Carlos interacted with other children. The sample was supplemented with comments he made while I read *The Very Hungry Caterpillar* (Carle 1979) in both Spanish and English. While he was expressing himself, word-finding difficulties were noted: he often mislabeled words from the same category, for example, he called a bus a "truck" and said "shorts" for long pants. Although it is not unusual for bilingual children to lack words for common items, Arturo's difficulty seemed more pronounced. His family had noticed the same type of language patterns at home. In the Spanish sample Carlos used language to request something as in, "Mami, quiero el carro" (Mom, I want the car), to ask something as in, "¿Dónde está la pelota?" (Where is the ball?), and to deny/negate as in, "No hay carros allá" (There are no cars over there). However, his ability to elaborate was significantly limited. His utterances were only about two words long in English. Conversations averaged two turns regardless of the language spoken, and most of his speech needed to be elicited. I took into consideration that Carlos was not used to me, but his parents and teachers reported that he did not speak very much at all in either language. His pronunciation of sounds was adequate in both languages.

In summary, four-year-old Carlos could understand and follow directions, and his overall comprehension skills appeared age-appropriate in both languages. His expressive language was a bit more extensive in Spanish, but verbal output in Spanish and English was minimal. Carlos responded in the language in which the interaction was taking place. Although Carlos is shy, there was a difference in his speech output in comparison with other children who had been exposed to a dual-language environment. Because of his speech delay and inability to communicate effectively with his family, teachers, and peers it was recommended that he receive supplemental assistance in speech and language development.

Arturo followed directions more easily in Spanish, but his knowledge of concepts such as colors, numbers, and labels for classroom items was more developed in English because they had been taught in that language. It was often necessary to repeat or rephrase requests to enable him to respond. Yet, it was almost impossible to sustain a conversation with him because he was unable to understand what I was saying, unless it was related to the here and now. His expressive language was minimal: two to three words on the average in Spanish and many formulaic phrases in English such as, "Look at it" or, "I don't want to." His pronunciation in Spanish revealed many errors, and his ability to repeat words when the correct model was provided was unsuccessful most of the time. I recommended that Arturo receive speech and language services.

Cecilia's ability to comprehend information presented orally was excellent in Spanish. She was able to converse on a variety of topics appropriately for her age. At times it was difficult to understand her because she made some developmental errors such as omitting or substituting /rr/ and /r/ for /ll/, and she reduced some consonant clusters by saying *pimo* instead of *primo* "cousin." Her ability to model words that included those sounds was excellent. Specific speech intervention was not recommended because the errors she made were considered developmental in nature. Instead, her teachers and parents were given suggestions on how to model the words for her without causing undue stress.

Improving Language Communication

Programs

The availability of bilingual Spanish-speaking speech and language clinicians and bilingual language programs are the two major challenges encountered in planning language intervention programs for Spanish-dominant children who have speech/language disorders. Although more Spanish-English bilingual programs for children are available, especially in certain states such as California, Texas, Florida, and others, finding Spanish-speaking speech and language clinicians is more difficult. The philosophy of how bilingual programs should be implemented has changed since the inception of the Bilingual Act of 1968. In the beginning the principal aim of the Bilingual Act was to foster bilingualism in children whether their native language was English or Spanish. At the present time, the majority of programs emphasize that the transition to English be made as fast as possible. Once the student is enrolled in an English program, the study of the native language is dropped (Langdon and Cheng 1992b). The implication of this philosophy is that only English counts. This attitude is particularly disturbing when the child is having difficulties learning his or her native language and when staff members who can communicate in that language are available. As mentioned earlier, unfortunately some staff members who are proficient in Spanish stop interacting with the children in Spanish because they believe that the more English they use, the better it will be for the child. In the case of young children it is particularly important to promote the main language spoken in the home whenever possible. It allows the children to gain a broader base in a language that they have heard since birth while they learn more English by interacting with peers, the environment, and the media. Intervention in the first language is preferable whenever possible. "To choose L_2 preference to the young language-handicapped child's mother tongue is to ignore six years of language development and to approach language intervention in a social vacuum. Most 'motherese' studies have shown that one of the most important predisposing factors in language acquisition is a positive social and emotional environment" (Duncan 1989, 185-86).

Intervention Strategies

Different intervention models can be followed depending on the availability of bilingual staff and bilingual speech and language clinicians. The most difficult scenario is when there is no available teaching support in Spanish. In this instance instruction and therapy will have to be provided in English. However, family and parents can be involved in the process by observing and participating in their child's program and by following up at home on some specific activities that are explained with the help of an interpreter. Although this is a time-consuming process, it can be an effective way to bridge the needs of the child at home and at school. If there are other family members or older children, they should also be involved in the process. Beaumont (1992) outlines strategies that the speech and language clinician can follow in collaborating with the teacher. If neither the clinician nor the teacher speaks Spanish, the main focus needs to be on English as a second-language development.

If one of the goals for the child is to enhance greater verbalization, the parents and families can be encouraged to model language for the child in Spanish. For example, when the child is doing something, the adult can verbalize the child's actions and expand on what the child says in Spanish. It is always difficult for families to accept that they can help their child by speaking their native language and that speaking English to the child will not necessarily improve the child's acquisition of the language. It is also important to give suggestions to parents and families at a level that is comfortable to them without imposing values that they may not be ready to accept at that particular time (Quinn 1995). The goals and level of participation need to be realistic and will depend on the parents' ability to help and on their level of formal education. For example, one should not advise a parent who is unable to read Spanish to read books to his or her child in Spanish. Alternatives should be offered such as suggesting that the parent look at books with the child and tell stories to develop the child's ability to listen to language in various contexts. The clinician and staff need to explain to parents and families the basis of such recommendations (Langdon 1994).

When the clinician can provide services in Spanish but the teacher does not speak Spanish, the clinician can assist the teacher by sharing areas that are emphasized during the sessions and by offering ideas on strategies that are appropriate for enhancing comprehension of the second language. Tabors and Snow (1994) suggest that language acquisition is facilitated when the teaching staff provides opportunities for language use and interaction through interesting activities, when teachers offer focused stimulation of particular language features such as the modeling of certain sounds or words, when they develop routines to help children connect events by providing scripts related to sociodramatic play activities, and when they stimulate social interactions between children, such as redirecting children's requests to other children (122).

For example, to develop Carlos's expressive language skills I followed the same thematic units that were used in the classroom, but in Spanish. During Thanksgiving time, I used the Spanish version of "The Little Red Hen" (*La gallinita roja*; López 1985), and I read the same book during three consecutive sessions. In the first session I asked Carlos to retell what each animal had said to the little red hen and expanded what he said when asked to describe what had happened from the time the little red hen found the seeds to when she baked the bread, using the pictures in the book. To enhance Carlos's interest I brought some toys: a small wooden house, a toy hen, and all the animals that were part of the story. While I read the story, Carlos spontaneously picked up each toy animal as we talked about what each one was saying. In the course of the second session I encouraged him to verbalize what would happen next, before turning the page. The third time we read the story to a small group of friends, and he had a chance to show them the pictures in the book and verbalize what each animal said to the little red hen. While we read the book, we discussed the reason that the animals did not want to help the little hen and why, at the end, the little hen did not want to share her bread with them. In a subsequent session we talked about different kinds of bread and which one was our favorite. I brought a few samples of different breads, and we named our favorite sandwich. In another lesson we could have talked about items other than bread that were baked and how they could have been eaten. Although the classroom teachers spoke primarily English, I encouraged them to read the English version of the story and discuss it with the children. I sent a note to the parents describing what we had read and encouraged them to go to the library to get the book. I also suggested that they let Carlos make or select the type of sandwich or dish he might like to eat and that they ask him to describe all the necessary ingredients. The basic principle I advocate is to reinforce the student's first language according to the concept of "common underlying proficiency": "Experience with either language can promote development of the proficiency underlying both languages, given adequate motivation and exposure to both either in school or in the wider environment" (Cummins 1984, 143). As Duncan states, "there is a growing amount of empirical data which supports the notion that offering a bilingually language-disordered system input in both languages promotes language learning in both languages. It could be that the disordered system needs more opportunities quantitatively and qualitatively to acquire language patterns" (1989, 186). In summary, I was trying to promote basic goals and activities in both languages: in Spanish during our sessions and at home, and in English in the classroom or day-care situation.

The scope of this paper does not allow me to elaborate on additional strategies; the speech and language clinician will have to adjust the goals to the children's needs and the availability of bilingual personnel who can serve those children.

How Parents and Families Can Help Their Children

- Observe the child closely. Although there are differences among children within the same family, determine if the child is developing like other children or if there are gaps.
- Ascertain that the child hears well. Seek medical assistance if children have prolonged colds or seem to have allergies, as these problems influence their hearing mechanism and may have a direct impact on language development.
- Follow up any concern with educational staff. Contact the home school district and request an educational or speech and language evaluation. These services are free of charge.
- Interact with the child as much as possible. Although each family may have some preferences about how to communicate best among its family members, it is important for children to have an opportunity to interact with different adults and other children in order to develop a wider range of language uses.
- The parents or family should be part of the evaluation and intervention process. If the family does not speak English fluently, it is important to request the collaboration of an interpreter. However, this person needs to be adequately trained so that communication between the family and the educational staff will be successful.
- If the child needs services in speech and language, the family should be involved in the process by following up on activities at home at their own comfort level. Caretakers and teachers need to be active participants in the process as well. For reasons stated above, it is important that parents interact in the language in which they are most comfortable talking with their children. What is learned in one language will transfer onto the other if and when there is opportunity to use and value each language.

How to Strengthen Collaboration between Mexico and the United States

Services for Preschool Children with Speech/Language Disorders

Most of the suggestions mentioned above can be followed by all families who have children with identified speech/language disorders. Children growing up in the United States have the additional challenge of having to learn a second language.

However, Mexico and the United States can collaborate by sharing practices that are effective with young children, which may vary due to cultural, linguistic, or socioeconomic differences, sharing research regarding Spanish language development and parent and family interactions, sharing materials, songs, and books that are used with young children in Mexico, sharing assessment and intervention strategies in language/learning disorders, encouraging medical and educational personnel to recognize signs of possible speech/language delays and referring children to the appropriate specialists, encouraging parents and families who have not had much formal education or who have limited English language proficiency to bring concerns about their children to the attention of the appropriate agencies, advertising on radio and TV about services and agencies that deal with assessment and intervention for young children who have language/learning problems.

References

Beaumont, C. 1992. Service delivery issues. In *Hispanic children and adults with communication disorders: Assessment and intervention*, ed. H. J. Langdon and L. L. Cheng, 343-72. Gaithersburg, MD: Aspen.

Bergman, C. 1976. Interference vs. independent development in infant bilingualism. In *Bilingualism in the bicentennial and beyond*, ed. G. Keller, R. Teshner, and S. Viera, 86-96. New York: Bilingual Press/Editorial Bilingüe.

Carle, E. 1979. *The very hungry caterpillar.* (*La oruga muy hambrienta* [Spanish translation by Scholastic, 1989]), New York: Philomel.

Cheng, L. L. 1991. *Assessing Asian language performance* 2d ed. Oceanside, CA: Academic Communication.

Cummins, J. 1984. *Bilingualism and special education: Issues in assessment and pedagogy.* Clevedon, England: Bilingual Matters.

Duncan, D. 1989. *Working with bilingual language disability.* New York: Chapman and Hall.

Erickson, J. G., and D. R. Omark, eds. 1981. *Communication assessment of the bilingual bicultural child.* Baltimore: University of Park Press.

Figueroa, R., S. H. Fradd, and V. I. Correa. 1989. Bilingual special education and this issue. *Exceptional Children* 56:145-62.

Gardner, M. F. 1990. *Expressive one-word picture vocabulary test* (revised) (EOWPVT-R), Level 1. Spanish and English versions. Novato, CA: Academic Therapy.

Goodz, N. S. 1994. Interactions between parents and children in bilingual families. In *Educating second-language children*, ed. F. Genesee, 61-81. New York: Cambridge University Press.

Grosjean, F. 1982. *Life with two languages: An introduction to bilingualism.* Cambridge, MA: Harvard University Press.

Hamayan, E. V., and J. S. Damico. 1991. *Limiting bias in the assessment of bilingual students.* Austin, TX: Pro-Ed.

Harry, B. 1992. *Cultural diversity, families, and the special education system: Communication and empowerment.* New York: Teachers College Press.

Huerta, A. 1977. The acquisition of bilingualism. A code-switching approach. *Sociolinguistic Working Papers* 39:1-33.

Kayser, H. 1989. Speech and language assessment of Spanish-English-speaking children. *Language, Speech and Hearing Services in Schools* 31:226-44.

_____, ed. 1995. *Bilingual speech and language pathology: A Hispanic focus.* San Diego, CA: Singular.

Langdon, H. W. 1992a. Language communication and sociocultural patterns in Hispanic families. In *Hispanic children and adults with communication disorders: Assessment and intervention,* ed. H. W. Langdon and L. L. Cheng, 99-167. Gaithersburg, MD: Aspen.

_____. 1992b. Speech and language assessment of LEP/bilingual Hispanic students. In *Hispanic children and adults with communication disorders: Assessment and intervention,* ed. H. W. Langdon and L. L. Cheng, 201-71. Gaithersburg, MD: Aspen.

_____. 1994. Meeting the needs of the non-English-speaking parents of a communicatively disabled child. *Clinics in Communication Disorders* 24:227-36.

_____. 1996. English-language learning by immigrant Spanish speakers: A United States perspective. *Topics of Language Disorders* 16, no. 4:38-53.

Langdon, H. W., and L. L. Cheng. 1992a. *Hispanic children and adults with communication disorders: Assessment and intervention.* Gathersburg, MD: Aspen.

Langdon, H. W., and L. L. Cheng. 1992b. Defining bilingual education in the United States. In *Hispanic children and adults with communication disorders: Assessment and intervention,* ed. H. W. Langdon and L. L. Cheng, 168-200. Gaithersburg, MD: Aspen.

Langdon, H. W., and B. J. Merino. 1992. Acquisition and development of a second language. In *Hispanic children and adults with communication disorders: Assessment and intervention,* ed. H. W. Langdon and L. L. Cheng, 132-67. Gaithersburg, MD: Aspen.

Langdon, H. W., V. Siegel, L. Halog, and M. Sánchez-Boyce. 1994. *The interpreter /translator process in the educational setting: A resource manual.* Sacramento, CA: Resources in Special Education (RISE).

Lindholm, K. J., and A. M. Padilla. 1978. Language mixing in bilingual children. *Journal of Child Language* 8:327-35.

López, L., trans. 1985. *La gallinita roja* ("The little red hen"). New York: Scholastic.

Merino, B. J. 1992. Acquisition of syntactic and phonological features in Spanish. In *Hispanic children and adults with communication disorders: Assessment and intervention,* ed. H. W. Langdon and L. L. Cheng, 57-98. Gaithersburg, MD: Aspen.

Ortiz, A. A., and B. A. Ramírez. 1988. *Schools and the culturally diverse exceptional student: Promising practices and future directions.* Reston, VA: Council for Exceptional Children.

Quinn, R. 1995. Early intervention: ¿Qué quiere decir eso?/What does it mean? *Bilingual speech and language pathology: A Hispanic focus,* ed. H. Kayser, 75-94. San Diego, CA: Singular.

Tabors, P. O., and C. E. Snow. 1994. English as a second language in preschool programs. In *Educating second-language children,* ed. F. Genesee, 103-25. New York: Cambridge University Press.

U.S. Bureau of the Census. 1990. Current Population Reports. *The Hispanic population in the United States, March 1990.* Washington, DC.

U.S. Department of Health and Human Services. 1993. Project Head Start. Statistical Fact Sheet. Washington, DC.

Werner, E. O., and J. D. Kresheck. 1989. *Structured photographic elicited language test* (SPELT) Level 1. Spanish version. Sandwich, IL: Janelle.

Wong Fillmore, L. 1991. Language and cultural issues in early education. In *The care and education of America's young children: Obstacles and opportunities,* ed. S. L. Kagan, 30-49. The 90th Yearbook of the National Society for the Study of Education. Chicago: Chicago University Press.

Zimmerman, I. L., V. G. Steiner, and R. E. Pond. 1992. *Preschool language scale-3* (PLS-3). San Antonio, TX: Psychological Corporation.

6

Indigenous and Informal Systems of Support

Navajo Families Who Have Children with Disabilities

*R. Cruz Begay, Richard N. Roberts, Thomas S. Weisner, and Catherine Matheson**

In the United States, many have come to believe that families and family involvement are the most important factors in supporting children with disabilities. Families exist within an ecocultural environment that is complex and powerful, and it is within the family context that development in all its forms begins and is nurtured. We cannot understand what family involvement means without understanding the culture of families and the informal systems that families use to adapt and operate. In this chapter, the example of Navajo families with children with disabilities underscores and shows in high relief the heavy reliance on cultural support for families that is part of any family system. As early-intervention and family support programs continue to grow in the United States, we need to understand and sustain those benefits of indigenous systems that provide support and relief to families even as we seek to engage families in the use of supports that may be offered by private and public agencies.

---

*Research was supported by a grant from the United States Department of Health and Human Services, Bureau of Maternal and Child Health.

Two complementary systems operate to fulfill the needs of Navajo and other American families who have children with disabilities: one is the indigenous adaptive system and the other is the public health system that has been established nationally in the United States with local options. One example is the Individuals with Disabilities Education Act (IDEA 1997), parts B and C, providing early intervention, preschool, and school-age services. The indigenous system was in existence long before the IDEA, but has not been recognized as such. Both systems attempt to increase the well-being of families, but because all adaptive systems have a cost, neither system is totally benign. Each system extracts some payment for the benefits it provides.

When discussing costs, our intent is not so much to point out financial costs, which are often involved, but to show that costs to families can be more subtle, such as the erosion of family responsibility and satisfaction with the efforts the family makes on behalf of the child with a disability. Thus, in the Navajo sample, families identified medical disabilities and sought help for medical problems from professionals but were sometimes unable to resolve their anxiety until they involved spiritual services or indigenous healing practices. Conversely, Navajo families did not identify learning disorders in the preschool age group that we interviewed. Learning and language disabilities were primarily identified by professionals and schools, who in turn sometimes found families apprehensive and reluctant to adopt an active role in early-intervention efforts that they had not sought themselves.

This chapter will examine the indigenous systems of support that a particular Native American culture uses to adapt to the situation of having a child with a disability. Families use spiritual and other informal supports to meet some of their needs. In addition, bureaucratic systems of support for Navajo families include: the Indian Health Service and other professional medical services, early-intervention programs, financial assistance programs, preschools and Head Start programs, housing programs, alcohol treatment services, and formal support groups. An examination of the indigenous systems of support is essential in any culture in order to understand family involvement and how public health programs might work to either foster, augment, or supplant informal systems. Space and time limitations preclude a thorough investigation of both systems, and this chapter only examines some of the costs and benefits of the indigenous system, leaving the evaluation of public health systems for another time and place. It is hoped that a study of the services provided in the United States and Mexico will explore the most beneficial and least destructive practices when implementing services.

Learning about Navajo Support Systems

The information for this chapter comes from ethnographic interviews of families on the Navajo Indian Reservation who have a child in an early-intervention program. The IDEA provides funds identifying children with "delayed learning" or who are at risk of being delayed so that they can receive education that will help them to catch up to normal children by the time they enter school. A total of twenty-nine children and their families was recruited for this study. Families were identified through program staff in three areas and programs: the school district in the Utah strip of the Navajo reservation; the Saint Michael's Association for Special Education, which included families in the southeastern area of the reservation in both Arizona and New Mexico; and the Navajo tribal program "Growing in Beauty" in the northwestern district of the reservation. Staff members in all three of the programs were asked to identify and recruit families who had children enrolled in their early-intervention programs.

Each agency provides a different program. The public school district providing services for children living in the Utah part of the reservation has identified many Navajo children as being at risk because of socioeconomic status and language. Saint Michael's Association for Special Education is a non-profit reservation school that provides direct services to children with disabilities and their families. The Navajo Nation "Growing in Beauty" program is primarily a referral service that works with the Indian Health Service and other programs throughout the reservation. The particular area served by "Growing in Beauty" in the study was the farthest from towns and the least accessible to services, though all three were rural. Ten families were referred from the St. Michael's program, ten were recruited from the San Juan School District, and nine families were referred by the "Growing in Beauty" program.

Agencies interviewed families in their own homes, using open-ended but directed topics. "Tell me about your child since he was born," for example, was usually one of the first questions. The primary caretaker of the child was interviewed, as well as other caretakers such as grandparents and spouses. Interviews were recorded so that the interviewer was able to listen and respond to the family. Several of the families were visited more than once, since the interview process was lengthy. The interviews were conducted primarily in English.

Among the topics that were addressed during the interview were: the resources the family used to adapt to the child's disability, the family's daily routine, and the supportive resources that family members used and how they used them. The focus was on the family's daily routine, with particular emphasis on how the child with disabilities was integrated into that routine. Family members were asked to describe typical days at home and normal routines with their children.

Participants

In the twenty-nine families interviewed we found a variety of living situations. The most common was the expanded family, in which more than one nuclear family was represented in the same household. Some families included grandparents or grown siblings who lived together. Other relatively common expanded families included nieces or nephews. The Navajo language uses the same terms for cousins and brothers and sisters. When speaking English, a Navajo might call a cousin "my cousin-brother" or just "my brother."

Over 65% of the families lived in "camps," or compounds, in which extended-family members lived in the same rural area or neighborhood but in separate households. Parents living with grandparents were as common as those living independently. Although 24% of the parents were not married, only 10% lived as the only adult in the family (see table 1).

TABLE 1 *Household composition of Navajo families interviewed*

TYPE OF HOUSEHOLD	*N*	%
Two Parents living independently	9	31.0
Two parents living in expanded family	11	38.0
Single parent living independently	3	10.3
Single parent living in expanded family	4	13.9
Other *	2	6.8

*Children in foster home.

Parents in any of the above situations may also live in a compounded family, or camp, so that the independent household might be living in a family camp. Nineteen families, representing 65.6% of those interviewed, lived in a family camp. Six families (20.7%) lived in a Housing and Urban Development, (HUD) project in a reservation town. The other families lived in trailer parks or employee housing on the reservation.

Mothers' ages ranged from 16 to 49 years, with a median age of 31.8. Fathers had a similar age range, but were slightly older. Education and employment are shown in table 2.

TABLE 2 *Education and employment of Navajo parents interviewed*

EDUCATION AND EMPLOYMENT	MOTHERS (%)	FATHERS (%)
Educational Level		
Less than high school	31.0	14.8
High-school graduate	37.9	51.8
GED[a]	17.5	14.8
Some college	6.8	18.6
College degree	6.8	0.0
Employment Status		
Not employed	62.1	33.3
Self-employed[b]	7.4	28.0
Intermittently employed[c]	13.8	37.0
Employed full time	24.1	33.3

[a]Passed general equivalency.

[b]Selling or trading own arts and crafts or ranching and selling or trading livestock.

[c]Employed on temporary basis either full or part time, such as in short-term construction, handiwork, or crafts.

*Some were *both* (b) self-employed and (c) intermittently employed.

Medical Profiles of Children with Disabilities

Most of the children in this study had major medical problems. It is presumed that any sample of children in early-intervention programs on the reservation would be medically involved, because the majority of children was identified by the Indian Health Service. Parents generally did not identify other disabilities or seek services for children who were not medically involved. Some schools in the San Juan School District enrolled children who were at risk. These programs worked with the home-based education program for adults, and they recruited the children in these families for the early-intervention program.

The average age of the target child was 24.7 months. Some 38% were girls and 62% were boys. The majority of children with disabilities had siblings living in the household. The median number of children in a family was 4, and the average number of siblings for the target child was 3.1. Nearly 38% of the households had more than 3 siblings, not including the target child, in the household. The children's diagnoses are displayed in table 3. (Diagnoses are not mutually exclusive. One child may have more than one disability.)

TABLE 3 *Identified diagnoses of Navajo children with disabilities*

DIAGNOSIS	%
Developmental delay	24.1
Chronic medical problem (heart, digestive, other)	24.0
Down's syndrome	17.2
Respiratory disorder	17.2
Seizures	10.3
Speech delay	10.3
Motor delay	6.8
Metachromatic Leukodystrophy	6.8
Fetal alcohol syndrome	6.8
Microcephaly	3.4
Cleft palate	3.4
Brain tumor	3.4
Emotional disorder	3.4
Neurological handicap	3.4
Spinal stroke	3.4
Unspecified syndrome	3.4
Normal/at risk	17.2

Sources of Support

Parents were asked to tell the history of their experiences with their child. Support sources were identified from the conversations as those resources that the family reported as having helped them either instrumentally or emotionally with their child. Descriptions were elicited by asking families to describe things that helped them or gave them strength with their child. If the family said that they sought support from religion, including traditional Navajo ceremonies, that was considered a support source only if they mentioned it specifically as support for coping with the child with the disability. Among this sample of Navajo families spiritual resources emerged as the leading source of support. Other family members and grandparents were the second and third sources of support for families. Relatively few of the Navajo families looked for support from professionals, and a large percentage of the Navajo families used more than three sources of support (see table 4).

TABLE 4 *Sources of instrumental/emotional support*

TYPE OF SUPPORT	%
Church/religious including Navajo traditional	88
Other family members	84
Grandparents	64
Friends	12
Professional therapy	8
Other families with children with disabilities	4

Spiritual Support

When asked if there had been any other help a Navajo woman received for her son, she answered, "Yeah, traditionwise. We had a ceremony about three times for him. . . . They just told me, you know, he's doing good and he'll do better. You know, just talking to me, and it's worked out OK. It took a lot off my mind. It took a load off my shoulders, you know."

Some 95% of the families interviewed mentioned spiritual services as part of their lives, and 88% said that they used spiritual sources in providing support to their child with a disability. Families made a distinction between two different kinds of spiritual services: traditional ceremonies and church services. Navajos used the term "traditional" for ceremonies based on the Navajo creation story, and also at times for Native American church ceremonies. It was clear that a "ceremony" and a "church service" were seen as different types of spiritual practices. One father explained, " I go to church whenever time permits, but I'm pretty traditional since my mother and my father were traditional Navajos. That was just their way. We had ceremonies for her [the child]. I know a lot of people that are . . . they perform different types of ceremonies. Traditional Navajo. And I think we went to one person who was NAC [Native American Church] who was over south of Gallup."

"Traditional" Navajo Ceremonies

Briefly, Navajo ritual services or ceremonies are based on the Navajo creation story, *Dine Bahane*, which may be compared to the Judeo-Christian Bible, though the Navajo story is still mainly an oral account. Each ceremony is based on a part of the story, and there are prayers and songs that accompany that section of the story. The Blessingway ceremony is considered by medicine men to be the basic ceremony from which all the others spring. There are variations of the Blessingway ceremony for different circumstances, usually blessings for places or persons. Other ceremonies mentioned by the families studied are the Enemy Way, which is performed in the summer and the Lightning Way and Red Ant Way, which are examples of ceremonies that are still performed, though not as frequently. Some ceremonies are rare, and, if needed, it would be necessary to find someone who would be able to provide them. A *Hataali*, or singer, performs a ceremony for a predetermined fee. The singer or medicine man may talk to the client and determine what ceremony is needed, but often uses a diagnostician to determine the appropriate ceremony. Families sometimes consult a diagnostician (a crystal gazer, hand trembler, or star gazer) before having a ceremony. The specific ceremony depends upon the underlying problem, but the underlying problem must often be determined by a diagnostician. Sand paintings and herbal preparations often accompany the ritual but are interwoven with the prayers and songs in a specific manner based both on the needs of the individual who is being prayed for and the creation story.

Native American Church (NAC)

This religion combines Christianity and Native American ceremonial chanting. The communion host is peyote. There are also NAC ceremonies that do not involve peyote. Services are conducted in the same manner as ceremonies; they are sponsored by a particular family or person requesting the ceremony. A large ceremony that is open to all the members of the church is called a "meeting" or "peyote meeting." Usually the sponsoring family asks for a ceremony for a certain reason or purpose, such as to help a family member who is sick or to give strength in time of need. There are no specific ceremonies as in Navajo religion, but the ceremony is dedicated to the purposes stated by the sponsors. There is a growing body of NAC songs, and they are sold on cassette tapes in some reservation stores. The services are Pan-Indian and open only to Native American Indians. NAC medicine men or ministers are called "roadmen." The religion started in the plains tribes, and for that reason meetings are held in tepees. Usually a tepee on the Navajo reservation means that there is a Native American Church meeting. These have become prevalent on the Navajo reservation.

Bible Churches and Pentecostal Churches

These are Christian churches, with individual ministries operating independently. Pentecostal Churches are also called Bible Churches at times, so it is not always clear which denomination a Bible Church represents. The ministers are often Navajo, and many have wide reputations for their preaching abilities. Pentecostal Churches are among the most common Christian churches on the Navajo reservation. The religion is characterized as one in which the members seek to be filled with the Holy Spirit. In addition to regular Sunday services, there are revival meetings all around the reservation during the summer.

Other Churches

Nearly every Christian denomination is represented on the Navajo reservation. One of the reasons for this is that when the governing body of the Navajo tribe was first set up, it made the process of acquiring land for church groups relatively easy. Often generations of a family stay with one church. Christian churches that were mentioned by the families interviewed were: Catholic, Baptist, Jehovah's Witnesses, Bahá'í (a non-Christian church), Seventh Day Adventist, Latter-day Saints (Mormon), Church of Christ, and Presbyterian.

Pattern of Religious Support

Of the families interviewed, 74% said that they had used Navajo ceremonies for support, 30% used Native American Church ceremonies, 33% used Bible Church or Pentecostal Church services, and 41% used other churches for support. For many of the families these were not mutually exclusive support systems. Fifty-two percent of the families practiced more than one religion or sought support from more than one spiritual source. In three of these families each parent practiced a different religion. In most of these households, however, both parents practiced more than one religion. The most common pattern was the practice of both traditional Navajo religion and a Christian religion. One Navajo mother said that at first she thought that it might be a problem to marry a traditional Navajo since she was raised as a Baptist, but now they get blessings from both sides, "intermingled or intertwined blessings." Approximately 30% of the members of Christian churches did not want their children to practice Navajo traditional religion. One mother explained, "I was never raised on the traditional ways . . . and from what I've heard from the people that go to church here, it doesn't help them at all . . . They start going to squaw dances [Enemy Way ceremonies] and learn how to drink and take up with boys at a younger age." A more prevailing view in the families was that Christianity was not in conflict with Navajo religion. This view was expressed by a father who said:

> We feel that in order to prepare a child for some of the hardships in life that you have to prepare them spiritually as well. And a lot of times we see that children who are not prepared spiritually, they encounter problems, and when they do encounter problems, they don't resort to religion of any type. And then we feel like it's only their choice, but yet we try to instill in them the forms of traditional *Dine'* [Navajo] at the same time as the Christian teachings, you know, so we instill in them that one day they, when they do encounter problems, they resort to either one of them.

Spiritual support was sought during times of crisis in which a child needed to be hospitalized, often away from the reservation. One mother described her situation and the two kinds of spiritual support her family gave:

> He just got weak, and we didn't know what to do, so we took him to the hospital over here [Indian Health Service], and I was up that night . . . They told me I had to go into Phoenix [with him] . . . Then my grandfather was down there, and he helped me. He prayed for the baby and me, and about a week later he [the child] was sitting up. Then my side of the family left, and I think they had ceremonies and all that done for the baby, 'cause they asked me for his pictures and all that, and his little clothes.

In the above example, spiritual support is interconnected with family support, medical services, and the extended family's resources. The mother's grandfather, a Christian minister, made a long trip to the hospital to pray for the baby, and the mother felt that her grandfather's prayers contributed to the improvement in the child. Other family members took pictures and articles of clothing so that they could have a ceremony for the child when they returned to the reservation, even though the child remained in the hospital.

Other Indigenous Support

Indigenous services are those that operate to provide services without government application. Examples of these kinds of services commonly found in all families are: baby sitting or emergency child caretaking; emotional support; financial and other help such as food and gifts for ceremonies; wood chopping; coal and water hauling; meal preparation; livestock care, including purchasing and hauling hay; and transportation to agencies for formal services and for shopping for needed items for the child or family such as dog food, diapers, or baby formula.

Indigenous services are encouraged by the kinship terms of the Navajo language for family and extended family. The reinforcement of family implicitly indicates both support and obligation for the family member. For example, when greeting family members it is appropriate to call them by their kinship term. A cousin might be called "my sister" or "my brother," an aunt is called "my little mother." In this way extended family or clan relatives are brought closer to the family. Brothers and sisters are not greeted by using their given names but as "my young sister" or "my older brother." Even people who are not directly related but are related by clan are greeted that way. This acknowledgment strengthens the bonds between family members. One of the strongest cultural tenets of Navajo society is that family members are obligated to one another. Family members are expected to take care of one another when help is needed. Asking for help from family members is normal and anticipated behavior. Typical favors family members ask are borrowing vehicles for necessary trips to town or paying for gas money, helping with ceremonies, donating money or groceries, chopping and hauling wood, butchering and cooking, and attending meetings of extended families.

In obtaining indigenous support, most of the families in the sample engaged in the same activities as Navajo families without children with disabilities. The frequency of activities, however, was greater due to intense needs. Ceremonies and other supportive activities are requested in times of stress such as funerals, weddings, and illness. When a child has a medical crisis, it is an accepted pattern for the immediate family to ask relatives for help with ceremonies and transportation. This is part of a system that existed before the public health and government programs for families were instituted and that still provides an extensive amount of support for families, though not without costs to the family.

Nearly 86% of the families said that they received financial help from their extended families. Thus several of the grandparents paid for ceremonies for their grandchildren by selling a rug or cattle. Grandparents and other family members also helped pay expenses for off-reservation travel to hospitals. One of the parents talked about her family having a meeting with extended family members in order to raise funds for the hospital visit.

Fifty-seven percent of the families said that the parents moved in order to be closer to their extended family for child care and support. One woman said that she moved in with her mother after her child was born with a disability, but later found that she wanted to move because her mother did not understand the demands of the disability. She found that living near the grandmother, but not with her, was better. Half of the families also talked about relying on siblings and grandparents for child care. A common pattern was for grandparents to become active caretakers for the child when one or both of the parents worked, and this also happened in families in which the child did not have a disability.

Benefits and Costs of Indigenous Formal Support Systems

Culture is not uniform for all families; each family forms its own interactive niche within the systems available. Families attempt to utilize the benefits of the culture familiar to them and to minimize the costs. The benefits of spiritual services for the families were many: parents felt that the services helped their child improve physically and developmentally, and they helped families to accept and cope with their child's disability and to provide material support by gathering their resources. In addition, the spiritual services interacted with formal medical systems in a positive way by helping parents to feel better about complying with medical procedures. There were also costs involved in using the informal services: money for ceremonies, demands on extended-family resources, and the more insidious cost of shame and guilt that developed in some etiologies of disability. In the following examples the families give insight into their interactions with these systems.

Many of the Navajo families we interviewed felt that spiritual services helped their child improve. Some examples are:

> Mother whose child was in intensive care at hospital: "Then my grandfather [a Christian minister] was down there and he helped me. He prayed for the baby and me, and about a week later he was—not even a week—he was sitting up. They [the doctors] couldn't believe it."

> Mother of child with Down's syndrome: "But now she's [child who had Navajo prayer ceremonies performed for her] gotten to the point she's about a month behind, and other than that she's pretty well up-to-date. So she's pretty alert, and the Doctors say that she wouldn't be."

> Grandmother of child with multiple disabilities: "Most the of the time she was in a daze . . . and I had a prayer done for her; then I had a couple of [large ceremonies] . . . and I took her back [to the doctor], and he told me right off, he told me that [the child] was more alert."

> Parents whose child was in off-reservation hospital: "We had a traditional ceremonial, and my parents, they mostly did the peyote meetings on her . . . On the peyote meeting, they just put her clothes or anything like that for her there, and on the ceremonial they just sat her there herself, so that she could get well real fast, and it helped a lot."

> Parents of child whose development was delayed and who was not sleeping well: "Families also spoke about the peace of mind these services gave to them as parents. All the nightmares went away after she [and older medicine woman] said that prayer over all three of us."

> Parent of child with Down's syndrome: "[Be]cause for a while there we were just going in all directions, we couldn't get our minds focused, but that [ceremony] helped. We were like going wild trying to figure out why, why, why, and we were trying to find out answers, but [after having ceremony] it doesn't matter now. I pretty much accept it now; I accept her whole to the point that, ya know, she's our child with special needs, she [just needs special things]."

Spiritual services sometimes gave families more hope and more positive expectations of their child than the medical doctors provided. A doctor, for example, told a parent that her child would need to wear leg braces in order to learn to walk, but the traditional healer told the parent that, "it is just a slow development in her. Other than that, she [the healer] checked from her legs on up to her spine. She said everything is working perfectly, she said, but its just that it is slow getting there. She is going to grow out of it, she said. So I believe that she will." Other parents said, "The doctors sort of like discouraged us. [Then we had a Navajo ceremony], not an all-night [full Blessingway ceremony], just a couple hours of prayers. So she's pretty alert, and the doctors said that she wouldn't be."

In another case, ceremonial healing helped the family to relieve their misgivings and thus increased their compliance with the medical system while their child was in a hospital. A prayer ceremony made them feel much better about the medical procedures, and they felt that the ceremonies helped to protect their child from harm during an operation: "The next morning they [husband and son] took back off to come up [to the reservation] to have more prayers done traditionally. We [mother and child] stayed in the hospital, and we told them [the doctors] to go ahead [with the operation]."

Spiritual services also functioned to provide support in terms of gathering resources for the family. When a family planned a ceremony or a church meeting was held, family and church members provided food and other material support. Groceries, wood, and money were collected for the use of the family in need. In the rural environment of the Navajo reservation, there are few regular meeting places for extended families to get together, but ceremonies and prayer services provided these opportunities.

Spiritual and Navajo family support systems are valuable for some, but not necessarily for all individuals in families. Some members of a family may pay the cost of keeping family harmony. The families we interviewed recounted cases of people with disabilities who paid the cost. At the same time, the recognition of the harm that these adaptations inflict seems to be a catalyst for change. A Navajo mother talks about what she remembers about people with disabilities when she was growing up:

> It's like they were, I don't know, like they had no mind of their own, and I remember when I was ten years old and there was this one handicapped that was tied to the middle of this hogan. I don't know what was wrong with him. I never thought about him until I had [my son with Down's syndrome], then I thought I wonder whatever happened to him. You know, it seemed like those days Navajos didn't understand. They were afraid that this person had a *Chindi* [spirit] in him. That's how I heard it described. I think people have to talk. There's this one lady over here. I keep telling her—I don't know if I'm getting through to her, 'cause I never see her take her baby anywhere. I know her baby's Down's. We need to help each other.

One family who had the Navajo ceremony and felt that it helped them also felt that there were things about Navajo traditional beliefs that were not helpful. When he first found out about Down's syndrome, the father wanted to find out the cause:

> When I got more frustrated was when I started talking to some of the elderly and even some of the people who worked in these various programs. [They told us] the only time that [genetic disability] happens is when you are actually related. Baloney, we're not even related . . . our clans did not at all relate in any manner whatsoever. [This person] just comes up to me and says, "Well, it's your fault because you were related or something like that or something that happened in your background." But that's not the case . . .

Another mother explains how her husband's extended family assigned blame when his son had a brain tumor: "That's how the extended family views him as being sick is that one of us did something that caused him to be sick. They will frequently ask questions like 'Did you drive past a cemetery or funeral parlor?' and stuff like that . . . But there was so many things that I was told that caused it . . ."

A few people talked about the financial costs of having ceremonies:

> Mother of child with disability: "My in-laws are traditional so they talk to us about it [having a ceremony for their son], but we just haven't had really anything done for him yet; we just don't have the time and money."

> Father of child with Down's syndrome: "I bought this real nice basket for her [to be used for a ceremony] because I wanted to get a blessing done, and it cost me a fairly outrageous price. I thought it was well worth it for [my daughter] ."

One of the heaviest costs of spiritual support for families, especially for those who used Navajo ceremonies, were the demands that were made on the families' time and resources. There were cases in which families did fund raising, sold grandparents' rugs and crafts, and provided groceries and other material goods for services. In the sample of families we interviewed, however, there were few negative comments about this. The common attitude was expressed by the parent who said it was well worth it.

Informal support is greater in families in which a family member provides the spiritual services, as in the case in which the grandfather prayed for the child, or in which the family contributes to a ceremony. This can both strengthen and stress families. When the demands on a family are too great, the stress has the potential to be detrimental. The challenges that families face are often daunting.

A woman whose daughter was born prematurely related how she stayed with relatives for over six months in order to be near her daughter. In this case several different families helped out, and there was no feeling expressed that families were distressed by this.

> I stayed with my cousin who lived there at Albuquerque . . . I didn't think she [the child] was going to make it out of the hospital. But [my cousin] said, "Oh, she will." She would talk to me, and she would give me a ride over to the hospital and then back to the house. And then she said that she went through the same thing with her daughter. Then, pretty soon, it was already five weeks went by. Then they said they wanted to send her [the child] to Gallup. We sent her to Gallup on a plane. Over there they put her back in the incubator because she had a few more IVs in her, and she needed to gain about two more pounds. I moved to my sister's over there in Gallup. We stayed with her for a month, and after that we went over to my brother's and stayed with him for three, four months.

Another woman spoke about how her nephews helped her take care of her child, but other family members were reluctant to help.

> I wasn't pushing nobody to try feeding him for me or, you know, do things like what I do, give him his treatment . . . They, more or less, you know, whenever they felt comfortable, they can come in and ask if they could do something. My nephew just picked him up and now feeds him through the G-tube, and he would feed him and he's real comfortable with him. And he doesn't even fight. He fights me when I feed him at times, but with his big brother [cousin] he would just sit there and take his feeding. But other than that, my mother and everybody, there's . . . I can tell at times when they're uncomfortable with something he does . . . You can see they just feel uncomfortable at times.

The pulling away of family and friends was extremely difficult for the Navajo families that we interviewed. The father of a child with cerebral palsy spoke about needing someone to talk to who could understand his situation.

> They told us he had cerebral palsy and that really hit me hard. It was the worst thing that could happen to me, you know. At that time I started thinking, "Why? Why me? Why is it?" I started having ceremonies done and I was doing everything. I went to church. I talked to people, but it seemed like nobody would understand. They would listen, but they didn't know what was going on inside, and that was harder to deal with than anything else. Not being understood.

The mother of a child with a brain tumor and other disabilities reported:

> There were so many things that I was told that caused it. Going past cemeteries, dead dogs . . . working in a special ed classroom . . . I mean, all kinds of things. I felt like I was overwhelmed, and I just felt like all of a sudden my friends pulled away, his family

> backed off, it was like there was no support of anybody coming around, nobody to talk to, nobody to get any other information or to share with, so it made it real, real hard.

The grandmother and legal guardian of a child with a disability complained:

> It was kind of hard for me to accept, you know, that [my granddaughter] was like that, you know, that her development was delayed. It was kind of hard because I never had any experience with my children like that . . . By talking to somebody with a child like that, it, all those things, it would have helped, you know, but I come a long ways after I experience all that through myself.

The mother of a child with respiratory problems spoke about the lack of family support:

> The only people I see a lot are my sisters-in-law. They say everything is my fault. I caused [my child] to be sick. I make my husband drink. There is no one I can talk to that understands. Now this one lady comes around from the Jehovah's Witnesses. She is really the only one that I can talk to now.

Another mother explained that she did not tell her parents and extended family that her baby had Down's syndrome, but she became increasing depressed and broke down crying during a clinic visit. The doctor at that point spent more time talking to her and convinced her to talk to the family. "We told our relatives and then we had some blessings done for us and then from that point [things changed for the better]." The formal help that this family received served to strengthen the family, which in turn allowed the parents to make a decision. In this case the parents had set up an appointment for genetic testing; after the family involvement and ceremonies, they canceled the appointment and said, "It doesn't matter now."

The above case is a good example of how service providers can have a positive and reinforcing effect on a family and work to reinforce the strength of informal support. In another family the mother avoided the service providers who had set up appointments for therapy with her son, and the service providers could not understand why she did this. The mother explained:

> You know, to me he knows what he's doing like when he wants something, so sometimes I think that I don't really have a Down's, and I'm just waiting for him to start walking and start talking. That's what I'm waiting for, you know. I always wondered when he's going to really start walking. At what age, you know. Two, three, you know. I know it's going to take time. I just have to have the patience for that.

This mother acknowledges that her child is delayed, but does not feel she can do anything to hurry him. She feels that patience is the best thing she can provide. She also feels that the outside service providers who come to her house mark her as having a Down's syndrome child. The same mother talks about how her other children take care of her son: "They're really enjoying him, you know. He gets all the caring, and he knows when he's going to get all that attention too. The twelve-year-old, she really helps me out. She knows what he's going through. She does treatment. She helps me out with doing treatment on him sometimes. I'm proud of her you know."

Being a parent of a disabled child drains people emotionally and physically to such an extent that it would probably be impossible to give too much help. The important thing for representatives of outside agencies to remember is that it is critical to bring the family groups together to help the child and not supplant the positive effects the family has to offer in order to achieve positive results. Thus a father whose son has cerebral palsy explained: "There were some ladies down there that were with, I think it was, early intervention. They really helped me out. They really encouraged me. They came out, and they just told me how to take care of him, physical therapy, everything." The father of a daughter with Down's syndrome reported: "I feel very confident in them helping too, the intervention program 'cause right now, the last time I had her evaluated she was maybe two weeks behind schedule over a normal kid."

Conclusions

Families within the study showed many of the common traits of Navajo families with children without disabilities. On the other hand they displayed many traits that form a common bond with families with children with disabilities from any culture in the United States.

First, these families reported, they needed to understand that their child was different from their other children in certain ways. They needed to understand the disability in a way that made sense to them within the context of their cultural traditions. This understanding grew out of interactions with both the indigenous and the public health support systems. Each family constructed its own set of beliefs about the disability or condition and its causes and effects on the child's development and its own sense of the future. Like any cultural group, the families who were interviewed did not share a universal vision with respect to any of these issues. A better understanding of both the cultural and ecological pressures on a family system leads to a better understanding of how the family comes to an understanding of disability. As family members are able to frame the disability in terms they feel comfortable with, they gain a sense of well-being and acceptance.

Second, each family developed accommodations to their daily routine based on the ecological and cultural pressures that they faced. Some families moved in with relatives. Others relied heavily on extended-family members for economic and emotional support. In some families, the extended family routinely took part in the caregiving of the child with a disability. In others, this did not happen. These accommodation patterns demonstrated both the expected cultural norm and the heterogeneity around that norm for the target families. The common features represented by the cultural norm suggested the need for service providers to understand the cultural expectations that operate in a consistent fashion within families. The heterogeneity of expression demonstrated that there is no universal pattern of adaptability rigorously followed by all members of a cultural group. Rather, it is a stereotype held up as a standard that families can recognize and react to even though it may not fit their particular conditions. The adaptive patterns generated by families are by definition the "best-fit" accommodations they are able to construct with the resources at their disposal. The disability of the target child has forced a redistribution of resources and their ways of getting things done. As Navajo families made these accommodations based on their ecological and cultural resources, so too would any family in any culture.

1. These findings carry powerful messages for service providers within public health services, social services, and education. Stated in simple terms, these messages are: Indigenous systems are constructed in response to enduring cultural and ecological constraints. They are sufficiently forceful so that they are not easily altered without serious consequences to family well-being.
2. Public health systems will be most helpful to families when the services they provide honor, respect, and support indigenous models of belief and interaction. To do otherwise creates conflict and demands further accommodations from families already experiencing high levels of stress. The goal of such programs should be to fit into the indigenous system and require as few accommodations as possible, consistent with the mutually agreed-upon goals of family and child well-being.

7

Overcoming Obstacles and Improving Outcomes

American Indian Children with Special Needs

Martha G. Gorospe

The two million Native Americans who live in the United States have been called the most neglected minority ethnic group in the country. The leading cause of death is accidents, and this group has a much higher rate of disabilities than the general population. Many Native Americans also experience poverty, substandard health care and housing, racial discrimination, and substance abuse. The poverty rate is twice that of the general population, and the unemployment rate is five times higher. The death rate from alcohol-related causes is three times greater for Native Americans than for the general population.

Of all the barriers to obtaining good health, poverty may be the most significant for Native Americans. Poverty, usually due to unemployment, is associated with increased rates of mortality, illness, disability, alcoholism, and suicide. Native Americans with disabilities are significantly poorer than other Native Americans. In areas with high unemployment for people without disabilities, the rate of unemployment for people with disabilities is much higher.

Isolation is another problem. Of course, Native Americans who still live on their traditional homelands in remote areas may not consider isolation a problem per se, since they are living where they want to live. But it becomes a problem in terms of receiving health and rehabilitation services, since it necessitates traveling long distances over poor roads. Emergency services may take much longer, so that vehicle accidents result in more disabilities than accidents in urban areas would.

If obtaining health care is inconvenient, it is also less likely to be sought. Public transportation is rare on reservations. Given the unemployment and poverty rates, it is not surprising that many Native Americans lack vehicles. Public transportation accessible to people with disabilities is particularly rare. Many reservations have dirt roads and lack sidewalks, making wheelchair use a problem. Even tribal and Indian Health Service buildings are usually inaccessible, and making them accessible for people with disabilities is considered a low priority. Many Native American homes on reservations lack telephones, electricity, and running water.

Lack of services and the lack of awareness of services is another major barrier. Although Native Americans have more disabilities than the general population, they are less likely to receive services. Many Native Americans with disabilities are unaware of the existence of programs for which they are eligible, and many service agencies do little outreach to reservations and urban areas. Outreach is made difficult by other barriers, such as isolation, lack of transportation, language differences, and differences in values and lifestyles. Many public agencies are already overburdened with large caseloads and have little incentive to do expensive and time-consuming outreach to find new clients in rural areas.

There are also cultural barriers that are unique to the Native American population. One must keep in mind that this group is not homogeneous; there are hundreds of distinct tribes and languages. Beliefs about health, illness, and disability may differ greatly from the European-American tradition. Often traditional-minded Native Americans have major disabilities but do not consider themselves disabled because they live in extended families that accommodate their needs. They may not be fully functioning, but they are fully accepted in the families and the community, and their contributions are valued. Some American Indian cultures do not even have a term in their language for disability; the closest term is "being different."

Some traditional Indian healers say that disabilities occur because the individual or one of his or her relatives broke a taboo or failed to follow prescribed codes of behavior. Often there is little emphasis on the "specialness" of the individual with a disability.

In the literature on Indian history there are some references to people with disabilities. The historian and author Dee Brown records many Indian names indicative of a disability, such as No-eyes, One-arm, and He-who-walks-with-a-limp.

Since some Native Americans think that disability results from breaking a cultural taboo, people with disabilities are sometimes stigmatized. Native American individuals may prefer not to bring attention to a disability. For example, a visually impaired woman on a rural reservation preferred not to use a cane for mobility; instead, she tied a string between the house and the garden and used it to guide herself. Other people with severe disabilities simply stay home as much as possible. In another case, a blind Indian woman who received corneal transplants from a cadaver became stigmatized because people said she had the eyes of a dead man.

Service providers should understand that when dealing with a culturally different group, special training and sensitivity may be required for it to be effective. Special culturally sensitive public-awareness activities may be necessary to make Native Americans aware that services are available. Outreach will be necessary to serve clients where they live, rather than expecting them to travel long distances for appointments. The client's family and extended family should be involved as much as possible to take advantage of their concern and support for the client.

Barriers such as intake paperwork, rigid appointment schedules, and psychological assessments should be minimized, and service providers should be trained to provide culturally appropriate services to Native Americans. Service agencies should hire more Native Americans to provide services. Services should be provided in the client's primary language.

Great strides can be made if administrators and providers make the necessary commitment to serve in a culturally appropriate way and strive to serve Indian people with disabilities in proportion to their population. It is important to note that Indian families, like all families who have children with special needs, face a variety of obstacles in obtaining specialized services or care for their children. Three principal barriers are: financial barriers, systems barriers, and knowledge barriers. Indian families with disabled children experience barriers with an overlay of additional difficulties arising from the inevitable conflicts between western culture and traditional Indian beliefs and values.

Mutual respect and understanding between the service provider and the family is the foundation for an effective program. Appreciation of Indian cultural values and beliefs, particularly those on child rearing, is a critical first step toward the development of a positive relationship between the provider and the Indian family. The provider must also gain the knowledge and skills necessary to work effectively with Indian families. These skills include techniques for improving cross-cultural communication, methods for determining the level of acculturation of the family, and methods for adapting a program to fit the lifestyle and values of the family.

There are many ways that non-Indian professionals can provide services while incorporating the family's cultural beliefs and practices on child rearing, health, and healing. For example, the Indian family may view traditional Indian healing services as their first priority and may not view early intervention services, particularly with a newborn infant, as important. Fischler and Freshman found that Navajo families could not relate to the concept of "developmental milestones." Their study reported that some families appeared to believe that if doctors or teachers diagnosed a problem, it was their responsibility to fix it. Other families felt that acknowledging their child's problem meant that they did not accept their child as he or she was born, an important Indian value. Consequently, the family would deny that the child had any special needs. In this situation, the early interventionist might focus on helping the family to get other nonintervention services and information such as financial assistance until the time that they are ready for early intervention.

The Individualized Family Service Plan (IFSP), a planning process mandated under the Individuals with Disabilities Education Act (IDEA), requires long-range goal setting for the child with special needs. However, the thought of setting up future goals may seem inappropriate for many Indian families. Asking a family a simple question such as, "What would you like your child to be able to do?" may cause the family discomfort. For many Indian families it would be more appropriate to focus on their immediate needs. Indian families want information on the services available for their child with special needs. Discussions can also focus on such needs as basic day-to-day care, special medications or therapeutic equipment, financial resources, and transportation.

The provider should not assume that the biological parents are the primary decision makers about the child's program. The parents should be asked whom they want to be included in meetings and be encouraged to bring along those family members. Whenever possible, location and space for a meeting should be based on the family's needs. Parents need time to go back to their families and discuss information with them. If time lines for services are controlled by regulations or standards, these should be explained to the family so they can take them into consideration.

Awareness of the Family's State of Acculturation

The provider must try to understand the Indian family's level of acculturation. Acculturation is frequently thought of as existing on a continuum. This continuum includes a wide range of Indian beliefs and values from very traditional to assimilated. The degree of acculturation is related to the family's behaviors and traditional beliefs, family, child rearing practices, health care practices, and language. Generally, the more traditional the family is, the less accepting of Euro-American methods or practices it is. In this situation, the family will primarily follow Indian healing customs and rituals.

This cultural continuum is dynamic for most Indian families. Many move back and forth along the continuum at different points in their lives. The family may also include individuals from different tribes, with different beliefs and practices. When various family members are at different places on the continuum or have different beliefs, there may be disagreement about whether the child needs early intervention. The process of coming to an agreement among the various family members may take additional time. The family may not be willing to accept early intervention services or move on to the next step in the early intervention process; for example, assessment or IFSP development, until they have had time to resolve their conflicting views.

It is not uncommon for more acculturated parents to become more traditional after the birth of a child, particularly a child with a disability or serious illness. There are a variety of reasons for this. Traditional Indian ways can provide the family with readily understandable explanations or causes for the disability or illness. Often medical science cannot provide an exact etiology for the disability. Even if a biological cause for the disability is known, traditional family members may not accept the explanation given by the doctors because it may conflict with their religious beliefs or customs. Knowing and accepting the cause helps all family members accept the disability or illness. They may then be ready for intervention.

Traditional Indian practices also provide the family with action steps that prepare them to meet needs their child might have in the future. Sometimes they are encouraged to follow all the recommended Indian practices before using non-Indian procedures or services. The parents may accept those recommendations, or they may seek to work out a compromise enabling them to use Euro-American and traditional services.

Historical Interaction between Indian Families and Professionals

Historically, Indian family involvement has not been encouraged by professional service providers. The Anglo-directed "service system" of educational, health, and social services has not involved Indian parents in the decision-making and planning process. Consequently, many families have had experiences that inhibit their active involvement with their children's service providers.

Following is an example of "trained non-involvement" by professionals. Until the 1960s, the Bureau of Indian Affairs took many Indian children, as young as five years of age, from their homes and bused them to boarding schools. Frequently, parents were not told which school their children would be attending. The educational system made all the decisions about their child's education and care for at least nine months of the year.

Historically, the Indian Health Service (IHS) has been the provider of Euro-American health care services for Indian people. Typically, these services are focused on episodic and acute care. In addition, IHS primary-care physicians have a relatively high rate of attrition (including transfers from one service area to another). This situation does not encourage the continuity of service necessary for an Indian family to develop a trusting relationship with their child's health care provider. Thus, the family may not want to get involved in the decision-making or planning process. This can be particularly detrimental for Indian children who have chronic health problems or developmental disabilities.

Relationships

Indian families usually consider relationships with individuals paramount to relationships with organizations or institutions. Families often build a relationship with a particular professional. However, they may not feel a strong tie or commitment to the agency or institution for whom that individual works. Family involvement is predicated more on the dynamics of the relationship with the individual than on the larger system of services. This can affect the way families respond to assigned case managers or early interventionists. For example, personnel changes resulting from staff turnover at a particular agency or from transitions from one early-intervention provider to preschool or another service provider may cause the family to withdraw from needed services.

Indian families have identified "service provider support" as a key requirement in obtaining services for their children with special needs. The type of support most frequently seen as significant was "emotional support and respect." This reinforces the idea that service providers must develop interpersonal skills that motivate Indian families to become more involved in their child's intervention program.

Additionally, agency administration must be aware that Indian families develop relationships with individuals, not agencies. This fact must be considered when making administrative decisions such as changing case assignments and assigning case loads.

Family Roles and Responsibilities

In American Indian culture, family is frequently defined in a broader sense than the nuclear, immediate family. Family may include immediate family and extended-family members, or it may be as broad as the family's clan or tribe. In many families, the roles and responsibilities related to the care of the child may belong to members of the extended family rather than the biological parents. Age and life experience are highly valued by most Indian families. The biological parents will seek the advice and support of their older brothers and sisters, their parents, their grandparents, and other elders in the extended family. For example, decisions to be made concerning health care or early intervention for a child may be deferred to a grandmother or elder aunt. In more traditional families, an extended-family member acts as a case manager. That individual takes an active role in identifying and coordinating traditional Indian services the child needs and helping the parents get those services.

In a family support survey conducted by Southwest Communication Resources, Indian families stated that "emotional support and respect" and "case management and advocacy" were key elements in improving services for Indian children with special needs. "Case management and advocacy" was also the most frequent response given by service providers. These results confirm the need of Indian families to have a supportive provider who will help them in accessing and using the health care system.

Health, Healing, and Intervention

In American Indian cultures, health is a state of combined physical, mental, and spiritual well-being. Because these cannot be separated, traditional Indian healers treat the "total person." The whole family is often viewed as being affected by the person who is unhealthy. Consequently, the entire family must become involved in the various aspects of treatment. Traditional Indian healing practices are usually less intrusive physically, mentally, and emotionally. For example, traditional healing techniques typically do not penetrate the body in an intrusive way. An Indian family whose child has multiple problems may express discomfort in going to several specialists, all of whom seemingly ask the same questions. The family may allow the appointments to be scheduled but not show up for them. They may ask why they can't go to one doctor who will take care of everything.

Communication and Interaction

The most obvious difference in communication between cultural groups is different languages. Some Indian families speak English as a second language, and some speak no English. Because English is the second language for some Indian families, they are still more comfortable hearing or discussing new information in their native language.

Another important issue involves cross-cultural communication patterns (interaction styles). Cultural groups have specific rules for appropriate communication and interaction. These depend on such factors as who is involved in a discussion, where the discussion is taking place, and what the discussion is about.

In many Indian cultures, the roles and responsibilities of individual family members affect communication patterns. For example, making eye contact during conversation may only be acceptable in certain situations. In traditional families, the listener typically looks down and does not ask questions when a healer or elder is speaking. Asking too many questions is not an acceptable behavior. In fact, silence is considered an acceptable and important part of conversation, allowing those involved time to think.

Another example may further serve to highlight a basic difference between non-Indian professionals and Indian families. Professionals are trained to communicate information about the child directly to the parents and expect the parents to communicate directly with them. In some Indian cultures it is not always appropriate to communicate feelings and concerns directly. Instead, the idea is communicated to another family member who takes responsibility for communicating the idea to the intended recipient of the message. Thus Indian parents have reported that they are not comfortable telling the doctor that they need to talk with other family members before agreeing to a surgical procedure for their child. Instead, they have communicated their reasons to an Indian nurse, who then communicated the information to the doctor.

Families cannot share some kinds of information with certain people. It may be because the person is not a family member or is viewed as an outsider. Or it may be because the person is of the same tribe and the family does not want to share personal information with someone from within their tribe. When a non-Indian professional selects a person from the family's tribe to act as an interpreter for the family, the family may feel that the interpreter chosen is not appropriate for confidentiality reasons and may become less communicative toward the interpreter. The professional may feel confused by the situation. Once again, the provider's well-intentioned effort to communicate with the family is not successful. The outcome might have been more successful if the choice of an interpreter had been discussed with the family.

Communication and interaction styles are complex. They affect decisions such as what a service provider should do when the family does not ask questions or gives indirect messages. Misunderstandings and uncomfortable interactions can occur when the service provider and the family have differing communication and interaction styles.

In contrast to non-Indian families, most Indian families view time as being plentiful; therefore the pace of actions and activities is slower. The family may place a high value on using whatever time is needed to make the right decision or accomplish a task correctly. Taking time is essential in developing trusting relationships. There are no time lines to predict or determine when something will be accomplished or completed. When deciding about a nonemergency medical treatment, a family may need time to discuss it with other family members. If there are differing views among family members, the family may take a long time (as much as a year) to decide what to do. This decision-making time is necessary, even if it means postponing treatment.

Some families may use traditional Indian healing ceremonies simultaneously with a medical treatment program. Other families may decide to have a traditional Indian healing activity done before they use a Euro-American treatment. However, they may have to wait for the right time to conduct a traditional healing ceremony. Because this information may be considered too personal or sacred to share with an outsider, the family may not tell the provider what is causing the delay. Instead, they may refuse the treatment, postpone the treatment, or continue to miss appointments scheduled by the service provider.

Professionals may be confused by this behavior or misinterpret it to mean that the family is not interested or does not care. If they suspect that this is the case, they may further explore the family's need for other services that may be acceptable. For example, the family may need help in applying for financial assistance to buy special equipment, or they may need help in enrolling in a commodity program such as WIC (Women, Infants, and Children). If nothing else, the provider can continue to visit the family on a regular basis to see how the child is doing and keep the family aware that services are available when they are ready. This expression of sincere concern and interest on the part of the provider is essential to the development of a trusting relationship with the family.

There are many environmental factors that may act as barriers that prevent Indian families from accessing services. Barriers include a scarcity of local service providers in certain areas, lack of transportation, and poor road and weather conditions. Many Indian families do not have transportation. This may make the scheduling of appointments difficult.

Another factor is the environment of the agency. This includes the physical setting and the psychosocial atmosphere. When Native Americans walk into an agency for the first time, they look for someone with whom they can identify (a person of color). They may sit and watch for that type of person to appear. If no one appears, they may feel discomfort. Discomfort may also result if the family is given a lot of paperwork to complete. Indian culture is not paper-and-pencil oriented.

Many Indian families are not comfortable if the facility is large and they are sent from department to department without someone to guide them. Again, this type of experience is incongruent with their cultural practice of accessing health care.

As a result, the family may leave before receiving the services they came for. In many instances, they may not return for further services. Finally, many families will not even go to a facility where they have experienced, or heard from others that they are likely to experience, discriminatory or disrespectful treatment by professionals or other staff.

Indian families must deal with many private, tribal, and governmental agencies. When trying to get services for a child with special needs, this maze of systems, each with different procedures and policies, can become overwhelming. Again, this contrasts with their custom of securing Indian healing services for a family member. When an Indian parent has a child with special needs, family members help them find and use traditional Indian services. There is no such resource to guide them through the complex system of Euro-American medical services. Indian families and service providers must face the task of working together despite many barriers. Effective cross-cultural communication is one of the essential elements in overcoming these differences and establishing a comfortable working relationship. Service providers must try to develop interpersonal skills that motivate Indian families to become more involved in their child's intervention program. Non-Indian professionals should identify someone who can help them when they have questions or when they want to check their perceptions about their interactions with Indian families. That individual might be an Indian parent liaison or another professional who has more experience working with the families.

Personnel preparation programs at institutions of higher education must address the need to train new professionals on working effectively with culturally diverse populations. Agencies and early-intervention programs should provide orientation and training for new personnel to help them learn about the culture and living conditions of the Indian families with whom they will be working. Learning about Native American culture and more effective ways to work with Indian families should be a dynamic, ongoing process. Indian families and service providers are striving to do what each feels is best for the child. If there is effective communication during their interactions, the result will be better understanding, mutual respect, and improved intervention outcomes.

Despite the support of the federal government, numerous cultural, financial, and institutional barriers exist that prevent families from obtaining the care their children require. This is especially true for culturally diverse families who have low incomes and live in rural areas such as American Indian families, whose access to health care for their children with special needs remains particularly restricted.

In 1955, Congress established free medical care through the Indian Health Service for all tribally enrolled Indians. IHS has provided health care services through a network of community clinics and Indian hospitals on or near reservations. Over time, most American Indians have come to depend on this system for their health care. However, the situation is rapidly changing. Due to reduced funding and higher health care costs, the IHS can no longer meet all the health care needs of American Indians. Indian Health Service has never been funded over 40 percent of its recommended level. Indian families are finding it necessary to use private and state health care agencies (including specialists and private practitioners). This has resulted in confusion, frustration, and misunderstanding for many families as they begin to access care through state and private health care systems for the first time.

Parents and service providers have similar suggestions for improving understanding between families and providers, and they have shared similar ideas about the changes needed to improve services. Improving service availability was most often mentioned as being important, followed by better sources and kinds of support.

Parents and providers have specified the need for a parent liaison or health educator who speaks the language and takes the time to explain the diagnosis, answer questions, and discuss concerns.

The finding that good service provider support enhances accessibility whereas the lack of it inhibits access is not surprising, as care for an Indian child with special needs is not traditionally provided by outsiders. Indian families report feeling more comfortable using services when they are treated with respect and given emotional support.

Agency administrators and case managers should consider the significance of the case manager's role, not just as a link, but as an advocate. It is recommended that agencies serving culturally diverse families examine their procedures to determine if they inhibit families from accessing their services. One method is to include representatives from targeted cultural groups, preferably the parents of children with special needs, on the advisory boards that review their policies and procedures.

Among suggestions for improving understanding between families and providers, "effective communication" was considered absolutely essential to avoid a breakdown in communication, which keeps Indian children from receiving the services they need.

To reiterate, the following are four types of communication obstacles, with suggestions for addressing each.

1. Most providers do not speak the Indian language. Although English is a second language for many Indian families, it is recommended that agencies employ interpreters.
2. Providers use professional language that is unfamiliar to Indian families and not easily translated into Indian languages. Professionals must explain things in a way that is easy for the family to understand and for an interpreter to translate. It is also recommended that agencies employ parent-patient liaisons or educators who can assist in explaining the information or follow up with further discussions with the family.
3. Different cultures have different nonverbal communication and interaction styles that are often misunderstood by someone outside the culture. For example, the use of silence in a conversation or the use of the lips rather than a finger to point may cause confusion between a family and provider. Preservice and in-service training for providers should address cross-cultural communication and interaction styles.
4. Providers typically ask questions and use handouts, booklets, or in some cases dolls and pictures as communication aides. However, Indian healers ask few questions and do not use forms. Providers need to learn from families and tribal representatives methods of communicating information without creating discomfort. When questions need to be asked, the family should be told why the questions are being asked, the way the information they provide will be used, and how it might benefit their child.

Families stressed the importance of culturally appropriate services to improve understanding. They emphasized changes in policies and procedures as a necessary step, including eliminating administrative barriers through improved scheduling, shorter waiting times, and easier access to specialized services.

Service providers should remind themselves regularly that becoming a culturally responsive person is a lifelong process. It is OK to say, "I don't know, and I want to learn." They should feel good about their accomplishments and learn from mistakes.

Through this process, it is hoped that providers will explore the positive and humanistic aspects of their own culture and the cultures of others. Over time, it will become easier to accept that there are no right or wrong ways of doing things, just different ways.

References

Gorospe, Martha J. *American Indian Perspective on Disability*. Education for Parents of Indian Children with Special Needs. Project (EPICS). Southwest Communication Resources.

Malach, Randi Suzanne, and Norman Segel. *Perspectives on Healthcare Delivery Systems for American Indian Families*. Southwest Communication Resources, 1990.

Overcoming Obstacles and Improving Outcomes: Early Intervention Services for Indian Children with Special Needs, Southwest Communication Resources.

Thomason, Timothy C. *American Indian Population Statistics*. American Indian Rehabilitation Research and Training Center, Northern Arizona University Institute for Human Development.

PART II

Education

8

Bridge over Troubled Waters

Collaboration between the United States and Mexico on Behalf of Individuals with Disabilities

Sofíaleticia Morales

"On behalf of my country, I express our deep concern—surely shared by other nations—with regards to some political movements including measures which limit human rights which are considered universal such as the right to health and education. We know that these are isolated incidents, alien to the sentiments of friendship and cooperation of the national governments. We know that they are desperate acts and products of a lack of faith in the potential for advancement of human beings."

—Dr. Ernesto Zedillo, President of the United States of Mexico
First session of the Hemispheric Summit December 9–11 of 1994, Miami, Florida

Difficult Moments

North American legislation, especially Proposition 187, once again threatens the educational future and well-being of the children of illegal immigrants, most of whom are Mexican. The incidents at Riverside are worrisome and compel us to renew our efforts so that respect for human dignity comes to play a major role in the formative process. Faced with this panorama of "río sin cauce," we come forward today to reaffirm bonds of friendship and collaboration between our two countries, bonds springing from a mutual commitment to work toward the inclusion of individuals with disabilities into society.

Binational Cooperation: Mexico–United States

Fifteen years ago the Mexico-United States Binational Commission was established to analyze collaboration strategies. Beside presidential meetings, the meetings of the Binational Commission are the most important consulting mechanism between our two nations. The Binational Commission meetings are held at alternate sites annually; they are cochaired by the Secretary of Education from each country and are attended by government cabinet members from each country. In 1990, the year of the eighth meeting of the Binational Commission, the "Memorandum of Understanding Regarding Education" between the government of Mexico and the government of the United States was signed. Since that date, discussions regarding the subject of education have intensified. Despite this progress, special education was not added to the agenda until the twelfth Binational Commission meeting which convened in October 1995 in Washington, DC. The recommendations made there as a result of these bilateral agreements were evaluated during the first week of May 1996, the date of the thirteenth Binational Commission meeting in Mexico City.

The coming together of the two countries on the subject of special education is due, in part, to the efforts of this group and the tireless energy and efforts of building bridges by Judith Heumann. Our conviction is that there exist ancestral bonds between our people. The indigenous inhabitants of our nations were brothers, and over the course of time our people have merged, and we are here to acknowledge the importance of the union of our two cultures.

There is no doubt that the Binational Commission meetings provide us with the framework for collaboration between the government of Mexico and the government of the United States using the "Memorandum of Understanding Regarding Education" as a guide. In its fourth annex for 1996 to 1998, the subject of special education is regarded as a priority on the agenda of both countries. However, as recognized in the memorandum, the principle role in this effort falls on the teachers and researchers. It is knowledge and technical experience and daily efforts that will permit us to realize our aspirations and build the future.

Special Education in Mexico—Long Road Journeyed

The tradition of special education in Mexico goes back to 1867 and the presidency of Benito Juárez, who issued decrees that resulted in the founding of the National School for the Deaf and the National School for the Blind in 1870. Since then, many services have been established to meet the needs of minors with disabilities. Between 1919 and 1927 two schools for girls and boys were established in Mexico City that offered orientation and mobility education. In 1935, the Medical Pedagogical Institute was created and in 1936, the Behaviour Clinic. However, it has been only fifty-five years since the reform of the Organic Law of Education established the institutionalization of special education. As a result, the Normal School of Specialization was created and inaugurated in 1943 to train teachers to specialize in the education of mentally retarded children and young offenders. In 1959, the Coordination Office for Special Education, directed by the State Higher Education and Scientific Research Office was created. Twenty-five years after the creation of the Medical Pedagogical Institute, two schools for "educable mentally retarded" children were founded. However, it was not until 1970 that, by presidential decree, the State Special Education Office under the direction of the Deputy Office of Basic Education was created. The creation of this state office was the *definite* setting for institutionalizing services for all atypical children and youth in Mexico.

Legislation

Although one may say that as of 1914 the project for an organic law that contemplated special education existed, it was not until 1993 that the General Education Law, as a federal regulating framework, established the government's obligation to satisfy by means of different strategies the fundamental learning needs of people with disabilities. It recommended that in regular schools the program include parents and tutors as well as teachers who were to provide services for students with special needs. Article 41 of the General Education Law states:

> Special education is earmarked for individuals with temporary or definite disabilities, as well as those that are talented or gifted. It will strive to educate students in accordance with their physical differences, with social equity. With regard to children with disabilities, this education will provide inclusion in regular elementary schools. For those who are unable to be integrated, this education will strive to satisfy general learning needs to achieve autonomous, social, and productive coexistence.

Legislation that favors the inclusion of children with disabilities in regular schools contributes to the challenges within our educational system. However, experience has shown that although regulating frameworks favor inclusion of children with disabilities, there is much to be done in order to gradually change segregated contexts to integrated ones. The existence of legislation does not reduce the controversy embedded in the decision. Research confirms that the key factor for promoting inclusion is accessibility to the curriculum, which will provide children with the complementary resources to facilitate the learning process. In addition, teacher training plays an essential role in the success of the process.

Inclusive Education: Reality or Promise?

With the creation of the State Office for Special Education came an awareness that people with disabilities should have the same privileges, rights, and obligations as any other person. However, at the time of its creation in Mexico, the concept of offering an equitable education to people with disabilities was to place them in specialized schools and in contexts that allowed them to coexist with children of their same age and similar levels of disabilities and to provide specialized teachers to meet their needs. We must recognize, however, that from its inception special education in Mexico has been implemented within a clinical-medical model and classified as an assistive service. Given the taxonomic characteristics of these children and the prejudice that exists with regard to them, the regular education system has impeded their access and promoted, by not offering other options for them, a subsystem of special education. This subsystem designed specific study plans according to two predominant service delivery models: the assistance model, which considers the special education student as a "handicapped" person requiring permanent assistance throughout life (i.e., a person with severe multiple disabilities or severe cognitive delay), and the therapeutic model, which considers the student with disabilities an atypical individual requiring an ensemble of corrective actions. In other words, intervention that will return the individual to normal functioning. In this model, teachers functioned as paramedic aides or therapists, displacing attention from the learning and teaching process to diagnosis, rehabilitation, and assistance.

In 1979, under the direction of Dr. Margarita Gómez Palacios, the "integrated groups" project was initiated as a strategic measure for the institutional inclusion described in the Elementary Education for All Children program. Inasmuch as special education was maintained as a parallel system to regular education, the members of its operating staff were on a higher professional level because of their specialization. They also participated in the Elementary Education for All Children program by serving children with learning disabilities in inclusive groups and later in psychopedagogical centers. The experiences derived from these programs were decisive steps toward school inclusion for individuals with disabilities. In 1980, the State Office for Special Education of the Department of Public Education (SEP), in a document entitled "Bases for a Policy of Special Education," outlined the principles on which its actions are sustained: (1) the "normalization" and inclusion of the child with special education requirements, (2) the acknowledgment that attention must be given to individuals who require special education at any time in their life, (3) the confirmation that special education will have its own special pedagogy, and (4) the conviction that special education should not be considered separate from general education.

In 1992, with the frim conviction that the road to follow was the gradual integration of minors with disabilities, the Directorate for Special Education under Lic. Eliseo Guajardo created the Units of Support Services to Regular Education (USAER) as an initial proposal for the reorganization of special education. The USAER became the techno-operative and administrative resource for special education and provided methodological support for attention to students with special needs in a regular school setting. Techno-operative attention uses two strategies: (1) attention to students and (2) attention to parents and school staff, in five areas: (a) initial evaluation, (b) intervention planning, (c) intervention, (d) continued assessment, and (e) monitoring. Each USAER supports an average of five schools, attending to students who have special education needs and orienting parents in addition to teachers. The USAER represents a new relationship between the services of special education and regular education within the framework of basic education. However, it is clear that the substantive challenge that the Directorate for Special Education faces is coverage, since it only provides specialized services to 5% of the students that need attention.

The Program for Educational Development (1995-2000) is a document that guides educational commitments of the federal government during President Zedillo's term and designates a separate branch to special education that defines inclusive education for students with disabilities as "the access to the basic curriculum and satisfaction of the basic necessities of learning." The strategies to gain access to such a curriculum can be provided by the services of special education in a regular school, with psychopedagogical support provided by specialized personnel in the school that the minor attends.

Cognizant that the process of scholastic inclusion of persons with disabilities is a gradual process that entails difficulties in responding equitably to specific requirements, the Educational Development program outlines progressive strategies in order to achieve educational integration: (1) diagnose and identify existing infrastructures to attend to these minors as well as the modalities and integration experiences in each federal entity, (2) design planning strategies for each zone and school region for the gradual incorporation of this population into the education system, (3) and, on the planning of each zone and school region, define the priorities for addressing the needs of specific diversities presented by the population, such as levels of disabilities, infrastructures of educational services, awareness level of parents, of teachers, and of the regular schools and communities, and professional competency of the specialist available in each locality and region.

Every scholastic option, special or regular, will be dependent on the conditions of the students, their families, and the services offered by regular or special schools. In both educational realms there exist opportunities to access the general education curriculum, providing for scholastic integration. Persons with disabilities cannot be isolated, as in many cases one disability masks another. In this sense, special education must respond to a continuum ranging from total integration in a regular school to segregated services in a special education center. This organizational model of special education services will be sustained on a sufficiently flexible basic education curriculum to allow for the integration of any minor independent of their place on the continuum.

Equilibrium between Extremes: Centrism versus State Independence

As indicated in the Program for Educational Development 1995-2000, the National Modernization of Basic Education Accord signed in 1992 implemented the process of federalization by way of transferring almost 100,000 schools to individual states and by establishing the bases for shared responsibilities between the states and the federal government with regard to education. General directions applicable to the diverse government systems as well as to equity in education were established.

It is important that we not lose sight of the fact that in many aspects these changes have only recently been introduced. Not all states of the federation have the same level of educational development, nor do their institutions share the same levels of consolidation and efficiency when providing for the needs of students with disabilities. Faced with this reality, much was gained with the Basic Education Accord and its judicial support of the General Law for Education. However, in 1993 a shift occurred at the national level with the change of the Special Education Directorate, which traditionally had been the normative agent in the operations area for the federal district. For the first time, special education has been elevated to constitutional status, but in Article 41 of the General Law for Education the obligatory nature of these services at the national level were diluted in terms of the unifying function and coordination efforts of special education. On the other hand, states shared the responsibility for offering varied initiatives and the possibility of making decisions at the sites where the problems arise. The state of Nuevo León initiated energetic processes toward educational integration (mainstreaming) in response to the outline of Article 41. Similar efforts were initiated in Sonora, Durango, Yucatán, and Aguascalientes to mention just of few of the states of the Republic of Mexico.

In 1995 President Zedillo confirmed his commitment to persons with disabilities by establishing the National Program for the Welfare and Development of Individuals with Disabilites (DIF). It was an unprecedented effort that brought together political willpower at the national and state level and fostered interagency collaboration with society for the benefit of persons with disabilities. This is the first time in the history of Mexico that a president created a program that establishes interagency cooperation on behalf of persons with disabilities. Taking advantage of the presidential political volition and the public sector's commitment, the Educational Development Program was put forward to coordinate the efforts of the states and of the federal government and to propel special education to the forefront of the National Coordinating Commission and of the thirty-one state commissions.

Under this program, the registration of minors with any sign of disability became mandatory and included all elementary schools throughout the country. This census was a joint effort by SEP, DIF, and the National Census (INEGI), as part of the National Information System Regarding Populations with Disabilities. The results of the registration delimited the areas requiring attention and provided a directory and a map that facilitated the identification and service needs of minors with disabilities. The data extrapolated from the census were surprising and made evident that it was not merely a matter of national coverage but that the fundamental challenge was to give specific attention to minors with disabilities who were already in school, which is the fundamental challenge to resolve. Of the 2,727,989 minors registered throughout the country, 2,121,365 are receiving some type of specialized educational service. This means that only 20% of the minors registered are not receiving any educational service. Of the total number of minors registered, almost 30% report having poor vision, 12% report having more than one disability, 12% report speech difficulties, 5.3% have hearing problems, 4.7% have a mental disability, and 2.1% have some type of physical malfunction.

Although we know that the 2,727,989 minors registered do not constitute all the minors with some form of disability in the country, the percentage of minors, six to twelve years of age registered (10.68%) does correspond to international estimates based on incidence figures of about 10%. Additional efforts will be undertaken to identify minors between birth and five years of age with some type of disability given that only 1.9% were registered.

The working model for special education in each federal entity was inspired by the National Association of State Directors of Special Education (NASDE) in the United States, particularly as it relates to the initiation of the formation of the National Network of Responsible Persons (staff) for Special Education at the state level. This work has been supplemented by the guidelines provided by the Department for Basic and Teacher Education of SEP and the guidelines established by state commissions in charge of welfare programs for persons with disabilities, as well as by the commitment and shared responsibility of governors and state secretaries of education to offer educational alternatives that provide social integration for minors with disabilities. The federalization of education is a key element in that it permits us to provide solutions in a concrete manner where problems for integrated education occur by responding to the diverse needs of each particular state.

Much remains to be done so that the efforts made by the states do not foster inclusive education at the cost of paralyzing actions because of the pretext of the complexity of the task to be accomplished. A lesson to learn, on our way there, is to support each other without hindering each other and to take advantage of social energy without permitting requirements to become demands that are attended to at the sacrifice of quality. We will not win the battle for children in regular schools if the appropriate conditions for them do not exist. We will not advance if we wait for ideal conditions to exist before initiating the process. The determination and will of all parties and effective planning are indispensable requirements of the process of inclusive education.

Society and Education: Mexico's Scenario

Mexico has achieved considerable historical advances in terms of education, given that in 1920 the average schooling of the population over fifteen years of age did not go beyond the first grade and by 1995 the average schooling had increased to seventh grade (in spite of the extraordinary increase in the country's population). This notable increment is attributable in great measure to the increase in the enrollment of students in basic education. In 1970, 10.7 million children attended preschool, primary school, and middle school, while today close to 23 million are enrolled in public schools. However, even with these advances, basic education still does not reach everyone. In 1990 the census bureau reported that 2,514,000 Mexicans between the ages of six and fourteen did not attend school. The differences between the states continue to be very noticeable. Only 6.9% of minors between the ages of six and fourteen do not attend school in the Federal District or in the state of Nuevo León. In states such as Guerrero and Chiapas that have a high rural and indigenous population the percentage of minors attending school is between 19.1 and 27.3%, which suggests that factors persist that maintain educational inequities. It is estimated that 35 million adults have not completed basic education in Mexico. Of the population over fifteen years of age in Mexico, 32% have not finished or never attended elementary school and 28% have not completed studies at the secondary level. The conditions of poverty in which a high percentage of the population lives restrict their opportunities to improve their living conditions and perpetuate the cycle of ignorance and poverty.

The schooling of females is another challenge that our country faces. The 1990 census indicated that the national percentage of illiteracy among men was 9.6%, while among females it reached 15%. Among the indigenous population the problem is even more grave given that more than half of the women do not know how to read or write. Although women's access to education has become more equitable and in most cases the number of girls and boys attending preschool, elementary school, and secondary school remains the same, census numbers indicate that among children twelve years and older, the number of girls attending school has decreased. This inequity is unacceptable in a society that confers equal rights to men and women; it translates into intergenerational educational injustices because of the critical role of the mother in the education of children. Their influence determines the adoption or rejection of healthy life practices, stimulates or limits children's school attendance, and has an important impact on the formation of habits and the acquisition of knowledge. There exists, for example, a high correlation between low maternal schooling and a high incidence of fertility and infant mortality. The enormous dispersion of the population of our country makes it difficult for education to reach all Mexicans; the isolation and extreme seclusion of small rural populations limit the offering of educational services. According to 1990 census data, there are 156,602 localities, of which more than 108,000 have a population of less than a hundred inhabitants. In the majority of cases these communities lack roads and passable trails by which to transport resources and provide assistance in a reliable and adequate manner to the inhabitants. Other services such as water, electricity, or sewers are few in number or nonexistent. On an average, each one of these communities has less than five minors between the ages of six and fourteen, of which approximately 35% do not attend school.

Added to the problem of a widely dispersed population is the challenge of providing education for indigenous groups. Although they represent 7% of the national population, they constitute 26% of the country's illiterate population. To date, the educational strategies directed toward the indigenous populations have not responded meaningfully to their needs or visions of the world despite the fact that in order to promote the initial teaching and learning of reading and writing in the mother tongue, texts and educational materials have been translated into forty-seven languages and dialects. Initial reading is to be provided in the mother tongue together with the oral teaching of Spanish as a second language. Efforts have been made to consolidate and extend compensatory programs in the indigenous communities and to maintain flexiblity in curriculum contents and organizational formats. This has been done in order to facilitate the integration of the indigenous population into national life by offering a relevant education in harmony with their traditions, beliefs and values, and ways of interpreting reality and relating to nature.

The community education model, which the National Council of Educative Furtherance (CONAFE) has been imparting for the past twenty years, is a response to the need of educational services for children living in rural communities with difficult access and limited population. This model is sustained by the social work of youth who have completed their secondary education and are summoned to work as community instructors in a rural community for one year. The community instructors receive intensive training during the months of June through August. They receive monthly economic help and upon completion of their year of service are given a scholarship to continue their studies at a *preparatoria* or technical school at a public institution of their choice. The instructor encourages the participation and shared responsibility of the community in educational tasks, with the help of the Association for the Promotion of Community Education (AEC). CONAFE supports community education with teaching aids, technical assistance, equipment, follow-up, and evaluations. The community provides food and lodging for the community instructor and shares responsibility for the task of educating its children.

For special education, these divergent realities present a complex scenario difficult to manage. It can be assumed that of the 2,514,000 minors between the ages of six and fourteen who are not in school a large percentage has some kind of disability. If close to 35 million adults have not finished elementary education, many parents who face the responsibility of supporting the integration of a minor with a disability into social life will not have the conceptual tools and skills with which to do so. If female illiteracy has increased in the last two decades and we recognize the fundamental role of the mother in the adoption or rejection of a healthy lifestyle, the children of mothers with little or no schooling will have to overcome more difficulties in order to achieve their social integration. If to this we add the fact that some children live in a small community of less than a hundred inhabitants, with only four or five children of their same age, and receive no basic educational services, and have few opportunities to receive early stimulation. Rehabilitation, isolation, and abandonment seem to be the only options. If the child with a disability is from an indigenous background or an Indian who lives in an isolated and secluded area and has parents who face language barriers to help their child, the situation is even more distressing. In spite of these conditions, we often find in these settings abundant feelings of solidarity and social support. Barriers to integration appear more often in urban settings accustomed to segregated parallel models than in rural indigenous communities where "all children are the same," where the basic law of the community is that the big take care of the small, the strong look after the weak, the learned assist the ignorant, because the community vision does not permit individualism or exclusiveness. This is the common vision we must adopt to carry out the objectives of justice and equity.

However, a review of the data of the National Registry of minors with any sign of disability suggests that the problem is not as severe as initially thought. Much has been gained with the directory and charts that INEGI generated as part of the results of the Registry; however, much remains to be done so that in every federal entity, in every municipality, and in every community or barrio public-sector brigades are formed to find and embrace the cause of minors with disabilities.

Educational efforts alone are insufficient to permit children and youth, with or without disabilities who are living in extreme poverty, to have access to a better life. Only strategies that link resources and efforts such as those put forth by the National Program for the Welfare and Mainstreaming of Individuals with Disabilites will make it possible to multiply the benefits for those groups. That it is why it is important to work together with the public and private sector as well as different social entities that operate in the poorest rural and urban sectors. This collaboration will enhance and strengthen efforts in the areas of health, education, rehabilitation, recreation, and material support.

Shortening the Distance: Communication via Satellite

The Mexican education sector has developed an important media infrastructure, the central feature of which, the Satellite Education (EDUSAT) system, is key. It consists of a telecommunication network that employs the Solidarity I satellite and is sustained by the use of digital technology for the transmission of images, sound, and data for television, radio, and other media. It has six television channels and twenty-one audio channels that can transmit twenty-four hours a day and can be used in a directed manner according to the needs of the site. To date, fourteen thousand parabolic antennas have been installed in schools throughout Mexico. This infrastructure will be expanded, diversified, and complemented during the next five years until it encompasses the majority of public schools in the country. The General Education Law, in Article 33, states that education authorities must promote the creation of distance education systems in order to facilitate the full execution of the right to education, more equity in education, and opportunities for access and permanence of educational services. The new network will be promoted and disseminated so that every home in the country will receive at least one channel with an open signal providing education and cultural content. In this way directed actions to promote essential values by strengthening learning and encouraging appreciation of diverse cultural practices will reach a larger audience. Processes that allow the linking of schools to communities will be investigated, using schools that receive the signal in the afternoons and on weekends, in order to transmit programs oriented to promoting community welfare. These programs will include: basic nonformal education, parental orientation regarding child care and development, family literacy, training for work, and information on how to take advantage of public services to defend the rights and improve the standards of living of the population.

The primary goal is to help Mexican families and their children with disabilities by providing educational programs and videos that will sensitize the general community to the challenge of integrating persons with disabilities into society. In addition, these programs will guide parents and teachers in the process of educational inclusion of minors with disabilities. The use of technology as a strategy for distance education, teleconferences, and special education programs with similar and different visions will facilitate teaching and learning, horizontally and jointly.

New Avenues for Binational Collaboration

Since the initiation of the binational meetings between the United States and Mexico we have taken advantage of contacts within the United States Department of Education, the National Association of State Directors of Special Education, and most recently with the South Atlantic Regional Resource Center (SARRC) and the Western Regional Resource Center (WRRC) to organize meetings of directors of special education from the bordering states of both countries. The Educational Development Program 1995-2000 specifies precise commitments that shall be utilized as a guide for possible avenues of collaboration and exchange of experiences between the United States and Mexico.

In order to strengthen the planning and operation of special education services we need to exchange experiences in the following areas:

The formation of teams, itinerant and intersectorial, for identification and diagnosis of minors with disabilities to work in dispersed and marginalized communities and verification of data from the National Registry of minors with disabilities.

Strategies for planning, monitoring and evaluation of inclusive education at state, municipal, community, barrio or neighborhood, zone, and school levels.

The design of flexible normative guidelines that will eliminate the restriction for minors with disabilities to have access to regular and special education settings and services.

Generating strategies that will allow us to offer adequate job-related training to persons with disabilities with the goal of helping them to become fully incorporated in society.

With regard to the orientation of parents and the general community we need to exchange experiences pertaining to:

The development of support modalities to regular schools that service children with disabilities.

The creation of linking mechanisms between regular schools and special-education schools.

With regard to strengthening the teaching-learning processes in the classroom we need to exchange experiences pertaining to:

The generation and use of individualized educational planning instruments (Individualized Education Program) that specify short-term and long-term learning goals for parents and teachers from regular schools and special education.

The elaboration of useful and practical adaptations to the basic curriculum.

The use of teaching materials that support school inclusion of minors with disabilities, facilitate the learning of all children and promote authentic collaboration.

With regard to the training of educational professionals it will be necessary to exchange strategies pertaining to:

The updating of teaching methods through in-service programs for special and regular teachers in inclusive educational settings.

The inclusion of special-education content in the basic training of teachers in order to sensitize them and prepare them to work with minors with special educational needs.

The roots that join the people of our two countries are becoming more evident each day: our commitments ensure future actions when we recognize that more than just being neighbors, the people of our two countries have common backgrounds and cultures that were flowering long before they were discovered. We have grown much since then, but our fraternal sentiments toward one another have not always been apparent. It depends on us to cultivate them so that they continue to prosper and flourish.

References

Chiu Velázquez, Y. 1997. Práctica docente e integración educativa. *Revista Básica*, Fundación SNTE, No 16, Mexico, D.F.

DIF. 1995. *Programa Nacional para el Bienestar y la Incorporación al Desarrollo de las Personas con Discapacidad.* Comisión Nacional Coordinadora. Mexico, DF.

MEC. 1992. Concepto de alumnos con necesidades educativas especiales. In *Alumnos con necesidades educativas especiales y adaptaciones curriculares.* Dirección General de Renovación Pedagógica, Centro Nacional de Recursos para la Educación Especial. Madrid, Spain.

ONU/MEC. 1995. *Informe final: Conferencia mundial sobre necesidades educativas especiales. Acceso y calidad.* Salamanca, Spain. 1994.

SEP. 1993. Artículo 3° Constitucional; artículos 39 y 41 de la Ley General de Educación. In *Artículo 3° Constitucional y Ley General de Educación.* Mexico, DF.

_____. 1993. *Ley General de Educación.* Mexico, DF.

_____. 1996. Atención a menores con discapacidad. In *Programa de Desarrollo Educativo* 1995-2000. Mexico, DF.

_____. 1996. *Programa de Desarrollo Educativo 1995-2000.* Federal Administration, Mexico, DF.

_____. 1997. *Documento base preliminar para la Conferencia Nacional de Huatulco.* Documento interno Asesoría del Secretario, Mexico, DF.

_____. 1997.*Unidad de Servicios de Apoyo a la Educación Regular.* In *Antología de_educación especial.* Carrera Magisterial, Mexico, DF.

SEP/DEE. 1997. Declaración de la Conferencia Nacional. In *Atención educativa a menores con necesidades educativas especiales: Equidad para la diversidad.* Huatulco, Mexico, DF.

SSA. 1995. *Programa Nacional de Acción en Favor de la Infancia.* Comisión Nacional en Favor de la Infancia. Mexico, DF.

UNESCO. 1992. *Seminario regional de la UNESCO sobre políticas, planeación y educación integrada para alumnos con necesidades especiales.* Informe Final. Caracas, Venezuela.

_____. 1994. *Declaración de Salamanca de principios, política y práctica para las necesidades educativas especiales y marco de acción sobre necesidades educativas especiales.* Conferencia mundial sobre necesidades educativas especiales acceso y calidad. Salamanca, Spain.

Special Education and Education Reform in Mexico

Providing Quality Education to a Diverse Student Population

Eliseo Guajardo Ramos and Todd V. Fletcher

Special education in Mexico, in keeping with international trends, is in the process of transformation. Educational reforms currently under way in Mexico have adopted and systematized the measures recommended by UNESCO (1994) to extend educational services to all students, accommodate the diversity represented in the special education population, and provide a high-quality education for all students. The 1994 World Conference on Special Educational Needs held in Salamanca, Spain, highlighted the importance of including all students in our schools, celebrating their differences and responding to the specific needs of each individual. The Declaration of Salamanca adopted at the Conference outlined the principles underlying inclusive education, discussed the political implications of the Declaration, and provided an action plan for the successful implementation of inclusive schools.

In addition to international declarations, forces within Mexico were calling for reforms designed to decentralize education and to provide quality instruction for all students. In Mexico, as elsewhere, this required legislative changes to meet the challenges of educating students from diverse backgrounds, including those with special educational needs. The goals of education recently adopted by the Mexican government focus on restructuring public education to enable it to respond to the basic learning needs of all students while attending to their cultural, economic, physical, and cognitive differences. This has led to a reconceptualization of the role of, and services provided by, special education and its relationship to general education. This, in turn, has led to systemic changes in the delivery of services for special needs students, the retraining of both general and special education professional, and new strategies and interventions to meet the demands of an integrated educational system.

Legislative Changes

Present-day Mexico is redefining its basic liberties. The senate of the Republic of Mexico, in consultation with the social and political protagonists of the country, has initiated reforms directed toward the creation of a new federalism. As part of these reforms, the powers of the federation, the states, and the counties were established, particularly with regard to the distribution of the public budget.

Based upon this changing situation, a new federal pact was established for the National Education System (SEN). In 1992, the National Agreement for the Modernization of Basic Education (Secretaría de Educación Pública 1992a, 1992b) was agreed to by the federal government, the 31 states of the Republic, and the Education Workers' National Union (Gordillo 1992). With the decentralization of the SEN, reform in education was initiated and restructuring begun. The restructuring consisted fundamentally of the decentralization of the SEN in an effort to return sovereignty to the states, allowing them to operate basic educational services according to the diversified conditions required by their particular populations, and to promote greater availability and completion of schooling (Pescador Osuna 1992). This movement toward a unique and diverse system of basic education created the need for constitutional reforms and legal ordinances regarding educational matters. Figure 1 provides a frame of reference outlining the different legislative and programmatic components that underlie the educational restructuring process currently under way in Mexico.

According to Article 3 of the Mexican Constitution, every Mexican has the right to an elementary education. Article 3 was previously interpreted as providing for the education of children with special needs, but not as mandating special education on a federal level (Dirección General de Educación Especial 1985). In 1993, Article 3 of the Constitution was amended, and a new General Education Law (GEL) replaced the previous Federal Education Law. For the first time in its history, Mexico had enacted national legislation that specifically provided for the education of individuals with disabilities. Articles 41 of the new law states:

> Special education is created for individuals with temporary or permanent disabilities, as well as for gifted individuals. It will attempt to provide services that are adequate to the needs of those served with social equality. As related to minors with disabilities, this education will promote their integration into general education. For those who do not achieve such integration, this education will attempt to satisfy their basic educational needs so they may achieve an autonomous, productive social life. This education

FIGURE 1 *Frame of reference of current educational reforms*

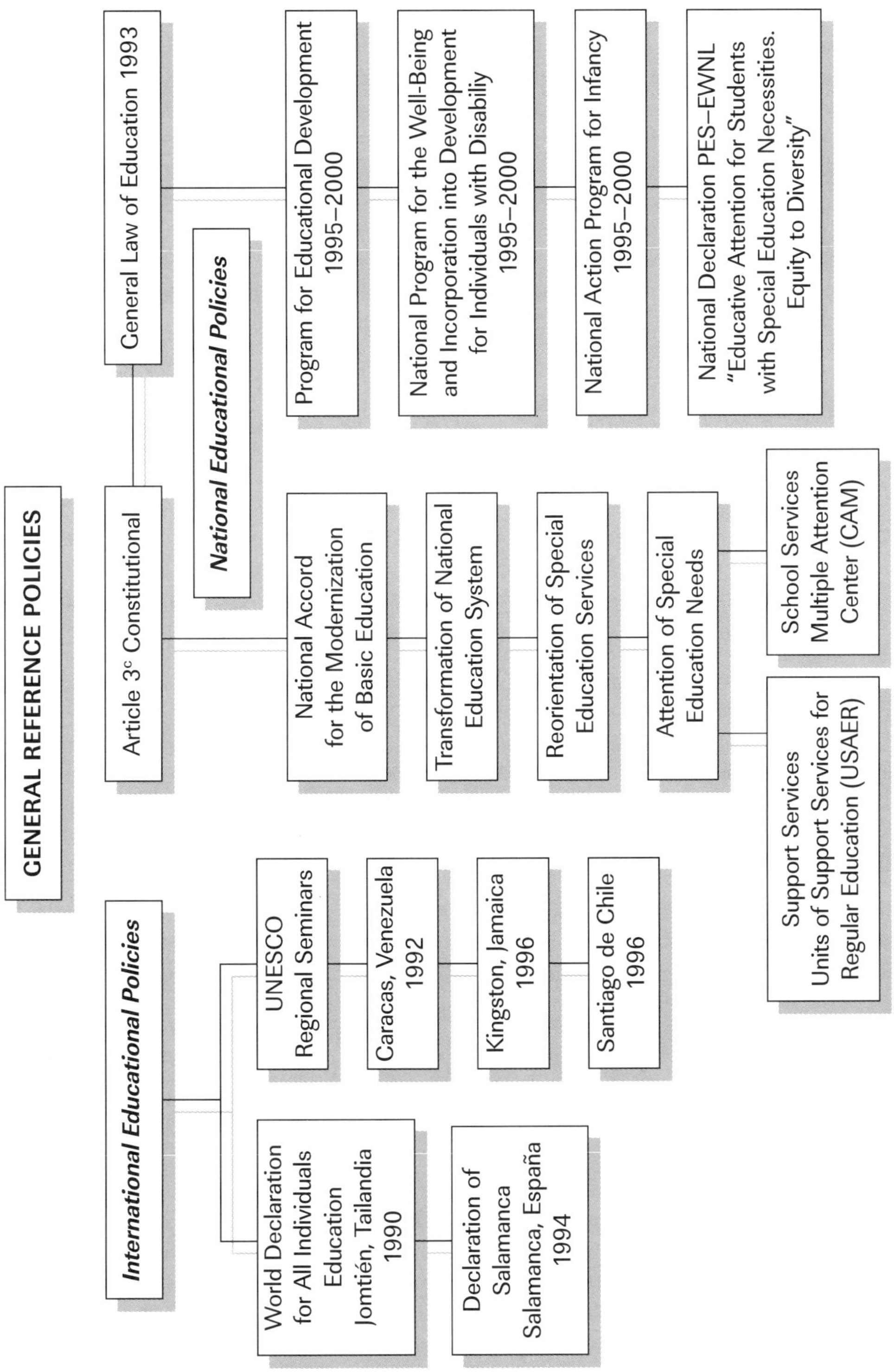

includes guidance for parents and guardians as well as for teachers and elementary, general school personnel where students with special educational needs are integrated.

The GEL is a legal ordinance that makes explicit the nonexclusion of students with disabilities. The general purpose of reordering basic education for diversity is to cease viewing special education as a separate, parallel system with its own curriculum. It contemplates the integration of special education with basic education and sharing the same broadened curriculum, albeit flexible and optional in many of its parts. Educational equity is widely assured, as is the involvement of society in education. Likewise, the protagonist and professional roles of teachers in educational reform and innovation are recognized.

The properties and conditions of Article 41 of the General Education Law, as they pertain to individuals with disabilities, include the following:

1. No one with a disability can be excluded from receiving basic education services.
2. The law no longer refers to "the disabled," but rather to persons with certain disabilities.
3. The law refers to total or partial inclusion in general education classrooms without restrictions, while continuing to provide the option of special schools.
4. Not only is the state obliged to provide special education services to students, but it also has responsibility to counsel families and provide training for general education teachers. This is based on the importance of working as a team to provide the best possible educational services in the context of the student's total ecology.

With the amendment of Article 3 of the Constitution and the passage of the new General Education Law, special education entered a new era. These legal changes recognized the existence of special education, defined its place within the basic educational system, and broadened the basic rights of all Mexican citizens.

Central Features of Change

The current reform of basic education in Mexico is designed to recognize the special educational needs of all students, preschool through eighth grade. As a result, four key areas are being emphasized in the restructuring process: (a) flexibility of the basic curriculum, (b) the preparation and professional development of teachers, (c) the implementation of new service delivery models, and (d) the participation of parents and the community (Guajardo Ramos 1993).

Meeting the challenge of the educational integration of students with disabilities begins with the development of a broad-based and flexible curriculum that is sensitive to the special educational needs of all students. Figure 2 illustrates the integration of all students into the basic core curriculum through abandoning the parallel curriculum that traditionally excluded and segregated some students based on their learning differences. This transformation has sought to minimize the impact of the learning difficulties exhibited by students with mild or moderate disabilities and to make general education responsible for meeting their educational needs. To date, this has only been moderately successful since most public schools have maintained their inflexible and rigid curricular objectives and

FIGURE 2 *Transition to educational integration*

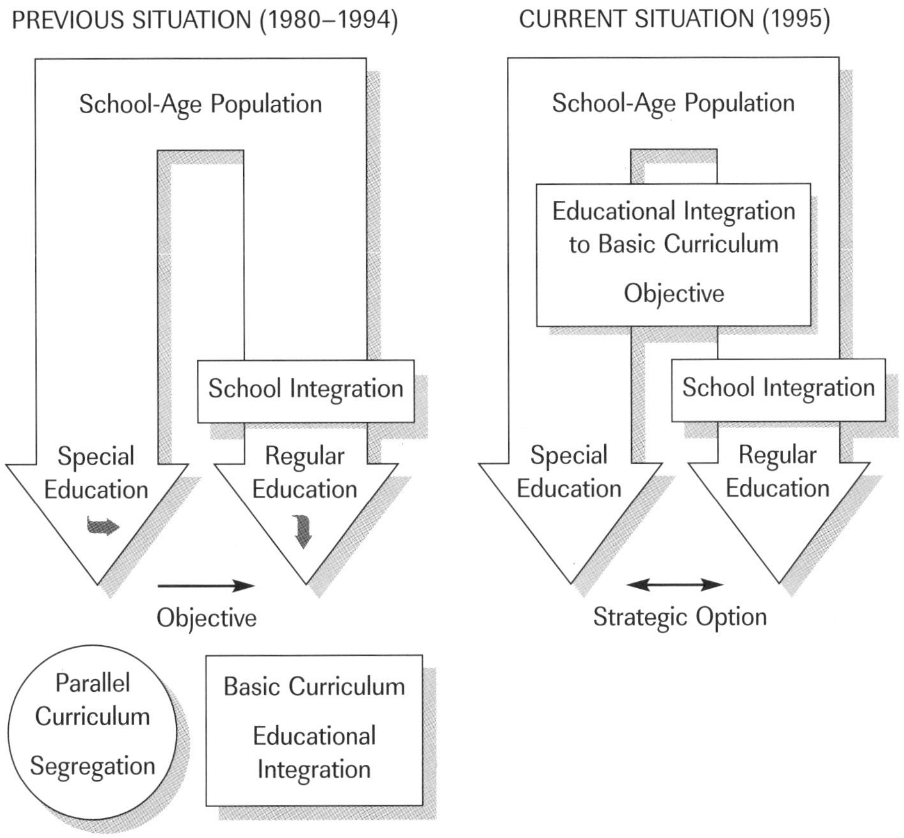

goals, as well as their traditional school organizational structures and practices. One of the greatest challenges facing this process is the provisions of a broad-based and coherent curriculum that is sensitive to the special educational needs of all students. This transformation will continue to require reciprocity and collaborative planning between general and special education. In addition to the transformation of general education, special education will need to become more flexible as to how it provides services, and will have to establish a professional development program to update special education personnel regarding the new realities of a common school for all students.

Program for Educational Development

Within the legal framework described above, the current administration sought to identify inequities in educational opportunities throughout the country (Dirección General de Educación Especial 1994). In 1995 the National Welfare and Incorporation for the Development of Individuals with Disabilities Program was established. This was an unprecedented effort to join political forces at the national and state levels to develop interagency agreements and to encourage communities to work together for the benefit of individuals with disabilities.

For the first time in Mexico, a president created a program that focused on the needs of individuals with disabilities. Using this presidential initiative, the Program for Educational Development was created for the purpose of propelling special education to the forefront of the National Coordinating Commission's agenda, as well as the agendas of the 31 state commissions (Comisión Nacional Coordinadora 1995).

Under the auspices of this program, and with the support of the Public Education Secretariat (PES), the National System for the Integral Development of the Family (DIF) and the National Information System regarding Populations with Disabilities (INEGI), a national census, called the Registration of Minors with Signs of Disabilities, was conducted. The purpose was to determine the number of children and adolescents with disabilities. Teachers throughout the country distributed forms to schoolchildren soliciting information regarding family members, friends or acquaintances who had disabilities. Contrary to expectations, results suggested that many students were already being integrated into schools throughout the country. Of the 2,727,989 minors registered in Mexico, over 2 million were receiving some form of educational service. This suggests that only 20% of registered minors were not receiving any educational services. Of the total minors registered, almost 30% reported having poor vision, 12% having more than one disability, 12% an inability to speak well, 5.3% having poor hearing, 4.7% having a mental disability, and 2.1% reported having some type of physical malformation.

Recognizing that the process of inclusion must be gradual, and that it must conform to equity standards, the Program of Educational Development outlined progressive strategies to achieve educational integration. These strategies included: (a) the identification of existing infrastructures for attending to the needs of minors, as well as the different modalities and integration experiences of each state entity; (b) the design of planning strategies that each school region could employ to undertake the gradual incorporation of students with special needs into the education system; and (c) the selection of each region's priorities for action according to the diversity presented by its population; and, in addition, the types of disabilities represented among its school-age children, the infrastructure of its educational services, the degree of sensitivity of the parents, teachers and communities within the region, and the professional competence of its teachers and other specialists.

The Program for Educational Development had a major impact on the design of educational innovations that provided for the scholastic inclusion of all students into the public schools in the Federal District of Mexico City. The following section describes the changes that are currently taking place.

Current Special Education Reform in the Federal District of Mexico City

In the Federal District, educational integration is being achieved through the reorientation of special education services, while simultaneously taking advantage of the innovations that basic education is putting into place to provide appropriate educational services for diverse populations within general education classrooms. In March 1993 the General Project of Special Education was developed and initiated in Mexico City (Secretaría de Educación Pública 1994). This project was comprised of ten basic components that provided, in general terms, a prospectus leading to the year 2010. The ten components were as follows.

1. In addition to being ethically unacceptable, the parallel system of education is incompatible with the new conception of quality in education and is incapable of meeting the demands posed by the population of students with special needs. Thus the parallel system must be eliminated and special education must be considered a modality of basic education, abandoning the practice of segregating students to provide "specialized" services.
2. It must be remembered that the institutions of special education originated more than a century ago, together with the pioneer institutions of public education. As special education was consolidated as a parallel system over a period of 127 years, we should not expect that it will be rapidly and easily integrated with regular education.
3. The current conception of quality education seeks to ensure that exclusion based on gender, ethnicity, territory, social class, special educational needs, etc. does not occur. Special education must not continue to be autonomous with respect to the criteria that define quality in general education.
4. The project did not intend to eliminate special education services and automatically integrate all students with special needs into general education. Rather, the intention was to establish a range of gradual options for integration such that students with special needs would enjoy access to different educational placements.
5. The program of integration should be viewed as a program of institutional development and as a means by which quality education is provided to all school-age children, with or without disabilities.
6. The decentralization of educational services, including those of special education, and the political reordering of the Federal District, makes it possible to resolve problems in their place of origin, using a site-based approach to management. This is important in terms of solving the complex problems created by educational integration. This was accomplished by Article 41 of the current General Law of Education, among other legislative acts.
7. It is of central importance to consider that the integration of a student with special educational needs requires a federal law prohibiting discrimination on the basis of disability. To achieve this it was necessary to amend the Federal Education Law to provide the legal basis for implementing new strategies for educational integration. This was accomplished by Article 41 of the current General Law of Education, among other legislative acts.
8. School integration is fundamental for the social integration of persons who have special needs. In view of this, the social integration of these persons must be part of an integral program that transcends traditional school programs. Integration should be promoted in the areas of health, education, recreation, culture, and employment. To achieve this objective, it is necessary to establish effective interagency cooperation.

9. It has been demonstrated that educational centers that achieve quality education are those that resolve their problems in a collegial and participatory manner through school councils. Thus it is of fundamental importance to establish school councils of social participation throughout the Federal District.
10. With respect to training and professional development of teachers, it is important that the fundamentals of inclusive education be taught in all institutes where teachers are prepared to work in elementary education.

The ten components outlined above provided the fundamental basis for the changes currently underway in the Federal District. As can be appreciated, with the implementation of federalization throughout Mexico, the provision of special education services in the Federal District has undergone significant restructuring. The goal of restructuring basic education is the creation of public schools that will respond to the learning needs of all students with social equity while attending to their cultural, economic, physical, and cognitive differences.

Twin Service Delivery Models

In the Federal District of Mexico City, the General Directorate of Special Education has restructured educational services in a manner that represents a new cooperative relationship between special education and general education (see figure 3). The function of special education under Article 41 of the GEL is that of a complementary service and support system for general education. Students are identified with special educational needs when, in relation to their peers, they encounter difficulties in learning grade-level content and, as a consequence, require appropriate adaptations to achieve the curricular objectives (Dirección General de Educación Especial 1994). Two new models for delivering services to individuals with special educational needs have been created and implemented, replacing the centers that formerly provided services in segregated settings. These new models are the Unit of Support Services for Regular Education (USAER) and Multiple Attention Centers (CAM).

The USAER represents a new relationship between special and general education within the framework of basic education in the public schools. Additionally, the USAER is responsible for providing guidance and orientation to students, parents, and public school personnel. It is based on the concept that the academic problems of students should be considered within the context of the learner and the classroom. The primary emphasis is on providing learners who have special educational needs with access to the core curriculum by modifying methodological approaches, objectives, content, assignments, or materials. The students served by this model typically include those with academic difficulties and learning disabilities that require only curricular adaptations (adecuaciones curriculares) or changes in methodological approaches to attain the objectives of the curriculum. It is expected that students who are deaf, blind, or mildly mentally retarded without additional complications would be educated in public schools under the supervision and assistance of the USAER.

The primary responsibilities of the USAER include: (a) initial evaluation, (b) intervention planning, (c) intervention, (d) ongoing assessment, and (e) monitoring. Evaluation procedures no longer require the administration of psychological

FIGURE 3 *Operational reorientation of special education services*

PREVIOUS SCHEMA	CURRENT SCHEMA
Center of Guidance, Assessment and Referral	Unit of Guidance to the Public
Unit of Integrated Groups A and B Center of Guidance for Education Integration Psychopedagogical Center Unit of Service for Children with Special Abilities and Talents	Unit of Support Services for Regular Education (USAER)
Center of Early Intervention Center of Professional Development in Special Education Special Education School	Multiple Attention Center (CAM)

or achievement tests but rather employ curriculum-based assessments to determine the student's current level of functioning and corresponding grade placement. Students who are determined to have special education needs using this procedure are no longer labeled and given "therapy," instead, curricular adaptations based on their specific needs are implemented within the context of the general education classroom.

The teachers who worked under the previous structure (see figure 3) are now serving primarily as resource and support personnel to general education classroom teachers, working with them in designing and implementing pedagogical modifications and curricular adaptations. In this new model, each special educator is responsible for monitoring about twenty children who have special educational needs. Most of the children remain in their respective general education classrooms for the greater portion of the school day. Students who require additional special attention receive alternate scheduling that provides them with individualized instruction or assistance outside of the regular school routine. For example, a student with emotional problems whose behavior interferes with his/her learning or that of others might be referred to one of many social agencies in the Federal District such as Mental Health, Social Security, or DIF. The student might continue to attend the public school in the morning and receive special attention in the afternoon from a selected agency targeting his identified behavior and emotional needs.

Within each school there is a support classroom (aula de apoyo) equipped to work with students and their families. The primary intent of this model is to include all students with special educational needs in regular education classrooms with support provided by USAER personnel. Special education teachers at each school site no longer teach special classes or provide "therapy"; instead, they work with the students' teachers in their classrooms. The general education classroom teacher, in collaboration with the resource specialists at each school site, determines which children will be served, where they will be served and the duration of their services.

Each USAER unit is comprised of a director, ten special education teachers, and a technical support team. The support team consists of a speech and language therapist, a psychologist, and a social worker. If other specialists are needed, they are called in on a case-by-case basis. Each unit serves five schools; two special education teachers are placed in each school. If the initial evaluation indicates that the special educational needs of the child require placement in a setting other than the regular school, the parents and school personnel are consulted and consent is obtained to move forward on the recommendation. A report is filed that includes the present performance level of the student, the reason for the change of placement and suggestions and recommendations for future instruction based on formal and informal evaluations.

The Multiple Attention Center (CAM) is an educational institution designed to replace the special education schools, centers of early intervention, and centers of professional development that previously served students with severe disabilities. Children who have special educational needs that cannot be accommodated in a regular school are educated in these centers. The goal of the CAM initiative is to provide the same core curriculum and quality education to students with disabilities who are unable to be successfully integrated into the public schools. These centers are operated much like the regular public schools with cross-categorical grouping of students by ability who are taught in classes of about twenty students each. Students ranging from preschool through high school are taught the basic core curriculum, with significant curricular modifications and adaptations. Parents, social agencies, and the USAERs are the primary sources of referrals to the CAM centers.

The primary functions of the CAM program are similar to those of the USAERs: (a) initial evaluation, (b) intervention planning, (c) curricular/methodological adaptations, (d) ongoing assessment, and (e) monitoring of progress. As in the USAERs, evaluations are typically performed using curriculum-based instruments to determine present performance levels in different academic areas. Depending on evaluation results, students are placed with other students according to their ability. There are no standard operating procedures as to how each CAM should function. Rather, each school maintains autonomy and flexibility in the organization, planning and delivery of instruction based on the needs of its student population.

The reorientation of special education services through the implementation of these twin-service delivery models has led to substantial structural changes in programs throughout the Federal District. As described below, many of the principles embodied in the reform of special education are evident in these structural changes.

1. Prior to the 1993/94 school year, the General Directorate of Special Education completed a self-evaluation of its effectiveness in enhancing the integration of all students. Based upon this evaluation, a decision was made to improve and strengthen the role of school supervision in the six regions of the Federal District. In-service training was provided to special education teachers in all schools and educational consultants (program specialists) with special education expertise were subsequently assigned and designated to function as a parallel administrative structure to the regional administrators; technical tasks were assigned to the consultants and administrative tasks to the regional special education administrators. The result of this demarcation of responsibilities resulted in a new

collegial relationship, eliminating the conflict that had traditionally existed between special education administrators and educational consultants.

2. During the 1993/94 school year, the six Orientation Centers for Educational Integration that had been operating within the six regions of the Federal Districts were eliminated. This was done because the primary functions of the centers were student referral and follow-up; they were not directly involved in the delivery of services in either general or special education. This superstructure was very superficial and led to the creation of bureaucratic barriers that impeded integration. The USAERs were given responsibility for providing follow-up services and support to students being integrated into the public schools.
3. During the 1994/95 school year, the provision of services to elementary school children using an "integrated groups" or pull-out service delivery model was changed and all the technical and human resources from these entities were transferred to the USAERs, broadening their distribution of services. Initially, a total of 90 USAER units were formed, working in 382 elementary schools. During the 1995/96 school year, 133 units were operating in 532 elementary schools and the number of units continues to increase every year.
4. Also during the 1994/95 school year, a basic core curriculum was adopted by all of the special education scholastic service centers, thereby eliminating the parallel curriculum.
5. Psychopedagogical centers were placed under the auspices of the USAERs. In this manner, the clinical services of these centers became a support system, providing intervention support to general education teachers.
6. All special education schools that provided services to students within specific disability categories, including the Centers of Special Training that served adolescents with mental retardation, became CAMs. This was done to enable each educational center to provide services to the students who were not integrated into regular schools, regardless of their disability.
7. The practice of awarding certificates of special studies to students with special educational needs when they graduated from high school was eliminated since all students are now studying the same core curriculum.
8. The curricula of vocational training centers, trade workshops and job skill development programs were redirected. Enrollment is now open to individuals with multiple disabilities whereas, in the past, only adolescents with mental retardation were admitted.
9. The Centers of Training for Industrial Work that were already providing services to adolescents with disabilities reached an agreement with the Office of Special Education and the General Office of the Center for Job Training to collaborate and support the integration of individuals in regular centers with support from special education.
10. One of the most challenging issues confronting schools was the professional development and retraining of preschool, primary, secondary, and special education teachers currently working in the field to better accommodate students with diverse special educational needs in public schools and the general education classroom. One solution has been an initiative entitled the "Reform of

Teacher Preparation Programs," which is designed to incorporate course work on "Attention to Diversity" into the curriculum of teacher preparation programs.

11. With respect to the professional development of preschool and elementary school teachers, the National Pedagogical University in Mexico City has developed a baccalaureate program in education with three concentrations: preschool education, elementary education, and educational integration. This new baccalaureate degree was inaugurated in September 1996 in collaboration with the Office of Special Education of the Public Education Secretariat in the Federal District (Secretaría de Educación Pública 1996).
12. Still to finish successfully. Even so, the most difficult stages had been carried out already. Among them the national consensus of special education reorientation with the Educational Worker's National Union, as the success that was attained in the National Conference PES-EWNU, "Educative Attention for students with special education necessities. Equity to Diversity." With all responsible for education—preschool, elementary, and special—the labor secretaries of all Union Sections, and the most recognized nongovernment organizations, raising the government policy to and state policy in according to the recommendation of the meeting at Kingston, Jamaica, 1996, (Principal Project for Latin America and Caribbean).

The unprecedented changes outlined above suggest that Mexico, as is true of other countries around the world, is dismantling and streamlining its excessive bureaucracy and challenging the status quo at the economic, social, political, and educational levels of society with the goal of attaining educational equity for all. B. Orozco Fuentes and S. Elizondo Carr (1993) acknowledge these changes and the need for reform by stating that "the excessively bureaucratized educational apparatus, inefficient and costly, is no longer sustainable. Given the new context, the discourse of modernization of education justifies and ratifies education's function as a social and political strategy to incorporate the excluded" (16).

Prior to the initiation of educational reform in Mexico, the first priority of the educational system was the provision of education to all children. Now, with these profound changes, a high-quality education is to be provided to all students by recognizing their special educational needs and by responding to their diversity.

Conclusion

Mexico is a multiethnic, multicultural, and multilingual nation intent on providing education aimed at accommodating diverse populations. Recent constitutional and legislative changes require that extraordinary efforts be made to provide educational services to individuals from diverse backgrounds. The current restructuring of special education in the Federal District of Mexico City is an integral part of this process. The following paragraphs summarize the desired goals and educational implications of providing a basic education for diverse populations in the twenty-first century.

Special education no longer subdivides its services by types of disabilities, but rather by educational performance levels, and services are provided on the basis of each student's learning capacity. As a result, the field of special education focuses on the special educational needs of children rather than on their disabilities. Developmental learning theory is now being employed in the education of all students regardless of their disability.

Educational integration, which is understood as access to the basic curriculum, constitutes an advance in how basic education will be configured in Mexico as it enters the new millennium. If regular and special education converge and are governed by one curriculum, the beginning of a gradual integration of services will have begun. Successful integration depends in large measure on family participation, collaboration between general and special education teachers, the leadership of the principal of each school, and the expertise provided by special education personnel.

The conceptual framework that serves as the basis for the restructuring process is attention to diversity supported by a new conception of basic education. Attention to diversity in this context is more broadly defined than just educational integration, although educational integration is assuredly an important aspect of it. As stated by Sofíaleticia Morales (1996), special assistant for special education to the Secretary of Education in Mexico:

> Much remains to be done so that the efforts made by the states do not accelerate the rhythms of inclusive education at the cost of neglecting the process or paralyzing actions with the pretext of their complexity. A lesson to learn while on our way is how to support each other without hindering each other, how to take advantage of social energy without permitting requirements to become demands that are attended to at the expense of quality. We will not win the battle by depositing children in regular schools if the appropriate conditions to receive them do not exist. We will not advance if we wait for ideal conditions to exist before initiating the process. The will of all parties and the planning, even though incipient, are indispensable requirements of the process of inclusive education.

The education integration of students with special educational needs should not be the sole objective of our reform efforts; rather, it must be one strategy among others that aims to provide a high-quality basic education for all students. Thus integration must shift away from being a pedagogically oriented objective to serving as a methodological strategy for achieving an ethical objective: equity in the quality of basic education.

References

Comisión Nacional Coordinadora. 1995. *Programa Nacional para el Bienestar y la Incorporación al Desarrollo de las Personas con Discapacidad* [National Program for the Welfare and Developmental Mainstreaming of Individuals with Disabilites]. Mexico, DF.

Dirección General de Educación Especial. 1985. *Bases para una política de educación especial* [Political bases for special education]. Mexico, DF: Grupo Editorial Mexicano.

_____. 1994. *Funciones, objetivos y servicios de la Dirección de Educación Especial* [Functions, objectives, and services of the General Direction of Special Education]. Mexico, DF: Dirección General de Educación Especial.

Gordillo, E. 1992. El SNTE ante la modernización de la educación básica [The Education Workers' National Union and the modernization of basic education]. *El Cotidiano* 51:12–16.

Guajardo Ramos, E. 1993. La educación especial en México en el marco de la educación básica: la integración educativa de los alumnos con necesidades educativas especiales. Paper presented at the sixth Encuentro Iberoamericano, March, Mexico, DF.

Morales, S. 1996. Bridge over troubled waters. Paper presented at the Union of the Mexican and Native American Cultures through the Collaboration of the United States and Mexico for Individuals with Disabilities and their Families Symposium (T. Fletcher, Chair), April, Tucson, AZ.

Orozco Fuentes, B., and S. Elizondo Carr. 1993. Educational reform in Mexico. *International Journal of Educational Reform* 2:12–18.

Pescador Osuna, J. A. 1992. Acuerdo nacional para la modernización de la educación básica: una visión integral [The national accord for the modernization of basic education: An integrated vision]. *El Cotidiano* 51:3–11.

Secretaría de Educación Pública. 1992a. Programas emergentes de actualización del maestro y de reformulación de contenidos y materiales educativos [Emerging programs for teacher development and the revision of educational material and content]. Mexico, DF.

_____. 1992b. Acuerdo nacional para la modernización básica [National agreement on the modernization of basic education]. Mexico, DF.

_____. 1993. *Ley General de Educación* [General Education Law]. Mexico, DF.

_____. 1994. *Cuadernos de integración educativa, no. 1: Proyecto general para la educación especial en Mexico.* Mexico, DF.

Secretaría de Educación Pública and Sindicato Nacional de Trabajadores de la Educación. 1997. Declaración Nacional SEP-SNTE. Atención educativa a menores con necesidades educativas especiales: equidad para la diversidad [National Declaration SEP-SNTE. Educational attention for students with special education needs: Equity to diversity]. Huatulco, Mexico.

UNESCO. 1992. Seminario Regional de la UNESCO. Sobre politícas, planeación y educación integrada para alumnos con necesidades especiales. Informe final. [UNESCO Regional Seminar. Policies, planning, and integrated education for students with special education needs]. Caracas, Venezuela.

_____. 1994. *Final report of the world conference on special needs education: Access and quality.* Salamanca, Spain.

_____. 1996. *Boletín 40: Proyecto principal de educación en América Latina y el Caribe* [Principal education project for Latin America and the Caribbean]. Santiago, Chile.

_____. 1996. *Perspectivas de educación especial en los países de América Latina y el Caribe* [Special education perpectives in Latin America and the Caribbean]. Viña del Mar, Chile.

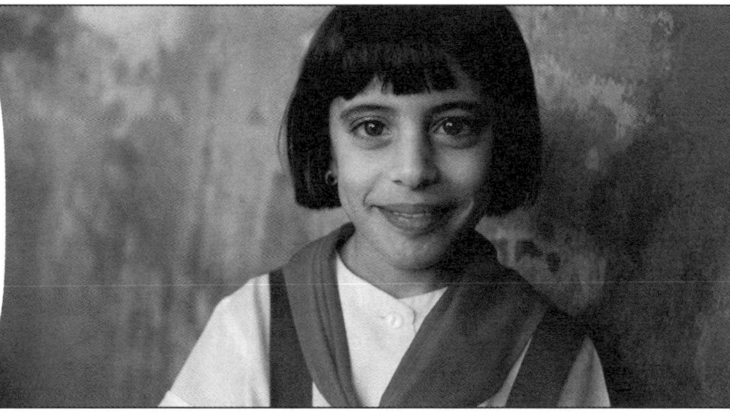

10

Educational Opportunities for Children with Disabilities in Mexico

Identification and Intervention

Georgina Reich-Erdmann

Education is a dynamic field in both the United States and in Mexico. One of the issues that have come up within this field is the merging of special education and regular education in order to provide an "inclusive education for all." This trend, which is currently taking place in both countries, began in the United States with Public Law 94-142 (Choate 1993). The law, known as the Education for All Handicapped Children Act, was enacted in 1975.

In Mexico, regular education and special education were, for several decades, two clearly separated entities. On 15 June 1993 a new general education law, which is in many ways similar in content and meaning to PL 94-142, came into effect. This law deals, among other things, with two important issues: the decentralization of education and educational integration.

It appears, then, that in Mexico the recognition of diverse characteristics and educational needs of children, as well as the merging of special education with regular education in search of an inclusive education, have started only recently. These changes are raising challenging issues that need close attention and prompt action. One of these issues relates to educational outcomes and their relation to expectations, which in turn have a close connection to identification, diagnostic procedures, and intervention strategies.

Mexico and Changes in Education

In regard to the decentralizing process, it should be pointed out that for many years Mexican education was organized, regulated, directed, and supervised by a central educational agency located in Mexico City. Educational norms and procedures, as well as educational planning, programming, and selection of content, were the responsibility of this governmental entity.

The objectives and educational decisions made by this central organ were uniform for all children and were to be equally applied throughout the entire nation. The principle behind this policy was to provide equal educational opportunities for all Mexican children. Identical teaching principles and identical materials were used regardless of location, population characteristics, ethnic and cultural backgrounds and values, and regional particularities. To ensure uniformity, a single set of free textbooks for elementary education was published by the board of education and distributed to every child nationwide (Villa 1988).

Private schools were able to add some specific goals and objectives, such as teaching a second language, but only after complying with the principles, objectives, and mandates imposed by the board of education. These schools were frequently inspected to ensure compliance with all regulations.

This kind of management and control of the public as well as private educational sectors did not allow for any individual accommodations; therefore, children who differed from the majority in any way were not offered opportunities in general education settings. This included children from native ethnic groups whose native languages were other than Spanish.

Currently, with the educational decentralization that is part of the new law, educational authorities of each Mexican state have theoretically been given the power to decide and implement educational plans, programs, and contents according to particular and regional characteristics and needs, and to assess their outcomes independently. As a result, these local authorities are beginning to incorporate diverse elements that are relevant to the population of each specific location and to recognize that educational diversity should be acknowledged and addressed appropriately. Likewise, private schools are finding that educational authorities are more flexible in accepting programs that implement minor or major differences in educational objectives and ways to approach them.

Educational integration has also brought about a radical change in the way children with special educational needs are treated within the general educational system. This includes children with different handicapping conditions as well as children who face other conditions that interfere with their learning and academic performance within the mainstream setting.

In Mexico, children who had a disability were legally banned from attending regular school facilities for a long time. Although integration of some special children into regular schools and classrooms was taking place, it was dependent upon the acceptance and goodwill of teachers, school directors, and administrators.

As it was illegal to have children who had disabilities in regular classrooms, schools were not obliged to provide any kind of special human or material resources for them to facilitate integration and foster academic performance. Whenever an official supervisor came around, these children were hidden. Parents had to accept whatever was provided for them and had no right to demand any special services, because their acceptance in a regular educational setting was considered a favor.

For the first time in Mexico, Article 41, chapter 4, of the new general education law recognizes the right of children who have a disability, or those with any other special educational need, to an appropriate education, without necessarily segregating them from "normal" children.

This law also states the right of these children to additional support services that facilitate the child's integration into the educational setting whenever possible. Therefore, the need to establish multidisciplinary professional support teams, known as Units of Support Services to Regular Education (USAER), has been recognized. The professional members of these teams are responsible for providing support and guidance to the child and his or her teachers within the regular classroom when possible. Otherwise, they may have to provide additional or alternate schooling if that is what best serves the child's special educational needs. These teams are also expected to provide information, guidance, and support to parents and to the teaching staff.

For those children who cannot be successfully integrated into a regular school setting, the new general education law keeps open the possibility to segregate them, temporarily or permanently. For this purpose, Centers for Multiple Attention (CAM) have been created (see chapter 2, Watkins "Family-Centered Early Intervention"). These institutions provide the children with the special education services they need and prepare them for future integration into regular classrooms whenever possible.

Issues and Challenges in the Mexican Educational System

For a long time the Mexican educational system has faced many problems. These unresolved problems prevail in spite of the enactment of the new general education law and present a challenge to the successful implementation of the new law.

In the last few years, the Mexican Ministry of Public Education has openly recognized the following four educational problems as priorities: (1) the greater demand for education in relation to nationwide availability, (2) the uneven quality of education among different regions in the country, (3) the number of children who fail to learn appropriately and who, as a result, are retained in the same grade at the end of each school year, and (4) the number of children who drop out of school before finishing their elementary-school education.

As regards the first problem, even though educational offerings have increased extraordinarily during the last few years and special attention has been given to support services in elementary education, there are still an important number of school-age children to whom educational facilities are not available (Schmelkes 1991). Statistics show that, at a national level, elementary education for children ages six to eleven provides 98% of the demand. Presumably the children who are left out are mostly those who live in remote, small rural communities that are often difficult to reach. At the secondary level, for children ages twelve to seventeen, only 53% of the demand is covered by education services. At the tertiary level, for individuals ages eighteen to twenty-four, educational facilities exist for only 14% of the population (Almazán-Ortega 1996; Rosas-Barrera 1995).

In relation to the disproportionate quality of education, Mexican educational authorities assert that on average Mexicans reach an educational level equivalent to seven years of schooling. While this is true for some regions of the country, others fall behind. Results from the 1990 national census (INEGI 1990) showed that although some of the northern states have an average educational level equivalent to seven years of schooling, in some of the southern states such as Chiapas, Tabasco, and Quintana Roo, the majority of the population has an average educational level of first grade. Many of these people are illiterate and live in poor economic conditions.

The retention of children in the same grade at the end of the school year, due to lack of adequate learning, and high dropout rates are recognized as serious problems. Educational authorities recognize that they are strongly related to factors such as poor socioeconomic conditions, inadequate attention to health factors that have negative impacts on learning, and the need for some children to help adults with their everyday labor instead of attending school.

Statistics show that currently only 62% of children who enter elementary education ever finish it (Safa and Nivón 1992). Following are the results of the 1990 census related to schooling for the population fifteen years of age or older: 13.4% never attended school, 23.8% did not finish elementary school, 19.3% completed elementary school only, 42.5% had some type of schooling beyond elementary school, and 1.0% entered college.

Some scholars strongly feel that the low socioeconomic status of a great number of Mexicans is one of the main causes of inadequate schooling. Poverty also brings with it poor nutrition, a factor that is closely related to poor educational outcomes. It is important to point out that eight years after the last census was taken, economic conditions in Mexico have worsened, and an increasing number of middle-class families have a standard of living that places them in the category of low socioeconomic status. Close to 40 million people, of a total population of approximately 98 million people, are currently considered to be living in conditions of poverty.

Other factors that may be interfering with academic achievement and may be contributing to high dropout rates have been largely ignored. Mildly disabling conditions such as the presence of minimal to moderate bilateral hearing loss or unilateral hearing loss have not even been considered as possible factors that interfere with academic performance, even though their negative effects on children's developmental and academic outcomes are well documented (Berg 1986; Blair, Peterson, and Viehweg 1985; Brandes and Ehinger 1981; Culbertson and Gilbert 1986; Davis et al. 1986; Matkin 1986, 1988).

In 1996, auditory screening was performed on 590 first-grade public elementary school students in a small town in Mexico (Reich-Novotny 1996). The purpose was to assess the hearing ability of children attending first grade in regular schools in a typical Mexican school district and to call to the attention of Mexican educational authorities the need to implement auditory screening programs nationwide, at least for children entering elementary school.

Of 590 children screened by using the auditory screening protocol (ASHA), only 349 (59%) fell within normal limits. Even though only 9 children (1.5%) were found to have a permanent, mild to moderate sensorineural hearing loss, either unilaterally or bilaterally, the condition of 232 children suggested the presence of factors that could have temporarily diminished auditory reception. In some children this condition might have been recurring. On the other hand, one-third of the sample population was found to have a copious accumulation of dark-colored earwax in the external auditory canal when observed through the otoscope. Although only 12 children had a complete wax obstruction of the external auditory canal in one ear, with a 40-db conductive hearing loss in that ear, many children explained how much more comfortable they felt after their ears were washed and the wax was eliminated. These excessive wax accumulations could have been causing some of the children's fluctuating hearing losses.

A history of variations in hearing thresholds due to fluctuating conductive hearing losses has been related to phonological defects (Abraham, Wallace, and Gravel 1996) and to language problems (Friel-Patti 1990).

The 590 children were observed through the entire school year. At the end of the school year, 96 of the children (16.3%) were retained in the same grade due to low academic achievement. Out of these 96 children, 58 (60%) had obtained abnormal measures in the auditory screening. The possible relationship between academic performance and the presence of abnormal measures in auditory screenings has yet to be investigated. However, these results should be an eye opener for Mexican educational authorities, who should recognize that minimal, mild, and moderate hearing disabilities in school-age children could be related to their failing or dropping out of school. In 1990, Ross stated that there is still a lack of understanding of the important role that hearing plays in communication and acquisition of information of all kinds, social as well as cultural and academic. This lack of understanding is highly prevalent in Mexico.

The possible influence of problems related to visual acuity have just begun to receive attention in Mexico. Recently an aggressive campaign has been started to help provide eyeglasses for those school-age children who need them and whose families cannot afford them. The slogan used in radio and television commercials invites people to "help see well for better learning."

Screening programs designed to detect other abnormal conditions that may be interfering with learning and academic performance in school-age children are nonexistent, so other factors that impede learning usually go undetected. Some extrinsic factors that affect educational outcomes, such as discrepancies between teachers' teaching styles and children's learning styles, are generally ignored as well.

It is also important to examine some of the conditions in which children receive regular education in Mexico. Not only are educational norms and procedures, devised by a central educational agency, applied indiscriminately throughout the nation, but there remains the problem of overcrowded classrooms with a single teacher instructing often more than 50 students. These children are expected to sit still in rows of desks for long periods of time and listen to teachers who frequently talk about things that are beyond their comprehension.

Problems Related to Special Education

Before the new general education law was enacted in 1993, quantitative data related to special education revealed a great difference between the capacity of existing facilities and the number of children who needed special educational services. This discrepancy has always been much greater than in regular education. Currently, there are no reliable statistical figures to show the number of children with disabilities that exist in Mexico. Demand for these services has been inferred from data obtained in other countries and those published by different international organizations.

The World Health Organization figures suggest that approximately 10% of the world's population of children have a disability that places them in need of special educational services. These rough figures have been used to arrive at an estimate of the number of children that require special educational services in Mexico.

Considering that Mexico has an estimated population of 18 million children from six to sixteen years of age, 10% of this total is equivalent to some 1.8 million children who have disabilities. According to Gómez-Palacio, 250,000 Mexican children were receiving special educational services, that is, these services were provided to about one out of seven children who required them.

In regard to the integration of children with disabilities into regular education prior to 1993, two main strategies were officially applied. One strategy consisted of the establishment of resource rooms on regular-school premises for children identified as having learning disabilities. This strategy, known as "integrated groups," was started between 1970 and 1973. A few of these resource rooms still exist today. Later, integrated groups for partially deaf and deaf children were established, and many are currently still in use.

As mentioned earlier, integration of individual children with disabilities into regular classrooms has been taking place for a long time; even though this practice was illegal prior to 1993, it has continued to increase at a steady pace for several years. Unfortunately, there were many individuals in this kind of setting whose academic accomplishments were very limited. In too many instances, students in these programs were issued elementary-school certificates although they had been unable to fulfill the basic learning requirements. The result of this practice is low expectations as to the potential of individuals with disabilities.

Problems Related to Educational Integration

The poor academic achievement of individuals with disabilities who attended either special educational institutions or regular classrooms during the past decades has led to the belief that these individuals are incapable of accomplishing anything worthwhile. As a result, society and general-school teachers have low expectations for children with disabilities.

With the enactment of the new general education law, the integration of children with disabilities into regular classrooms is being implemented. Children with different special educational needs are being placed in regular classrooms without general-teacher preparation or training. USAER teams have been established to provide the additional support that is required under these circumstances. Different special-education facilities are being closed, and the teachers previously employed in these schools have become part of the USAER teams. However, the multidisciplinary professionals included on the USAER teams have not been adequately prepared, and their different roles, even though well defined on paper, have not been completely understood. Although some schools have a USAER team that gives all the needed support, in many cases a single USAER group serves several schools, with each school getting only meager support. Finally, there are many schools that get no help at all.

The new general education law was enacted five years ago. Educators from different sectors and educational authorities nationwide are slowly becoming aware that several important modifications need to take place if integration of children with special needs into the mainstream of education is to be successfully accomplished in Mexico. The first issue that needs to be addressed, if the integration of students with disabilities into regular schools and into society is to succeed, is related to the concept of "normalcy" and "abnormalcy." Individual differences have to be viewed as an inherent component of the human race. Attention has to be drawn to the strengths of each individual, and everyone has to be given the opportunity to fully develop these strengths in order to overcome and complement as best as possible individual disabilities and other weaknesses. The concepts of normalcy and abnormalcy need to be seen in a continuum delimited by these two extremes, with each individual forming part of the spectrum. The specific characteristics of each individual in this continuum will have a different impact depending on the context in which he or she is being educated and the tasks that are being required.

Once this diversity inherent in the human race is recognized, the need arises to open up curricular planning and programming and to implement curricular flexibility, allowing teachers to be freer and more creative in their teaching. Teachers should be able to feel that they have the possibility to modify educational plans and programs and be allowed to make curricular adaptations according to the specific needs and abilities of the children in their classrooms. Even though this change is included in the new law, implementation has been difficult. The trend to maintain central norming and control continues, and too many teachers find it difficult to develop individualized and collaborative strategies in their classrooms. In those groups that are still managed as a whole, children are forced to sit and passively follow the teachers' instructions, and it is difficult to provide an adequate environment for a child who needs individualized instruction and management.

Teacher training programs need to be modified. Information about diversity in school-age children's characteristics and needs and basic strategies to cope with them have to be included. Teachers need to learn that special educational needs in children exist as a result of both disabling conditions and cultural and socioeconomic differences. A basic knowledge of the various disabling conditions and their most important consequences, management needs, and intervention strategies has to be incorporated into teacher education. In-service training related to these issues has to be provided for working teachers, school administrators, and other staff members, so they will become active participants in the process of educational integration. Teachers have to learn that what they expect from children has an important influence on their achievement. The positive relationship between teachers' expectations and students' achievement has been well documented (Schumm and Vaughn 1998).

Another issue that has to be addressed is the need to inform "normal" peers as well as their parents, family members, and other members of society about the characteristics and attributes of children who have special educational needs. This knowledge will facilitate a better understanding of what goes on in a regular classroom when a child is disabled or has other special educational needs.

Children who achieve appropriate learning outcomes have to learn to interact with and become resources for children who are different. They need to learn to work in collaborative environments, to provide guidance, support, and tutorship to other children, and to share their learning strategies and techniques.

Along with these changes, expectations regarding the potential of each individual, including those who have disabilities, have to be reviewed. It has to be recognized that most individuals who have disabilities have many attributes that allow them to become members of society in every way. They can be as productive as anyone when given the opportunity to develop their skills. Therefore, appropriate opportunities for the full development of everyone's potential have to become available at an early age.

Finally, programs for the early detection of disabling conditions and for early intervention need to be in place nationwide. This will improve developmental and educational processes that in turn will improve educational outcomes. These will lead to a rise in expectations and foster understanding that if the proper resources are assigned and adequately used to open up better opportunities for disabled individuals, the results will benefit everyone.

An Ecological Perspective

Kirk and Gallagher (1994) explain that in the United States the perspectives from which individuals with disabilities are viewed have changed. An ecological perspective has taken the place of a reductionist medical perspective.

From this new perspective, the objective is to identify and develop individual strengths as early and fully as possible. Individuals with disabilities are increasingly being provided with better opportunities to demonstrate what each one is capable of accomplishing. This has led to the recognition of the enormous strengths and potential that exist in these individuals. As a result, elements such as early detection and intervention, availability of needed support, the optimal use of human and material resources, and the development of appropriate educational provisions from an early age up to adulthood with a view to eliminating all social and physical barriers have become the legal rights of individuals with disabilities. These rights, among others, are clearly stated in laws such as PL 94-142, Education of All Handicapped Children Act of 1975, and PL 101-476, Individuals with Disabilities Education Act of 1990 (Gearheart, Mullen, and Gearheart 1993).

A similar change in perspective is strongly needed in Mexico. Although the new general education law was written from this new perspective and includes a number of updated and positive propositions, the medical perspective is prevalent throughout Mexico. It is widely accepted among general and special teachers, pediatricians, medical doctors, psychologists, and members of society in general.

From this perspective, the individual who has a disability is conceived of as a sick or incapable person with all the limitations that are believed to be inherent in his or her illness or physical condition. As a result, individuals who have a recognized disability are considered to have limited ability and to require either therapeutic intervention to correct or diminish their limitations or long-term care.

Two examples are provided by Macías-Pimentel (1998) and Gálvez-Aguilar (1998). Macías-Pimentel, after working for several years with children with severe and profound hearing losses, asserts that they never attained the use of language symbols, either oral or written. She states that she came to this conclusion after observing twenty-seven, seven- to fifteen-year-old deaf students and trying to measure their reading competency. Most of the students had been diagnosed as deaf before the age of three and some as early as at one year of age. After attending a special program for deaf children for several years, they were unable to communicate significantly with other people. Their communication was limited to elements that allowed them to indicate only their most basic needs. Macías-Pimentel does not question intervention approaches and their effectiveness nor analyze other factors that might have accounted for these poor results; instead, she concludes that their limitations are inherent in their deafness. This view is shared by too many educators of the deaf in Mexico.

In a speech she gave at the Universidad de las Américas on 21 October 1998, L. Gálvez-Aguilar, counselor in special education, asserted that it was very important to integrate deaf children into regular classrooms and stressed their need to communicate. Yet she stated that once they finished elementary school, they had to be directed to develop a skill that did not demand the use of language, as they were unable to attain its use at a competent level; however, they could become excellent computer specialists or carpenters.

Toledano-Landero (1995), Robles-Robles (1995), and Fleischmann-Loredo (1995), among many others, clearly state the urgent need for individuals with a disability to be treated with dignity and respect and to be allowed to participate in society like any other human being.

It is important to stress that there is great lack of programs in Mexico for early detection of disabilities in children and of children at risk for developmental delay. Appropriate educational facilities for children who need special education are scarce, and when parents suspect a problem that is not evident at first glance, it may take several years to find help for their children. Many never find it. In too many cases, when help is found, the possibility of benefiting from early intervention has passed.

Too many institutions and specialized services offer educational approaches and methods that are obsolete, so outcomes are poor and only serve to reinforce the low expectations that exist in relation to individuals with disabilities. Every time low expectations are confirmed, they reinforce the idea that these children are not worth the economic and human resources and efforts spent on them. As these children grow up and reach adulthood, the lack of education makes them ill prepared to become productive members of the labor force; this once again reinforces the low expectations that surround them. The inclusion of a child with a disability in a regular school or of an adult with a disability in an employment context is often seen as an act of charity.

The vicious cycle continues and has a negative impact on the possibilities of early and appropriate intervention and education. The generation of resources needed to provide opportunities for success in integrated contexts and in an integrated job market is also jeopardized. These individuals are disqualified a priori from the possibility of participating in the mainstream of society and schooling; the result is a self-fulfilling prophecy that begins with low expectations.

Only a few individuals who have had a severe disabling condition from an early age have been able to succeed and accomplish high levels of performance in society. Most of them have done so because they had extraordinary parents who were committed to the development of their child's potential. Whereas from the medical perspective it is society that decides what an individual who has a disability is allowed and expected to do, the ecological perspective recognizes the individual's right to get involved in any type of activity according to his or her abilities. Compensatory strategies and the use of adaptive methods determine what the individual will be able to accomplish.

From an ecological perspective, a handicap is not considered an existing difference that sets the individual apart, but rather the combination of an individual's differences, strengths, and attributes. These are combined with opportunities to develop the individual's potential and with the elimination of obstacles and barriers imposed by society in order to facilitate the development of the individual's potential regardless of his or her difference.

It is urgent to promote in Mexico the concepts of this ecological perspective and to implement conditions that will assure that children who have a disability have access to optimal opportunities that will allow them to develop their full potential regardless of their disability or other difference. It is also important for Mexicans to have contact with successful individuals who have been disabled since an early age, so that they understand the potential these people have to become fully integrated and productive individuals on their own and not as a result of charitable acts or some "miracle."

Conclusion

Dynamic changes are taking place in special education on both sides of the border. The United States has mandated inclusive education since 1975, and Mexico has taken the same position with the new general education law of 1993, eighteen years later. Inclusive education has become the current trend also in many other countries around our world.

For Mexico, a country that has gone through three profound economic crises in the last twenty years and has experienced a substantial increase in its population, the challenge to provide appropriate education for all of its children has become an enormous task.

In order to successfully promote an inclusive policy, it is critical that a profound reexamination of current beliefs, expectations, and general educational practices, particularly in relation to children with disabilities, accompany the legal changes that are mandating the educational integration for children with special educational needs. There has to be an extensive promotion of the potential and accomplishments of individuals who have disabilities. This is the only way to make society aware that with optimal educational opportunities for all children, and especially for those with special needs, society as a whole can profit from the enormous potential of all its people.

References

Abraham, S. S., I. F. Wallace, and J. S. Gravel. 1996. Early otitis media and phonological development at age 2 years. *Laryngoscope* 106:727-32.

Almazán-Ortega, J. L. 1996. ¿Cómo está la educación en México? *Entorno* (May):17-22.

American Speech-Language Hearing Association. 1990. Guidelines for screening for hearing impairment and middle-ear disorders. *ASHA* 32 (suppl. 2):17-24.

Berg, F. S. 1986. Characteristics of the target population. In *Educational audiology for the hard of hearing child*, ed. F. S. Berg, J. C. Blair, S. H. Viehweg and A. Wilson-Vlotman, 1-24. New York: Grune and Stratt.

Blair, J. C., M. E. Peterson, and S. H. Viehweg. 1985. The effects of mild sensorineural hearing loss on academic performance of young school-age children. *Volta Review* 87:87-93.

Brandes, P., and D. Ehinger. 1981. The effects of middle ear pathology on auditory perception and academic achievement. *Journal of Speech and Hearing Disorders* 46:301-7.

Choate, J. S. 1993. *Successful Mainstreaming: Proven Ways to Detect and Correct Special Needs*. Needham Heights, MA: Allyn and Bacon.

Culbertson, J. L., and L. E. Gilbert. 1986. Children with unilateral sensorineural hearing loss: Cognitive, academic, and social development. *Ear and Hearing* 7:38-42.

Davis, J. M., J. Elfenbein, R. Schum, and R. T. Bentler. 1986. Effects of mild and moderate hearing impairments on language, educational, and psychosocial behavior of children. *Journal of Speech and Hearing Disorders* 51:53-62.

Fleischmann-Loredo, F. 1995. Barreras físicas, culturales y sociales que impiden la integración del discapacitado. Paper presented at Primer Congreso Internacional de la Discapacidad en el Año 2000. Mexico, DF: Lotería Nacional para la Asistencia Pública.

Friel-Patti, S. 1990. Otitis media with effusion and the development of language: A review of the evidence. *Topics in Language Disorders* 11:11-20.

Gearheart, B., R. C. Mullen, and C. Gearheart. 1993. *Exceptional Individuals: An Introduction*. CA: Brooks/Cole.

INEGI. 1990. *XI censo general de población y vivienda, 1990*. Mexico, DF: Instituto Nacional de Estadística, Geografía e Informática.

Kirk, S. A., and J. J. Gallagher. 1994. *Educating exceptional children*. 6th ed. Boston: Houghton Mifflin.

Macías-Pimentel, A. G. 1998. El proceso de aprendizaje de la lengua escrita en el sordo profundo. Master's thesis, Universidad de las Américas, Mexico, DF.

Matkin, N. D. 1986. The role of hearing in language development. In *Otitis media and child development*, ed. J. F. Kavanagh, 3-11. Parkton, MD: York Press.

_____. 1988. Re-evaluating our approach to evaluation: Demographics are changing—are we? In *Hearing Impairment in Children*, ed. Fred H. Bess. Parkton, MD: York Press.

Reich-Novotny, G. 1996. Demographic study of hearing status of first grade elementary public school children in a Mexican school district. Ph.D. diss., University of Arizona.

Robles-Robles, I. L. 1995. Legislación y derechos: La legislación en México. Paper presented at Primer Congreso Internacional la Discapacidad en el Año 2000. Mexico, DF: Lotería Nacional para la Asistencia Pública.

Rosas-Barrera, F. 1995. David contra Goliat: La educación mexicana ante el TLC. *Educación 2001* 3:34-37.

Ross, M. 1990. Implications of delay in detection and management of deafness. *Volta Review* 92:69-78.

Safa, P., and E. Nivón. 1992. La educación y el tratado de libre comercio: De la crisis a las perspectivas. In *La educación y la cultura ante el tratado de libre comercio*, ed. G. Guevara Niebla and N. García Canclini, 49-72. Mexico, DF: Editorial Patria.

Schmelkes, S. 1991. Problemas y retos de la educación básica en México. In *Cambio estructural y modernización educativa*, ed. M. T. de Sierra, 147-64. Mexico, DF: UPN, UAM-A, COMECSO, A.C.

Schumm, J. S., and S. Vaughn. 1998. Introduction to special issue on teachers' perceptions: Issues related to the instruction of students with learning disabilities. *Learning Disabilities Quarterly* 21:3-5.

Toledano-Landero, J. E. 1995. Abran cancha, el mundo también es nuestro. Paper presented at Primer Congreso Internacional de la Discapacidad en el Año 2000. Mexico, DF: Lotería Nacional para la Asistencia Pública.

Villa, L. L. 1988. Los libros de texto gratuitos. Guadalajara, Mexico: Universidad de Guadalajara.

11

Special Education for Latino Students in the United States

A Metaphor for What Is Wrong

Richard A. Figueroa

This chapter is about bilingual special education. The joining of bilingual education with special education provides an interesting example of what should *not* happen in terms of educational reform and evolution (Skrtic 1991; Elmore 1996). However, the flawed interface between bilingual and special education in the United States provides the basis for a unique form of critical dialogue between the United States, Mexico, and Latin America about the education of children who do not thrive in general education programs and who subsequently wind up in remedial classrooms or in special education.

The fundamental premise of this paper is that the medical and psychological underpinnings of the current special education modus operandi in the Western Hemisphere has outlived its usefulness. It is time for an educational paradigm to guide the conduct of special educators in meeting the learning needs of disabled students. It is time for the diminution of the role of regulations, the importance placed on diagnostic and predictive assessments, the emphasis on a ritualized and elaborate system for creating Individualized Educational Programs (IEP) and the belief in the power of drills, skills, and contingent reinforcements as necessary and sufficient conditions for actuating higher-order mental processes. A different vision is needed for underachievers, and a new skepticism should be applied to many, if not most, current practices and beliefs in special and bilingual special education.

Bilingual Special Education

In the early 1970s Leonard Baca almost single-handedly launched bilingual special education as a new area of research and development. In *The Bilingual Special Education Interface*, he set out to meet the needs of bilingual children who were eligible for special education services (Baca and Cervantes 1984). Ironically, however, this undertaking was clouded by the fact that special education had a long history of diagnosing too many Latino children as mentally handicapped (Reynolds 1933; Shotwell 1945; Anastasi and Cordova 1953; Palomares and Johnson 1966; Chandler and Platkos 1969; *Diana v California Board of Education*, 1970; U.S. Commission on Civil Rights 1974; *José P. v Ambach* 1979; Heller, Holtzman, and Messick 1982; Valdés and Figueroa 1994). In the 1970s and 1980s, the predominant area of inquiry in this field was the phenomenon of overrepresentation, and one of the most interested consumers in this regard was the federal judiciary system. In *Diana, Covarrubias, José P.*, and other cases, the courts examined the issue of overrepresentation and indicted the assessment methods used for determining who was and who was not mentally disabled.

In Public Law 94-142, the judicial inquiries were "answered" in the provision that all assessments and diagnoses in special education were to be culturally nondiscriminatory. Nonbiased assessment was pressed into the service of searching for the "real disability" without any contaminating effects of culture and bilingual abilities.

Mercer, in her study *The System of Multicultural Pluralistic Assessment* (SOMPA), created the most elaborate answer to how to do nondiscriminatory, nonbiased assessments (1979). Using some eleven tests that could generate twenty-one scores from what were supposedly three separate assessment models, the SOMPA battery of tests essentially established one "metaprinciple" in the assessment of minority children. This principle is: when cultural and linguistic factors apply in testing, do *more* testing. Others answered the same call for nonbiased assessment by "doing more" in creating supposedly parallel forms of tests in Spanish (e.g., the Batería Woodcock Psico Educativa and the Mexico City WISC-R) or parallel Spanish instructions for nonverbal tests (e.g., the K-ABC).

The "do more" principle, by the time Baca and Cervantes published the second edition of *The Bilingual Special Education Interface* (1989), was well established and applied to elongated models of prereferral activities and to elaborated due-process regulations enacted to serve bilingual disabled learners across many states. California, Illinois, Florida, and New York are the front-runners in this regard.

Over the last five years, annual professional conferences on bilingual education or on special education for bilingual children have included an increasing number of presentations in which the "do more" principle is recommended. The prereferral models are getting longer, the "innovative" uses of tests are increasing, and the state-based regulatory edifices are being discussed with an eye to enlarging them.

The interface of bilingual and special education or, more precisely, the piling-on of bilingual theory and practice on top of the regulatory, diagnostic, pedagogical, and structural system that is special education, provides one of the more interesting approaches to educational reform or, rather, one of the clearest examples for the continued failure of systematism. As Skrtic noted, adding more boxes to the assembly line of programs that constitutes American education does not change the underlying industrial paradigm that has both survived a century of efforts at reform and delivered progressively less and less education to those who need it the most (1991).

Contemporary bilingual special education in the United States lacks two components: a theoretical grounding that would serve to explain and guide bilingual special education and a clear acknowledgment of the thirty-year-old literature that questions the regulatory, diagnostic, pedagogical, and structural foundations of special education (Mercer 1973; Tucker 1980; Ysseldyke et al. 1982; Coles 1987; Cummins 1984; Rueda et al. *Performance,* 1984; Rueda et al., *Examination,* 1984; Mehan, Hertweck, and Meihls 1986; Poplin 1988; Taylor 1991; Skrtic 1991; Valdés and Figueroa 1994; Skrtic 1995; Poplin and Cousin 1996). The omission of this critical literature may be central to understanding why bilingual special education has not progressed intellectually and why disabled and nondisabled bilingual children in special education in the United States, together with their nonbilingual peers, have little hope for any academic achievement once they qualify for special education services.

For example, in a study of California's premier special education program, the Resource Specialist Program (RSP), Figueroa found that the corpus of available studies on this program together with the results of the statewide California Assessment Program (CAP) conducted on over forty thousand pupils in special education over five years (1986-1990) generally indicated that objective evidence of academic progress was negligible. He concluded that

> On standardized tests of academic achievement, on CAP test scores and on two studies on teacher judgments about the academic achievement of RSP students, the data paint a bleak picture. RSP pupils not only do poorly, they get worse with each progressive grade. On the other hand, according to data on proficiency exams, meeting IEP goals and educators' judgments on RSP pupils' academic achievement, these students are supposedly doing well. What augurs badly in terms of these latter, positive outcomes is the fact that several studies report that the RSP suffers from a lack of clear direction, philosophy and teaching methodology. RSP teachers and the educators who work with them see role conflicts. In conjunction with the "hard data" on RSP underachievement, this suggests one conclusion: the program is ineffective and the majority of pupils are being subjected to "dead end" educational classes. (1992, 4)

A Critique of Special Education

The Rituals

The regulatory and due-process provisions in special education in the United States are the most elaborate of any educational program. Many, if not most of these, have their genesis in a series of court cases initiated by parents of disabled children who were, often by state statute, denied access to public education because of their alleged uneducability. The parents fundamentally wanted one thing: that their children be taught. To achieve this, however, they needed to ensure the children's access and protection. The settlements won by the parents in the *Pennsylvania Association for Retarded Children (PARC)* (1971), the *Mills* (1972), and the *Knight* (1969) cases were codified in Public Law 94-142 precisely as access and protection provisions. As Mehan, Hertweck, and Meihls showed in their ethnographic study of the Oceanside School District in California, and as most parents of physically disabled children who have attended IEP meetings will attest, these provisions are routinely circumvented by special education bureaucracy (1986).

The implementation of the elaborate decision-making processes laid out in Public Law 94-142 is not rational. It is irrational insofar as it is governed by exigencies, such as class size, personnel availability, class undersize, funding, student reputations, and so on, that are important to special educators but not the law or the children and their parents. Ironically, even in their ineffectiveness they remain among the most expensive rituals in U.S. public education.

The clearest example of how these rituals have come to dominate special education and how they have come to threaten the fundamental goal of the parents in the *PARC*, *Mills*, and *Knight* cases is the agreement reached in 1996 in the *Chanda Smith* complaint in the Los Angeles Unified School District (LAUSD) (Barber and Kerr 1995). This class action suit could require the LAUSD to live up first and foremost to the access and protection provisions under 94-142 and to California special education laws in their entirety and with full paper documentation and paper compliance. The assumption is that it is possible to actually do every ritual (search, student study team, parent permission for assessments, testing, IEP meeting, IEP implementation, complaint hearings, due-process hearings, placement in special education programs, annual evaluation, triannual evaluations, record keeping systems, matriculation, transportation, and so on) for every student and, most critically, that paper compliance in these will effect what the *PARC*, *Mills*, and *Knight* parents wanted: that their children be taught.

Currently, there is little in the Chanda Smith Consent Decree and Order Thereon that speaks of diminishing the impact of children's disabilities, providing the best learning environments, affirming educational goals that are similar to those of general education, or holding anyone accountable for children's learning. Ironically, in 1974, these ideals formed the foundation for California's Master Plan for Special Education (California State Department of Education 1974) before the ritualized legalese of Public Law 94-142 ushered in the current irrational application of processes and procedures (Mehan, Hertweck, and Meihls 1986) that now define special education. If *Chanda Smith* only focuses on access and protection provisions, it could represent the worst possible educational scenario for disabled children. They will receive access and protections, but as the national secretary for special education recently acknowledged (Merrow 1996), they will not be taught under the current system.

Potentially, *Chanda Smith* could go beyond mere access and protection compliance. Unlike the major testing cases of the 1970s (e.g., *Diana* and *Larry P.*), *Chanda Smith* could provide a unique opportunity for reforming one of the largest special education public school systems in the country. All it needs to do is return to the fundamental goal of parents of disabled children, that their children be taught. With the support and authority of the federal courts, the *Chanda Smith* case could even help to rewrite the current versions of the *Individuals with Disabilities Education Act* (IDEA) by demonstrating how the primacy of instructional reform can diminish the need for exaggerated procedural practices. For bilingual children, *Chanda Smith* could even bring about a new vision of bilingual special education in the school district with the largest number of bilingual children in the country.

Practicing Medicine without a License

The medical model origins of special education are now manifested in the most interesting and flawed manner in the assessment processes used to diagnose what are overwhelmingly nonmedical conditions, such as mild mental retardation, learning disabilities, speech and language problems, behavioral disorders, and attention deficits.

The mythology supporting the assessment processes maintains that it is possible to diagnose these conditions with the available corpus of normative-psychometric tests and procedures on a decontextualized, immediate basis (similar to what emergency room doctors do) and that the results are useful for instructional goals, objectives, and methods. For bilingual children, the data, particularly as synthesized in the current *Standards for Educational and Psychological Testing* are quite clear (American Educational Research Association, American Psychological Association, National Council on Measurement 1985, chap. 13). Most tests are linguistically confounded or contaminated. As the *Standards* note: "For a non-native English speaker and for a speaker of some dialects of English, every test given in English becomes, in part, a language or literacy test" (73), and, concurrently, for bilingual learners a test in Spanish becomes in unknown degrees a Spanish test. Moreover, tests are basically unable to diagnose because of their exceedingly weak power to predict anything in either English or Spanish (Valdés and Figueroa 1994). They seldom account for anything more than 25 percent of the variance of real-life outcomes (Figueroa and García 1995), and they are further limited because of the lack of empirically validated definitions of mental conditions such as "mild mental retardation," "learning disabilities," or "attention deficits." As Skrtic notes in his exhaustive review of the research that has been done in special education (1991), the professional literature on special education is fairly unanimous in conceding that special education diagnosis is not useful.

The New Pedagogy of the Oppressed

Similarly, when Skrtic consulted special education literature on whether special education instruction was effective, the answer was no. In 1988, Poplin provided one of the most insightful explanations for this phenomenon. In her analysis of the four methodological changes in special education curricula and instruction over the last fifty years, she concluded that the changes were essentially ephemeral. There has always been only one paradigm in special education: reductionism. There has always been the belief that for learners who have problems in general education classrooms, the best course of action is to break learning, lessons, and curricula down into small bits and pieces. In our own ethnographic work in California's resource specialist classrooms, we concluded that Poplin had no real appreciation of how much special education classrooms acted like mental repair shops trying to fix little broken mental processes by drills, repetition, exercises, and nonacademic "sensorimotor" activities (Ruiz et al. 1992).

At its core, special education is a tracking system. It shares all the structural traits of classical tracking programs and, like them, it produces the same marginal outcomes for children (Oakes 1985). A fundamental premise that undergirds tracking is the belief that an aptitude treatment interaction (ATI) is possible. This belief is carried to a unique extreme in special education, insofar as the ATI is to be effected at the ideographic level of the IEP and at the generalized level of the disability. The basic belief is that disabled children learn differently and that they therefore require different teaching and curricula. As Rueda (1989) and others suggest, this is an unsupported belief for the overwhelming majority of disabled students. Furthermore, as ATI literature has shown over the last twenty years, ATI effects are rarely ever produced in groups and much less in individuals (Slavin 1991).

The Reform of Bilingual Special Education

As noted, bilingual special education has not only adopted all of the regulatory, assessment, pedagogical, and structural characteristics of special education, it has also embellished them with more provisions as well as with the theoretical and applied-knowledge base particular to bilingual education. Nowhere is the "adding-on" quality of bilingual special education more evident than in the following list of assessment principles suggested for testing bilingual pupils that have been referred for special education (Baca and Cervantes 1989).

1. You need to do a psychoeducational assessment in order to make decisions.
2. You need to make a diagnosis of the disability before you can determine the instructional treatment.
3. Accurate and comprehensive psychoeducational assessments are important, useful, and possible.
4. It is difficult to identify the educational needs of bilingual multicultural pupils.
5. It is necessary to know about the student's "behavioral, cognitive, and academic strengths and weaknesses" in order to develop useful instructional plans.
6. It is important to know whether underachievement is due to a disability or to "level of acculturation and language acquisition."
7. It is possible to assess and use an individual's "learning style."
8. The more you test, the more accurate the "diagnosis."
9. Testing in the primary language "works" for bilingual children.
10. "Improved assessment capabilities and identification of students' needs are critical for minority (plurality) populations."
11. There are assessment instruments that are linguistically and culturally appropriate for bilingual, multicultural populations.
12. There is such a thing as "nondiscriminatory assessment."

One of the interesting aspects of the assessment principles shown in this list is that they all seem perfectly reasonable and potentially useful. They are neither. It is impossible with current technology to control culture and bilingualism so as not to contaminate test scores (Valdés and Figueroa 1994). It is also impossible on an immediate basis to "diagnose" a disability without taking learning contexts into account. The National Academy of Sciences suggested as much in 1982 (Heller, Holtzman, and Messick 1982) when it recommended that before testing a child an assessment of the current instructional program had to be done to see if the curriculum was appropriate for the pupil in question and, if so, to determine whether it was being implemented effectively in that classroom.

The same futility as in bilingual special education generally pertains to the adoption and enhancement of special education regulations, pedagogy, and organizational structures.

So where do the solutions lie? The parents in the *PARC*, *Mills*, and *Knight* cases had it right. The focal point of special education and now, by extension, for bilingual special education should be that bilingual children who struggle in the general education classroom *should be taught*. To accomplish this, our own work in this field has suggested that a new set of paradigmatic principles be considered (Ruiz 1989; Rueda 1989; Figueroa and Ruiz 1993; Ruiz and Figueroa 1995; Ruiz et al., *Bilingual*, 1996; Ruiz, García, and Figueroa 1996).

First, educators have no business practicing medicine without a license. Currently, we are incapable of determining educational needs outside of enriched, effective, instructional contexts and outside of longitudinal observations and social interactions with the learner (Taylor 1991). For example, it is educationally useless to diagnose auditory, visual, kinesthetic, or field-dependent "learning styles" since evidence of their effective aptitude treatment interaction has not reliably been shown. The only learning style that has ATI validity is, ironically, what bilingual educators have been proposing since the *Lau v Nichols* Supreme Court decision: primary-language instruction for limited-English speakers (Thomas and Collier 1995).

Second, the money currently used to guarantee access and protection (which has been marginally achieved) should be redirected toward increasing instructional resources. Special education classes are literature-poor and technologically unsophisticated in supporting literacy (both in language arts and mathematics) (Ruiz et al. 1992). We have found in California that shifting the bilingual special education classroom to look and act more like the classroom for the gifted produces levels of achievement of anywhere from one to three years' growth in literacy for up to 70 percent of "learning-handicapped" bilingual learners and "cures" up to 25 percent of them annually (Ruiz and Figueroa 1995). This is a considerably higher degree of improvement than the one- to two-percentile annual level of academic achievement at all grade levels for learning-handicapped students in California (Figueroa 1992).

Third, the premier focus for the bilingual special education classroom should be the instructional events and contexts created by the teacher. The Optimal Learning Environment (OLE) classrooms that we have helped to set up in California reflect this philosophy and use not only a set of very specific nonreductionist instructional strategies but also a different set of instructional principles than what is currently found in the Skinnerian classrooms for the learning-handicapped

(Rueda, Ruiz, and Figueroa 1996; Ruiz, García, and Figueroa 1996). A list of the OLE instructional principles follows.

1. Give students as much choice as possible in what they learn, read, write, and work on in the classroom, as opposed to always having the teacher select the topic, book, or project.
2. Be constructive. Build on the cultural knowledge and the interests of the student, as opposed to providing prepackaged materials, exercises, and drills.
3. Use a whole-part-whole approach to literature, writing, the arts, science, and mathematics, as opposed to requiring work on parts, fragments, or prerequisite skills.
4. Set up conditions for active student participation, as opposed to activities in which students are passive receptacles of "knowledge."
5. Attend to ideas first and then to mechanics, as opposed to giving issues of form, such as phonics, spelling, or grammar, a primary or exclusive focus.
6. As much as possible, have the students work for an authentic purpose, as opposed to teacher evaluation.
7. Immerse the students in a language- and print-rich environment, as opposed to an impoverished one in terms of the quantity and quality of books and the amount of reading, writing, listening, and speaking.
8. Provide multiple opportunities for demonstrations of how to do the work, as opposed to giving verbal instructions.
9. Understand and accept the role of approximations in getting at the right answer, as opposed to reinforcing the "correct" answer on the first try.
10. Always give an immediate response to students' work products, as opposed to a future grade for the "right" response.
11. Create an atmosphere in which the classroom becomes a learning community, as opposed to a collection of individuals working on their individualized learning programs.
12. Have high expectations. Believe that the social and academic potential of underachieving pupils and of persons with disabilities is truly unlimited, as opposed to focusing on what they cannot do or on their previous grades, test scores, or labels.

A crucial proposition in all this is that the regulations that currently drive so much of the ritualistic nature of special education should be replaced by a mandate for a different, enriched instructional program. This is not quantitatively "more of" what already exists in special education but the insistence on a qualitative sea change (Ruiz 1996a, 1996b). The sort of reform we propose requires a long-term commitment to help teachers create learning communities to guide their own change, namely, a model of in-service support. As we have found in our work, the process of such a change is multivariate and to a certain degree unpredictable at the individual level (Ruiz et al., *Bilingual,* 1996). It is not an easy process. It is considerably more difficult to create optimal learning contexts that rely on choice, constructivism, holism, cooperative groups, and so on, which reflect OLE principles, than to transmit information, assign work sheets, or repeat last year's lesson plans.

Finally, bilingual special education should actively consider an ethnomethodological theoretical foundation. Bilingual special education began with the problem of overrepresentation and with the hypothesis that the disabilities of many bilingual pupils placed in special education were socially constructed. We propose that, for all learners who are underachieving in the general education classroom, a theoretical base that seeks to explain learning problems in terms of the educational/social construction of a "learning disability" is apt to deal more effectively with the current levels of underachievement of children placed in special education and in bilingual special education.

The Special Child in the Americas

The historical merger of special and bilingual education on behalf of students who are both bilingual and considered eligible for special education provides a solid example of how *not* to reform. Piling-on is not a good way to change.

Instead, we need to deconstruct the systematic and paradigmatic barriers to academic achievement and life success for students in special education, no matter how entrenched they are historically, legislatively, and philosophically. We must begin to construct in their place a system that is wholly preoccupied with the contextual, versus psychological, features that define good instruction, create classrooms for gifted students, and generate student and teacher behaviors such as interest, tenacity, emotion, and excitement about all forms of literacy. It should be a system that has at its core the view that the social and academic potential of persons with disabilities is truly unlimited.

In the continuing dialogue among the United States, Mexico, and Latin America concerning the education of exceptional and emergent learners, the example of bilingual special education, in its attempt to simply incorporate the structure, technology, and procedures of special education, should serve as an excellent example of what *not* to do and a promise of what might be done, particularly in those bilingual special education programs that have broken away from the old paradigm and have chosen to concentrate on the pedagogical and educational mission of special education (Ortiz and Wilkinson 1991; Rueda, Ruiz, and Figueroa 1996).

Over the last fifteen years, the research and development that have taken place in Mexico's special education programs have been extremely influential throughout Latin America. Some of this, however, has recreated parts of the system used in the United States, particularly those aspects involving tests, testing, and "diagnosis." Many Mexican versions of psychometric tests have been developed, and these have fostered the growth of testers and the perpetuation of various medical model procedures and definitions.

One other consideration is worth noting. The need for a powerful pedagogy for children who are disabled or have become disabled by the severe economic dislocation occurring throughout Latin America and Mexico has never been greater. As recently noted by the United Nations Children's Fund, 40 percent of the world's population of children lives in Latin America (Albarrán de Alba 1996). There, 16 to 18 million of them work in order to survive. In Mexico, 16.9 percent of the children work. Anywhere from 3 to 13 million of them live and work on the streets. For many of these children, the one arena of possible government intervention that may preclude the virtual certainty of intergenerational poverty is literacy.

In this regard, what is remarkable about the Mexican special education system is its research and applied contributions on how to teach literacy to special learners. In a series of groundbreaking studies on mathematical literacy (Gómez-Palacio Muñoz and Farha Valenzuela 1987, 1988a) and writing/reading literacy (Ferreiro and Teberosky 1979; Ferreiro and Gómez-Palacio Muñoz 1982; Gómez-Palacio Muñoz, Moreno Carbajal, and Espinoza Monzón 1989) as well as on pedagogy and model programs (Dirección General de Educación Especial 1988), the Mexican Dirección General de Educación Especial and the Secretaría de Educación Pública predicted much of the new paradigmatic revolution in special education in the United States.

Mexico is uniquely situated to contribute to the reform of bilingual special education in the United States and to model a system of teaching literacy, such as the one advocated in this chapter, to all of Latin America. If the temptation to practice medicine without a license, to give access and protection provisions priority over teaching and optimal classrooms, or to set up a new pedagogy of the oppressed via behaviorism and reductionism is resisted in Mexico, bilingual special education and the emerging programs in special education in Latin America can initiate an unprecedented dialogue in the Western Hemisphere on how to diminish the impact of disabilities in children's lives and futures.

References

Albarrán de Alba, G. 1996. En el Distrito Federal la infancia no es prioridad: Se multiplica la producción de niños que viven, crecen y mueren en las calles. *Proceso* 1024:16-23.

American Educational Research Association, American Psychological Association, National Council on Measurement in Education. 1985. *Standards for educational and psychological testing.* Washington, DC: American Psychological Association.

Anastasi, A., and F. Cordova. 1953. Some effects of bilingualism upon the intelligence and test performance of Puerto Rican children in New York City. *Journal of Educational Psychology* 44:1-19.

Baca, L., and H. Cervantes. 1984, 1989. *The bilingual special education interface.* St. Louis, MO: Times/Mirror Mosby.

Barber, L., and M. M. Kerr. 1995. *Chanda Smith et al. v LAUSD* consultants' report. El Dorado Hills, CA: Lou Barber.

California State Department of Education. 1974. *California Master Plan for Special Education.* Sacramento.

Chandler, J., and J. Platkos. 1969. *Spanish-speaking pupils classified as EMR.* Sacramento: California State Department of Education.

Chanda Smith et al. v Los Angeles Unified School District et al., USDC Central District of California, CV 93-7044 LEW (GHKx 1996).

Coles, G. S. 1987. *The learning mystique: A critical look at "learning disabilities."* New York: Pantheon.

Covarrubias v San Diego Unified School District, No. 70-394-T, San Diego, CA. 1972.

Cummins, J. 1984. *Bilingualism and special education: Issues in assessment and pedagogy.* San Diego, CA: College Hill Press.

Diana v California Board of Education, San Diego: College-Hill, C-70-37 (ND CA 1970).

Dirección General de Educación Especial. 1988. *Estrategia psicopedagógica de integración a la escuela regular de niños con problemas en el desarrollo: Los grupos integrados B*. Mexico, DF.

Elmore, R. F. 1996. Getting to scale with good educational practice. *Harvard Educational Review* 66:1-23.

Ferreiro, E., and M. Gómez-Palacio Muñoz. 1982. *Nuevas perspectivas sobre los procesos de lectura y escritura*. Mexico, DF: Siglo XXI.

Ferreiro, E., and A. Teberosky. 1979. *Los sistemas de escritura en el desarrollo del niño*. Mexico, DF: Siglo XXI.

Figueroa, R. A. 1992. *The failure of the special education reductionist paradigm: The unique case of California's Resource Specialist Program*. Santa Cruz, CA: California Research Institute on Cultural Diversity and Special Education.

Figueroa, R. A., and E. García. 1995. Issues in testing students from culturally and linguistically diverse backgrounds. *Multicultural Education* 2:10-23.

Figueroa, R. A., and N. T. Ruiz. 1993. Bilingual pupils and special education. In *Recent advances in special education and rehabilitation*, ed. R. C. Eaves and P. McLaughlin. New York: Andover.

Gómez-Palacio Muñoz, M., and I. Farha Valenzuela. 1987. *Estrategias pedagógicas para niños de primaria con dificultades en el aprendizaje de las matemáticas*. Mexico, DF: Secretaría de Educación Elemental, Dirección General de Educación Especial.

_____. 1988a. *Estudio comparativo sobre la generalización de las nociones de lectura, escritura, y matemáticas en la escuela primaria, entre medios rural y urbano*. Mexico, DF: Dirección General de Educación Especial.

_____. 1988b. *Estrategias pedagógicas para superar las dificultades en el dominio del sistema de escritura*. Mexico, DF: Secretaría de Educación Elemental, Dirección General de Educación Especial.

Gómez-Palacio Muñoz, M., S. Y. Moreno Carbajal, and M. Espinoza Monzón. 1989. *Panorama histórico de la educación en Mexico y sus influencias en la enseñanza de la lengua escrita*. Mexico, DF: Universidad de las Américas.

Gómez-Palacio Muñoz, M., G. B. Villareal, and L. González Guerrero, eds. 1988. *Simposio: Pedagogía y didáctica de la lengua escrita*. Mexico, DF: Universidad de las Américas.

Heller, K. A., W. H. Holtzman, and S. Messick. 1982. *Placing children in special education: A strategy for equity*. Washington, DC: National Academy Press.

José P. v Ambach, C-270 (EDNY 1979).

Knight v Board of Education of the City of New York, 48 FRD 108 (US Dist. Court, 1969).

Larry P. v Riles, 495F. Supp. 926 (N.D. Cal. 1979).

Lau v Nichols, 414 US 563. 1974.

Mehan, H., H. Hertweck, and J. L. Meihls. 1986. *Handicapping the handicapped*. Palo Alto, CA: Stanford University Press.

Mercer, J. 1973. *Labeling the mentally retarded*. Berkeley, CA: University of California Press.

_____. 1979. *The system of multicultural pluralistic assessment*. New York: Psychological Corporation.

Merrow, J. 1996. What's special about special education? Columbia, SC: Educational TV.

Mills v Board of Education of the District of Columbia, 348 F., Supp. 866 (1972).

Oakes, J. 1985. *Keeping track.* New Haven, CT: Yale University Press.

Ortiz, A. A., and C. Y. Wilkinson. 1991. *Aim for the BEST: Assessment and intervention model for the bilingual exceptional student.* Arlington, VA: Development Associates.

Palomares, U. H., and L. C. Johnson. 1966. Evaluation of Mexican American Pupils for EMR Classes. *California Education* 3:27-29.

Pennsylvania Association for Retarded Children (PARC) v The Commonwealth of Pennsylvania, 334 F., Supp. 279 (1971).

Poplin, M. 1988. The reductionist fallacy in learning disabilities: Replicating the past by reducing the present. *Journal of Learning Disabilities* 21:389-400.

Poplin, M., and P. T. Cousin. 1996. *Alternative views of learning disabilities.* Austin, TX: ProEd.

Reynolds, A. 1933. *The education of Spanish-speaking children in five southwestern states.* Bulletin No. 11. Washington, DC: U.S. Department of the Interior.

Rueda, R. 1989. Defining mild disabilities with language-minority students. *Exceptional Children* 56:121-29.

Rueda, R., D. Cardoza, J. R. Mercer, and L. Carpenter. 1984. *An examination of special education decision making with Hispanic first-time referrals in large urban school districts.* Los Alamitos, CA: Southwestern Regional Laboratory for Educational Research and Development.

Rueda, R., R. A. Figueroa, P. Mercado, and D. Cardoza. 1984. *Performance of Hispanic educable mentally retarded, learning disabled, and nonclassified students on the WISC-RM, SOMPA, and S-KABC. Final report, short-term study 1.* Los Alamitos, CA: Southwestern Regional Laboratory for Educational Research and Development.

Rueda, R., N. T. Ruiz, and R. A. Figueroa. 1996. Issues in the implementation of innovative instructional strategies. *Multiple Voices for Ethnically Diverse Exceptional Learners* 1:12-23.

Ruiz, N. T. 1989. An optimal learning environment for Rosemary. *Exceptional Children* 56:29-41.

_____. 1996a. The social construction of ability and disability I: Profile types of Latino children identified as language learning disabled. In *Alternative views of learning disabilities,* ed. M. Poplin and P. T. Cousin. Austin, TX: ProEd.

_____. 1996b. The social construction of ability and disability II: Optimal and at-risk lessons in a bilingual special education classroom. In *Alternative views of learning disabilities,* ed. M. Poplin and P.T. Cousin. Austin, TX: ProEd.

Ruiz, N. T., and R. A. Figueroa. 1995. Learning-handicapped classrooms with Latino students. *Education and Urban Society* 27:463-83.

Ruiz, N. T., R. A. Figueroa, R. Rueda, and C. Beaumont. 1992. History and status of bilingual special education for Hispanic handicapped students. In *Critical Perspectives on Bilingual Education Research,* ed. R. V. Padilla and A. H. Benavides. Tempe, AZ: Bilingual Press.

Ruiz, N. T., E. García, and R. A. Figueroa. 1996. *The OLE curriculum guide: Creating Optimal Learning Environments for students from diverse backgrounds in special education and general education.* Sacramento: California Department of Education.

Ruiz, N. T., R. Rueda, R. A. Figueroa, and M. Boothroyd. 1996. Bilingual special education teachers' shifting paradigms: Complex responses to educational reform. In *Alternative views of learning disabilities,* ed. M. Poplin and P. T. Cousin. Austin, TX: ProEd.

Shotwell, A. M. 1945. Arthur performance ratings of Mexican and American high-grade mental defectives. *American Journal of Mental Deficiency* 44:445-49.

Skrtic, T. 1991. The special education paradox: Equity as the way to excellence. *Harvard Educational Review* 61:148-206.

_____. 1995. *Disability and democracy.* New York: Teachers College Press.

Slavin, R. 1991. *Educational psychology.* Englewood Cliffs, NJ: Prentice Hall.

Taylor, D. 1991. *Learning denied.* Portsmouth, NH: Heinemann.

Thomas, W. P., and V. P. Collier. 1995. *Language minority student achievement and program effectiveness.* Washington, DC: National Clearinghouse for Bilingual Education.

Tucker, J. A. 1980. Ethnic proportions in classes for the learning disabled: Issues in nonbiased assessment. *Journal of Special Education* 14:93-105.

U.S. Commission on Civil Rights (1974). *Toward quality education for Mexican Americans.* Washington, DC: GPO.

U.S. Department of the Interior. See Reynolds, A.

Valdés, G., and R. A. Figueroa. 1994. *Bilingualism and testing: A special case of bias.* Norwood, NJ: Ablex.

Ysseldyke, J. E., B. Algozzine, M. Shinn, and M. McGue. 1982. Similarities and differences between low achievers and students classified learning disabled. *Journal of Special Education* 16:73-85.

Effective Literacy Instruction for Latino Students Receiving Special Education Services

A Review of Classroom Research

Nadeen T. Ruiz*

In dealing with far-reaching policy initiatives regarding Latino students with disabilities in Mexico or the United States, it is easy to become focused on macro contexts of education, and with good reason. Macro contexts associated with education, such as regulatory agencies, help ensure that due process rights of students with disabilities are acknowledged and available to them and their families. Without the legislative, litigious, and broad social mandates as a base for educational equity for students with disabilities, we could not effectively proceed with our efforts toward widespread reform of special education services for Latino students.

*This paper was supported in part by a grant from the California State Department of Education, Migrant Education, the Optimal Learning Environment (OLE) Project, California State University, Sacramento.

However, what sometimes gets lost in discussions of due process rights and systemic educational reform is precisely what leads many of us to continue our work with Latino students with disabilities: the quality of educational services provided to them and their families on a daily basis. Those of us who spend time in classrooms with teachers and students occasionally see reason for hope, but most often we see reason to criticize: Spanish-speaking students in special education receive instruction that does not take into account their linguistic needs, that is linked to minimal academic growth, and that is the epitome of "dead end" classes (Figueroa 1986; Figueroa, this volume; Rueda, Cardoza, Mercer, and Carpenter 1984).

Consequently, we need constantly to remind ourselves that while the admirable and crucial work in the macro contexts of special education for Latino students in the United States and Mexico must continue, there are millions of Spanish-speaking students who show up daily to a teacher and a classroom. Furthermore, it is on that teacher and classroom that families of Latino students pin their hopes for their children's academic success.

This chapter, then, concentrates on the micro context of special education for Latino students—the classroom. Specifically, it synthesizes a body of research on Latino students in U.S. special education classrooms and relates that research to recent pedagogical directions in Mexico. From this synthesis of the research, principles of effective literacy instruction for Spanish-speaking students in the United States and Mexico emerge. These principles can in turn guide us in constructing those daily classroom contexts that promote acquisition of literacy skills among students with disabilities.

Classroom Research with U.S. Latino Students Receiving Special Education Services

Within the last ten years a number of studies looking closely at Spanish-English bilingual students in special education classrooms have appeared in the professional literature. In an earlier article I briefly described those studies and pointed out the striking communality of themes across them, despite their disparate locations and researchers (Ruiz 1995b). Since then, two other studies have taken place. Once again, in locations as different as Chicago and East Los Angeles, and with research teams who proceeded independently of each other, the results of these studies further validate earlier findings.

To become part of this review, studies had to meet the following criteria: (1) students had official designation as students with language learning disabilities; (2) the majority of focal students were Latino; (3) students were directly observed in the course of classroom interaction; and (4) the study explored covariant relationships between students' communicative and academic performance, and contextual features of classroom events. Eleven studies met the criteria.

Table 1 combines the data from these studies of U.S. Latino students in special education classrooms in a way that highlights their research themes and outcomes. In this chapter I describe in depth the two more recent studies as a way of illustrating the themes running through this corpus of studies. (For an in-depth description of the earlier studies, readers are referred to Ruiz 1995b.)

TABLE 1 *Bilingual special education classroom studies*

AUTHORS	SUBJECTS	OUTCOMES				CONTEXTUAL FEATURES OF OPTIMAL PERFORMANCE/INSTRUCTION						
		Reading	Writing	Oral Language	Engagement	Classroom Orientation	Teacher Practices	Teacher Beliefs	Background Knowledge	L1	Meaningful/ Authentic	Increased Interaction
Cutiérrez & Stone, 1997	1 grade 5 boy, fully included			X								X
López-Reyna, 1996	14 students 7-10 yrs, SDC*	X	X	X	X	X	X		X	X	X	X
Beaumont, 1995												
Rueda, et al.												
Ruiz, 1995 a & b	10 students, SDC		X	X	X		X		X	X	X	X
Ruiz et al., 1995	5 RSP** teachers					X	X	X	X	X	X	X
Echevarría & McDonough, 1994	12 students SDC			X	X		X		X	X	X	X
Coldman & Rueda, 1988	40 students RSP		X						X	X	X	X
Trueba, 1987	20 students RSP		X		X							
Willig & Swedo, 1987	120 students RSP/SDC				X				X	X	X	X
Flores, Rueda, Porter, 1986	1 grade 2 boy, RSP		X		X				X	X	X	X
Rueda & Mehan, 1986	1 grade 6 boy, RSP	X							X		X	
Viera, 1986	1 grade 2 boy RSP	X								X	X	

*SDC = special day class setting wherein students receive the majority of their academic instruction in a self-contained learning handicapped classroom with other students with disabilities.

**RSP = California's Resource Specialist Program. Historically, students with disabilities are served by Resource Specialist Teachers using a pullout (from their general education classroom) model of instruction. Currently, there is a move toward serving students within their general education classroom.

López-Reyna (1996)

López-Reyna (1996) and her research team began by studying at a special day classroom for Latino students aged seven to ten in a large urban school district in the Midwest. After extended observations, the researchers found that there was a skills-driven orientation, sometimes referred to as *reductionism* (Poplin 1987a), pervading the classroom. Briefly, reductionist instruction is based on the belief that reducing learning to small, discrete segments helps students acquire competency in the target area. Reductionist instruction is very appropriate for learning certain skills, and all teachers, even self-identified "holistic" teachers, employ reductionist instructional techniques for particular aspects of their curriculum. On the other hand, many literacy scholars have questioned exclusive reliance on reductionism for such complex, social, and strategic processes such as learning to read and write. Practice and drill in the subskills of literacy do not seem to add up to competence in an range of literacy practices (Flurkey 1997; Poplin 1987b; Taylor 1998). This is particularly true for second language learners (Tharp 1997; Krashen 1996). The dismal record of reading and writing achievement of U.S. students with language learning disabilities makes a strong case for rethinking reductionist, traditional, special education instruction associated with this underachievement (Figueroa, this volume; Skrtic 1998, 1991).

The reductionist orientation in the classroom studied by López-Reyna was operationalized through the primary literacy activities of the students: copying words and stories from the board and reading isolated words from lists. Under these conditions, students showed little growth in acquisition of oral language and literacy skills, and reduced engagement with academic tasks. However, when the research team helped change the reductionist orientation of the classroom through introduction of very different instructional strategies, there was marked growth in the students' language and literacy skills.

One of the research team's interventions consisted of purposely focusing on connections between literacy lessons and the students' background knowledge through a well-documented method of effective reading instruction for culturally and linguistically diverse students called the Experience-Text-Relationship method (Au 1979). The team also expanded the students' reading materials from worksheets to trade books. Furthermore, they allowed bilingual students to use their language of preference and to write extended text on self-selected topics.

Results of the intervention showed that students made great improvement in knowledge and use of reading strategies, analytical responses to literature, oral language initiations and questions, and overall engagement.

Table 1 represents the López-Reyna study in the following way. First, the study focused on three aspects of literacy skills: oral language use, reading and writing, and a broader dimension of learning—engagement. A quick perusal down table 1 shows that the other, earlier studies of bilingual special education classrooms have also looked at these four dimensions of literacy and learning as outcomes. The López-Reyna study further examined the classroom orientation and how beliefs about instruction were related to the daily activities of the students. Other studies, such as Ruiz et al. (1995), have also looked at the connection between teacher beliefs and classroom practices, as indicated in the table under the more generic category of orientation. Finally, the López-Reyna study determined a co-variant relationship between the outcomes (increased language and literacy skills) and the features of the instructional context (inclusion of students' background knowledge in literacy lessons, use of the students' native language, meaning-based literacy instruction, and promotion of increased interaction among students). These situational features of the classroom's social organization are indicated on the right half of table 1.

Gutiérrez and Stone (1997)

The other recent study of bilingual, special education students' classroom interaction was undertaken by Gutiérrez and Stone (1997) in the Los Angeles area. These researchers closely examined the classroom interactional patterns of a fifth-grade Latino boy, Billy, in an inclusion setting, the only study in table 1 to target such a placement option. Billy was experiencing his first general education inclusion classroom after a series of special day class placements.

The general education classroom was unique in that it had a community of learners orientation based on cultural historical theory (Rogoff, Radziszewska, and Masiello 1995). Briefly, in a community of learners classroom less experienced students (here, less experienced in terms of academic uses of language and literacy) participate in "apprenticeship experiences" with others who have greater proficiency. In contrast to traditional, teacher-active/student-passive instructional patterns, responsibility for teaching and learning is shared among students and teachers. This shared responsibility multiplies opportunities for students to move on to complex skills; rather than depending solely on the teachers, students can also rely on more expert peers to provide additional bridging experiences (guided participation) to academic competence. Operating within this theoretical framework, Gutiérrez and Stone point out the danger of isolating low-performing students with each other (traditional special day classrooms), or of traditionally organized, general education, inclusion settings that inhibit student-active forms of participation.

Gutiérrez and Stone tracked Billy's participation in Book Club, an instructional approach to reading that mirrors book clubs of avid adult readers. In book clubs, also known as literature study circles, students meet in small groups to discuss, analyze, and in other ways respond to literature (Ruiz, García, and Figueroa 1996; Samway and Whang 1995). Using videotapes, field notes, interviews, and an analysis of student work products, Gutiérrez and Stone found that over the academic year Billy progressed from participating with gestures only in book discussions, to making fledgling linguistic contributions, to tentative participation, to actually taking the lead in his group's interpretation of the meaning of a literature book. The researchers documented that in a nontraditionally organized, general education classroom, this first-time, fully included Latino student with learning disabilities became what they term an "emergent expert." They attribute his growing academic competence to participation in a social organization that "minimized differences in that it used each member's resources" (29). Table 1 reflects this study's focus, outcomes, and co-varying features of instruction that resulted in Billy's increased oral discourse competence.

These two recent studies differ on the surface. For example, the Gutiérrez and Stone research is a case study located within a larger ethnographic classroom study, while the López-Reyna work can be characterized as a classroom intervention study, comparing differing methods of literacy instruction. Furthermore, Gutiérrez and Stone focused primarily on oral discourse development, while López-Reyna looked at a range of oral, reading, and writing skills. However, both studies support a recurrent, working theory that I have pointed out in an earlier analysis of bilingual special education classroom studies. This theory holds that certain contextual features of instruction—features which radically differ from traditional special education approaches (again, with an almost exclusive reliance on English, reductionism, skill drills, and relative student passivity)—result in marked, positive language and literacy gains for Spanish-speaking students receiving special education services for language and learning difficulties. Consequently, a close look at the commonalties running through the studies listed in table 1 can be generalized to form a set of working principles for the effective instruction of Spanish-speaking students identified as having language learning disabilities.

Working Principles for Effective Literacy Instruction for Spanish-Speaking Student with Language Learning Disabilities

To the extent possible, I have collected from major special education and bilingual education journals all of the currently available studies of classroom interaction among Spanish-English bilingual students with language learning disabilities.[1] I also located research articles in edited books on bilingual and bilingual special education. In addition, I included widely cited, unpublished manuscripts meeting the previously delineated criteria. As noted earlier, there is remarkable convergence among these studies as to contextual features of instruction that promote increased language and literacy skills in this target population.

It is important to note, however, that the results of this body of studies are further validated by work proceeding from the most prestigious center for research in second language and literacy acquisition, the Center for Research on Education, Diversity, and Excellence (CREDE, University of California, Santa Cruz). CREDE, too, has conducted a meta-analysis of classroom studies, specifically looking closely at twenty years of research on effective instruction for students who speak English as a second language. Through this extensive meta-analysis, CREDE has developed a list of five principles for effective instruction—principles that are strikingly similar to those emerging from this review of bilingual special education studies. As I list the working principles from bilingual special education research, I also note the principles from second language research as put forth from CREDE (Tharp 1997).

Principle I: Connect Students' Background Knowledge and Personal Experiences With Literacy Lessons

The teachers in the López-Reyna study operationalized this principle by preceding reading with questions and conversation that linked or built up students' background knowledge with the book's key themes or information. After reading, students critically analyzed literary elements of the stories, e.g., they compared the story elements with earlier connections to their own lives. The teachers also encouraged students to write extended texts that brought their life experiences into the curriculum.

In the Gutiérrez-Stone study the teacher gave Billy and his classmates the opportunity to socially construct their understandings and interpretations of children's literature in book clubs. Once again, students were invited to connect the literacy curriculum with their own life experiences and personal knowledge.

This principle is reinforced by CREDE Principle III, as derived from their meta-analysis of second language and literacy research: Contextualize teaching and curriculum in the experiences and skills of home and community.

Principle II: Foster the Use of Students' Primary Language (L1) in Literacy Lessons

In the intervention phase of the López-Reyna study, teachers increased opportunities for the students to use their primary language in classroom literacy activities. The teachers also brought in many children's books in Spanish to use as resources for more cognitively complex skill building and literary discussions.

In the Gutiérrez and Stone study, Billy and his classmates chose to use English in the particular book discussions reported in the article. However, as in the classroom from the López-Reyna story, students could exercise a choice of language during literacy events. Consequently, students' oral discourse skills in both studies showed surprising growth.[2]

Principle III: Create Opportunities for Students to Meaningfully and Authentically Apply Their Developing Oral Language and Literacy Skills

Rather than requiring students to complete worksheets that only dealt with subskills of literacy, the teachers in the intervention phase of the López-Reyna study took a very different approach. They asked students to use oral and written language that accomplished a range of communicative purposes. As in the Gutiérrez and Stone study, students' oral language contributions also increased in both number and quality when there was an authentic reason to communicate.

One part of this principle deserves special mention: literacy skills. Teachers applying this principle to their classrooms take very seriously the charge to teach literacy skills and subskills such as phonemic awareness, phonics, spelling and punctuation, grammar, reading comprehension strategies, and so on. However, they acknowledge the last twenty years of research in second and foreign language education that unequivocally establishes the link between meaning-driven, communicative instruction and second language and literacy development.

CREDE Principle I: Develop Competence in Language and Literacy Instruction Throughout All Instructional Activities

The narrative accompanying the principle elaborates: "Language/literacy development should be fostered through use and through purposive conversation between teacher and students, rather than through drills and decontextualized rules" (p. 13).

Principle IV: Foster Increased Levels of Interaction (Oral Language, Reading, and Writing) among Students and Teachers

The teachers in both classrooms discussed in this article enacted this principle by increasing the opportunities and authentic reasons for students to collaborate on literacy and other academic tasks. Through these collaborations students dramatically increased their productive and receptive oral language interactions as well as their opportunities to read and write for a range of purposes.

CREDE Principle II: Facilitate Learning through Joint Productive Activity among Teacher and Students; and

Principle V: Engage Students through Dialogue, Especially Instructional Conversation

At least two nationally recognized literacy programs for Spanish-speaking students with language learning disabilities have based their instructional strategies on these principles: the Optimal Learning Environment (OLE) Project based at California State University Sacramento (Ruiz, García, and Figueroa 1996) and AIM for the Best, based at the University of Texas at Austin (Ortiz and Wilkinson 1992).

The appendix of this article shows an example of how the OLE Project has incorporated these principles through the selection of key instructional strategies. The appendix contains an excerpt from the *OLE Curriculum Guide* that describes interactive journals, an instructional strategy that clearly enacts the four principles of effective instruction. When writing in their interactive journals, students take pen in hand to communicate with either teachers or peers on the topic of their choice, and receive written responses to their journal entries. Hence, students are able to bring their life experiences to the literacy event (Principle I); to use the language of their choice (Principle II); to exchange messages with real communicative intent with a real audience (Principle III); and to be the most active agents in the literacy event, initiating extended turns of writing and talk (Principle IV).

Connections to Recent Literacy Instruction Trends in Mexico

The most heartening aspect of these principles and practices for effective literacy instruction is their strong connection to recent pedagogical reform in literacy education in Mexico. Largely based on the work of Latin American scholars such as Emilia Ferreiro and Margarita Gómez Palacio, Mexican educators in both general and special education have applied similar principles and their associated instructional techniques with deaf students (Ruiz and Obregón 1999), students with mild to severe language disabilities (García 1997; Obregón 1998; Valencia 1998), students at risk of failing the first grade (Gómez Palacio, Antinori, Lus, Maldonado and Uribe 1984), and primary literacy education in general (Gómez Palacio, Villareal, González, Araiza, and Jarillo 1995). The result is a convergence of theory and practice from both sides of the border about what constitutes effective literacy instruction for Spanish-speaking students who are struggling to learn to read and write.

Conclusion

This chapter has begun to map out principles of effective literacy instruction based on classroom research with Spanish-speaking students receiving special education services. A number of educational researchers, myself included, would expand this list of principles based on their own and others' work. However, I have striven here to keep to those principles which have the most extensive theoretical and empirical base, as exemplified in the studies listed in table 1.

Our task, however, as Mexican and U.S. educators is unfinished and ongoing. We need to continue our joint research and programmatic efforts to optimize literacy instruction for students struggling with Spanish and English literacy. We also must keep forefront in our minds what I highlighted in the beginning of this chapter:

> There are millions of Spanish-speaking students who show up daily to a teacher and a classroom. And on that teacher and classroom, families of Latino students pin their hopes for their children's academic success.

Appendix

Excerpt from the *OLE Curriculum Guide.*

Instructional Strategies for Optimal Learning Environments

Interactive Journals

In *Interactive Journals,* students write about what is important to them. They share their life stories and their burning interests. In return, teachers are able to say to their students through their oral and written responses, "What goes on in your life is important to me." *Interactive Journal* writing also promotes the development of written conventions through written demonstration by teachers as they respond to student's entries. Furthermore, the emphasis on the message (and not the mechanics) encourages students to take more risks with their writing topics and skills. *Interactive Journals* in which students write and teachers respond on a daily basis create a developmental record of writing progress (Flores & García, 1984).

Recommended Procedures:

1. The *Interactive Journals* procedure has at least three basic parts:
   (a) the student draws and writes; (b) a teacher/paraprofessional/parent volunteer or peer responds with a written question about the student's entry; and (c) the student answers the question either orally or in written form.
2. Before beginning this instructional strategy, it is helpful to demonstrate the three basic parts of the interaction. In a large format, such as an overhead transparency or chart, write the date, brainstorm a topic out loud, draw, and then

vocalize the words as you write your entry. Then, if possible, ask another teacher or parent to write a written question to your entry. Finally, orally respond to the question.

3. Ask students to follow the same procedure that you have demonstrated. As they finish their entries, students bring them to the teacher for a response in the form of a question. Students in turn orally or in written form answer the teacher's question.

   For emergent readers and writers: When students bring you a journal entry that you cannot read (i.e., it is scribbled or in letter string form), simply ask them to "read" it to you. As you respond with a written question, be sure to vocalize as you write so that the students can understand the question and respond to you.

   For independent readers and writers: Experiment with buddy journals. Pair students up with a buddy (either randomly or by allowing students to suggest their top choices for a writing partner with you making the final decision), and ask them to write to each other. OLE teachers suggest, however, that teachers occasionally collect and respond to the journals to provide both a model of writing and to monitor students' progress.

Reminders:

- Students, not teachers, choose topics for journal entries.
- Students receive a response each time they write.
- During journal time, teachers write in their own journals and ask a student to respond.

Assessment: Interactive Journal Matrices

Students' journals become an authentic record of their writing development. You may want to use a version of the portfolio matrices in figure 1. These have been used by OLE teachers to analyze and track their students' writing development. They should be accompanied by sample journal entries and placed in students' portfolios.

Which of the optimal conditions listed in table 1 does the Interactive Journals strategy help create in your classroom?

Your notes:

FIGURE 1 *Teacher example of an Interactive Journal assessment.*

INTERACTIVE JOURNAL ASSESSMENT/
EVALUACION DE DIAROS INTERACTIVOS

Name/Nombre: Roberto

KEY/CLAVE
NE = No evidence/No hay evidencia
B = Beginning/Está comenzando
D = Developing/Está en desarrollo
C = Controls/Tiene control

Date/Fecha	2/15/99
Takes risks/Se arriesga	B
Reads entry/Lee su escritura	D
Spacing/Segmentación	B
Letter formation/Formación de letras	D
Punctuation/Puntuación	B
Conventional spelling/Deletreo convencional *Conventional/Total, Convencional/Total*	7/18

Comments/Comentarios:

For the first time Roberto began to use spaces between some words.

Notes

[1]Not included in this list is research that was primarily self-reporting in nature and in other ways not based on systematic and intense observation of classroom interaction. Though those studies make general contributions to our knowledge base of effective instruction for Spanish-speaking students with disabilities, they do not include the level of detail needed confidently to connect instructional innovations with increased language and literacy achievement.

[2]CREDE's omission of this principle is surprising given the well-documented effectiveness of L_1 education (Cummins 1998; Greene 1998; Ramirez et al 1991; and Thomas and Collier 1996).

References

Au, K. H. 1979. Using the experience-text-relationship method with minority children. *Reading Teacher* 32, no. 6:667-79.

Cummins, J. 1998. Cognitive, linguistic, and organizational issues. Presentation at the California Reading and Literature Project's conference on the Reading and English Language Learner, Sacramento, California, March.

Echevarría, J., and R. McDonough. 1995. An alternative reading approach: Instructional conversations in a bilingual special education setting. *Learning Disabilities Research and Practic* 10:108-119.

Figueroa, R. A. 1986. *Diana revisited.* Bilingual Education Paper Series. Los Angeles, CA: California State University, Dissemination and Assessment Center.

Figueroa, R. A., N. T. Ruiz, and E. García. 1994. The Optimal Learning Environment (OLE) Research Project in the Los Angeles Unified School District. *Report 1: Reading outcome data.* Sacramento, CA: The OLE Project, California State University Sacramento.

Flores, B., R. Rueda, and B. Porter. 1986. Examining assumptions and instructional practices related to the acquisition of literacy with bilingual special education students. In *Bilingualism and learning disabilities,* ed. A. C. Willig and H. F. Greenburg, 149-65. New York: American Library.

Flurkey, A. 1997. Inventing learning disabilities. In *Teaching and advocacy*, ed. D. Taylor, D. Coughlin, and J. Marasco, 211-32. York, MN: Stenhouse.

García, A. 1997. Proyecto OLE: Una alternativa para el enriquecimiento en el proceso de adquisición de la lecto-escritura en niños con bajo rendimiento escolar. Masters thesis, Colegio Superior de Neurolingüística y Psicopedagogía, Mexico, DF.

Goldman, S., and R. Rueda. 1988. Developing writing skills in bilingual exceptional children. *Exceptional Children* 54, no. 6:543-51.

Gómez Palacio, M. et al. 1984. *Integración escolar de niños repetidores con problemas en el desarrollo.* Mexico, DF: Dirección General de Educación Especial.

_____. 1995. *El niño y sus primeros años en la escuela.* Mexico, DF: Secretaría de Educación Pública.

Greene, J. P. 1998. A meta-analysis of the effectiveness of bilingual education. Manuscript sponsored by the Tomás Rivera Policy Institute, University of Texas at Austin.

Gutiérrez, K., and L. D. Stone. 1997. A cultural-historical view of learning and learning disabilities: Participating in a community of learners. *Learning Disabilities Research and Practice* 12, no. 2:123-31.

Krashen, S. 1996. *Every person a reader: An alternative to the California Task Force Report on Reading.* Culver City, CA: Language Education Associates.

López-Reyna, N. 1996. The importance of meaningful contexts in bilingual special education: Moving to whole language. *Learning Disabilities Research and Practice* 11, no. 2:120-31.

Obregón, M. 1998. Proyecto OLE. *El buzón del lector* (newsletter), fall.

Ortiz, A. et al. 1991. *Aim for the BEST: Assessment and intervention model for the bilingual exceptional student.* Arlington, VA: Development Associates.

Poplin, M. 1988a. The reductionist fallacy in learning disabilities: Replicating the past by reducing the present. *Journal of Learning Disabilities* 21:401-16.

_____. 1988b. Holistic/constructivist principles of the teaching/learning process: Implications for the field of learning disabilities. *Journal of Learning Disabilities* 21:401-16.

Ramírez, J. D. et al. 1991. *Final report: Longitudinal study of structural immersion strategy, early-exit, and late-exit transitional bilingual education programs for language-minority children.* Aguirre International (Report to the U.S. Department of Education). San Mateo.

Rogoff, B., B. Radziszewska, and T. Masiello. 1995. Analysis of developmental processes in sociocultural activity. In *Sociocultural psychology: Theory and practice of doing and knowing,* ed. L. W. Martin, K. Nelson, and E. Tobach, 125-49. Cambridge: Cambridge University Press.

Rueda, R., and H. Mehan. 1986. Metacognition and passing: Strategic interaction in the lives of students with learning disabilities. *Anthropology and Education Quarterly* 17:145-65.

Rueda, R. et al. 1984. *An examination of special education decision making with Hispanic first-time referrals in large urban school districts.* Los Alamitos, CA: Southwest Regional Laboratory.

Ruiz, N. T. 1995a. The social construction of ability and disability, I : Profile types of Latino children identified as language learning disabled. *Journal of Learning Disabilities* 28:476-90.

_____. 1995b. The social construction of ability and disability, II: Optimal and at-risk lessons in a bilingual special education classroom. *Journal of Learning Disabilities* 28:491-502.

Ruiz, N. T., and M. Obregón. 1999. Hacia una enseñanza óptima del lenguaje y la lectoescritura para niños sordos: El Proyecto OLE. Unpublished manuscript. Sacramento, CA: OLE Project.

Ruiz, N. T., E. García, and R. A. Figueroa. 1996. *The OLE Curriculum Guide.* Sacramento, CA: California State Bureau of Publications.

Ruiz, N. T. et al. 1995. Bilingual special education teachers' shifting paradigms: Complex responses to educational reform. *Journal of Learning Disabilities* 28:622-35.

Samway, K. D., and G. Whang. 1995. *Literature study circles in multicultural classrooms.* York, ME: Stenhouse.

Skrtic, T. 1991. The special education paradox: Equity as the way to excellence. *Harvard Educational Review* 61:148-206.

_____. 1995. *Disability and democracy: Reconstructing (special) education for postmodernity.* New York: Teachers College Press.

Taylor, D. 1998. *Beginning to read and the spin doctors of science.* Urbana, IL: National Council of Teachers of English.

Tharp, R. 1997. *From at-risk to excellence: Research, theory and principles for practice.* Washington, DC: Center for Research on Education, Diversity and Excellence/ Center for Applied Linguistics.

Thomas, W., and V. Collier. 1996. Language Minority Student Achievement and Program Effectiveness. Unpublished document, George Mason University.

Trueba, H. 1987. Cultural differences or learning handicaps? Towards an understanding of adjustment processes. In *Schooling language minority youth: Volume III, Proceedings of the University of California Linguistic Minority Research Project Conference*, 45-79. Los Angeles: University of California.

Valencia, L. 1998. OLE: Un espacio estimulante. *ARARU* (November): 24-25.

Viera, D. 1986. Remediating reading problems in a Hispanic learning disabled child from a psycholinguistic perspective: A case study. In *Bilingualism and learning disabilities*, ed. A. C. Willig and H. F. Greenburg, 81-92. New York: American Library.

Willig, A., and J. Swedo. 1987. Improving teaching strategies for exceptional Hispanic limited English proficient students: An exploratory study of task engagement and teaching strategies. Paper presented at the annual meeting of the American Educational Research Association, Washington, DC.

13

Many Ways Is the Way

Supporting the Languages and Literacies of Culturally, Linguistically, and Developmentally Diverse Children

Pamela J. Rossi*

Setting the Stage

The primary purpose of this exploratory study is to show some of the observable features of an enriched, holistic, and constructivist curriculum that builds on the strengths of children within a bilingual context. This classroom portrait vividly illustrates how educators can create classroom contexts that support the languages and literacies of culturally, linguistically, and developmentally diverse children (Ruiz, chap. 12). It is hoped that this curricular innovation, an opera project, will invite educators, researchers, parents, and policy makers to put away their assumptions and perspectives about what it means to live a literate life; to reconceptualize language arts/literacy as being more than simply the ability to read and write

*The author wishes to thank Amy Hazelrigg, doctoral student at the University of New Mexico, for her critical help in the final preparation of this chapter.

words; to transform the way they think about meaning making and curriculum, intelligence and knowledge, perception and expression; and to ask new questions.

Critics of language and literacy curricula in schools point to the gap between a reductionist, deficit-driven paradigm and the way they believe children learn naturally. In the past fifty years, particularly in the field of learning disabilities, school children have typically been viewed as passive recipients of information who learn primarily from part to whole in a decontextualized, linear, verbocentric, or language-dominated manner (Poplin 1988b). Culturally and linguistically diverse children, often in families with fewer socioeconomic opportunities than mainstream families, are frequently presumed to be less capable and in need of remediation or repetition through rote learning and drill-like mastery of fragmented subskills, resulting in further marginalization (Flores, Cousin, and Díaz 1991).

However, concurrent research on learning and teaching focuses on a strengths-based, contextualized, and collaborative process of constructing learning (Ruiz and Figueroa 1995; Poplin 1988a). Scholars and teachers/researchers are building on the principles of holistic, language, and learning-centered philosophies and are advocating culturally relevant curricula based on multiple ways of knowing (Eisner 1994; Leland and Harste 1994; Kasten 1992; Fueyo 1991; McCarty et al. 1991; Goodman, Bird, and Goodman 1990; Short 1989). The instructional alternatives suggested by this body of research offer opportunities for expanding the communicative, expressive, and learning potentials of all children. One way to support the development of multiple literacy potentials is to create enriched learning environments in which children can create and produce original operas based on their personal experiences.

In this particular opera project, Dr. Carroll Rinehart ("Dr. R"), a retired music educator well known in Tucson for facilitating hundreds of successful opera projects in the local schools since 1983, has invited two teachers and their students to work with him on creating and producing an opera. Subsequently, with the approval of the school principal, Dr. Rinehart, Mrs. Hood, and Mrs. West have invited me to participate in what will be a nine-week partnership and project in collaboration with Very Special Arts Arizona (VSAA), a non-profit arts organization that has been providing opportunities in the arts for children with and without disabilities since 1977. Because the arts are so often considered an expendable frill in schools, one of VSAA's long-term goals is to work toward the centralization of the arts throughout the curriculum. Teachers, students, and artists engage in open-ended inquiries based on real problems in a supportive learning environment.

As a participant observer, I want to know what a literature-based opera project looks like and how it relates to students' learning and literacy (Spradley 1980). Along with the field notes I write two times a week (three times a week in the production and performance stages of the process), I collect and analyze the teachers' and artist's written documentation forms, one teacher's audiotape journal, and the children's writings and drawings to create a thematic portrait of a classroom experience (Merriam 1988). This portrait is part of a larger ethnographic and arts-based study that looks at the nature and uses of multiple literacies in young children's opera (Rossi 1997a). New understandings were rendered as an opera libretto to challenge the way we think about language arts (Rossi 1997b) and revealed that young children's opera was a metaphor for the authoring/inquiry cycle (Short, Harste, and

Burke 1996). Young children's use of multiple literacy processes, forms, and functions in the context of an inquiry-based apprenticeship demonstrated the diversity and complexity of meaning making in a classroom opera project and its contribution to the children's language and literacy growth.

In this exploratory study, Dr. Rinehart visits two collaborating classrooms for twenty-four one-hour sessions. The teachers develop a holistic-constructivist learning environment, curriculum, and experience based on the integration of the opera project within their general education classrooms throughout each day (Poplin 1988a; Goodman 1986; Dewey 1934). The kindergarten class comprises nineteen children: five girls and fourteen boys. The first grade consists of twenty-six children: eighteen girls and eight boys. The primarily Latino and Anglo children range in age from five to eight years with varying levels of Spanish and English proficiency and preferences. Two of the nineteen kindergarten children have been identified as needing special education services and are fully included in the classroom and opera project. All of the children will have expanded opportunities to listen, speak, read, write, sing, draw, and dance their understandings of their lived experiences through an extended response to literature (Rosenblatt 1976).

Scene One: Choosing a Culturally Relevant Story

It's midwinter in the southwestern United States. Kindergarten and first-grade students are embarking on the creation of an opera. Outside, the air is filled with the fresh smell of sage and creosote produced by the recent rains. The prominent and rocky hillside that borders the school is dotted with yellow flowers. Crows and hawks glide above the playground; roadrunners dart from prickly pear to saguaro.

Love of Reading Week is underway at the school. Wendy Hood, the bilingual first grade teacher, and Karen West, the new kindergarten teacher, have chosen the newly released picture book *Coyote: A Trickster Tale from the American Southwest* by Gerald McDermott (1994) to share with their students. They are hoping the children will like it so it can become the basis for an opera project.

Mrs. Hood, a veteran facilitator of four previous children's opera projects, has seen the potential of *Coyote: A Trickster Tale* from the start. It is a narrative with clear-cut episodes adaptable to dramatic form, and it has sufficient roles to go around. But it is also important to Mrs. Hood that the book has appeal for the children. She holds the colorful picture book open to face the two classes of children seated on the rug in a large area of the first-grade room and reads in English and Spanish. (I urge you to first read Gerald McDermott's version of the Zuni tale, as it will make the description and interpretation of the opera process more comprehensible.) The children become excited. Of the many books they have read, they decide they like this one best. A blue coyote with a "nose for trouble" longs to fly like the crows. At first, they each share a feather from one of their wings with him. Out of balance, he falls. The crows balance him with a feather from their other wing. When Coyote tries to fly a second time, he becomes arrogant and boastful. Deciding to trick the trickster, they take back their feathers and Coyote falls so fast that his tail catches on fire. He lands in a pool on the mesa, rolls through the dirt, and turns gray, the color he remains today. Mrs. Hood notes, "The kids love it. It's them. Here we are where the kids see mesa-like mountains. They're not as big as the Hopi mesas where people live on top of them, but we live in this desert setting."

What will happen in this classroom as this literature-based opera process unfolds is that Coyote's singing, dancing, and flying his way into trouble from atop a desert mesa will become a metaphor for the children's own lives. Dr. Rinehart arrives in Mrs. Hood's classroom with a keyboard under his arm and says with excitement, "When do we start?"

Scene Two: Composing Lyrics and Music

Dr. R, now settled behind his keyboard, pencil in hand, asks, "Who's the character in it?" The children say, "It's a coyote; it's a blue coyote." Dr. R prods, "What will he say?" One of the children half sings, "I'm a blue coyote." Dr. R accepts this line enthusiastically and writes it down. In this scene, the opera libretto and the musical score are created simultaneously (Purrington, Rinehart, and Wilcox 1990).

Scene Three: Using Alternative Sign Systems

One child is counting the crows on the mesa top, and soon they are all counting. Children's arms flap as Coyote tries to fly. Dr. R plays descending notes on his keyboard as Coyote falls to the ground, providing a musical demonstration of Coyote's action in the original narrative. Mrs. Hood asks what it means when Coyote "sang out of tune." Alberto responds, "He didn't sing the right thing," and Dr. R illustrates with a discordant series of notes. The students giggle and look with interest at the keyboard. Once again, Mrs. Hood reads aloud from the book about how arrogant Coyote tries to fly and falls to the ground. The students bend down to the floor and laugh.

In this class, as in Mrs. West's kindergarten across the hall, the children have many opportunities to extend their response to the book by using other sign systems. The communication potential has been expanded. The concept of sign systems is a perspective that "defines communication and literacy more broadly as all the ways we use to construct and share meaning with others including language, mathematical symbols, music, visual forms, and movement or performance" (Short 1989, 1).

Scene Four: Making Personal Connections

The children are making connections across the story, their own lives, and various art forms. The discussion in this first grade bilingual classroom continues with Sarah sharing a personal experience. Others join in as they look at an illustration and demonstrate the beginning sensibilities of visual literacy.

Sarah:	We [her family] went on a mesa. We had to drive out of Tucson. We also got to go hiking.
Mrs. Hood:	Can you tell everybody what it was like?
Sarah:	Brown, green, and yellow.
Mrs. Hood:	How did it feel?

Sarah: Like on a mountain.

Rodney: Was it scary?

Sarah: No. There was a little water and we got to go in it.

Mrs. Hood: Oh, was that [what] the poor Coyote fell in?
(Opens the book and shows the illustration to the children)

Rodney: He is bigger than the cactus. How could he be as big as a mesa?

Dr. R: Yes, why did the illustrator do that?

Berto: So we could see it.

Andy: They're important.

Dr. R: Yes, they're the most important.

Mrs. Hood: Sarah's dad is an artist.

Sarah: But the mesa is littler than the one we walked on.

Sarah, Berto, and Rodney's careful reading of the images shows they are drawing upon their prior experience (Harste, Woodward, and Burke 1984). Their discussion of scale relationships in an illustration generates an illustrating study. After reading a number of Gerald McDermott's picture books and looking at the visual elements common in his work, the children create collages in his style. Their visual literacy grows.

Scene Five: Composing Their Own Mesa Song

In creating their mesa song, Spanish- and English-speaking children apply their experience, imagination, and primary language, which shape the content of their songwriting and make it authentic and personally relevant (Ruiz, chap. 12; Freeman and Freeman 1994; Edelsky, Altwerger, and Flores 1991; Harste, Woodward, and Burke 1984).

Dr. R: What does Coyote say? I see a . . .

Bradley: Mesa.

Mrs. Hood: *(Writes)* Mesa. I see a mesa.

Andrea: Mesa mesa. Yo veo una mesa. I see a mesa.

Mrs. Hood: We can repeat mesa twice. *(Writes)* Can you put that heartbeat in your legs?
(The children read and slap the rhythm on their legs.)

Dr. R: How does that feel?

All: Happy!

Dr. R: Will we sing it in major or minor [key]? *(Demonstrates both)*

All: Major!

Andrea: *(Takes a risk and sings)* Mesa mesa *(Gives the melody a fresh direction)*

Mrs. Hood: ¡Qué buenos cantos! "What nice songs!"

(Applause and nods of approval from the children, some singing. Dr. R adds Andrea's melody to the score. Mrs. Hood writes on large chart paper as the children look on and help her spell in Spanish and English.)

During the composition, a small group of boys have been playing off by themselves. Dr. R says, "Do you want to sing it from the top, the beginning?" After the go ahead, he begins playing. The boys settle on the rug and begin singing softly. Some of the girls drape their arms over each other's shoulders and sway to and fro. The boys' eyes glisten with quiet attention. Dr. R says, "It's beautiful."

Music can communicate to us in a way that oral or written language cannot. The linguistic and musical composition had not seemed to resonate with the small group of boys until it was sung as a whole. Verbal language is only one of the sign systems that people use to express themselves (Langer 1957). In this case, opportunities for growth were expanded as some read, some wrote, some sang, some moved, and some were moved to tears.

Scene Six: Celebrating the Composition of an Original Coyote Song

As the scene opens, Mrs. Hood tells me that Rodney is an "energetic and highly focused boy who sometimes forgets that he isn't the only one in the classroom." However, now he is sitting on Mrs. Hood's lap, a real-life, comfortable, and safe version of an author's chair (Harste, Short, and Burke 1988). Mrs. Hood announces that Rodney will be reading the coyote song that he had written with Joey's help the previous afternoon. The book is written using invented spelling (Goodman 1994). Mrs. Hood says to me, "This is a first for Rodney, who can write and is just discovering he can read." Rodney half-sings:

I wet to the Palt sAlP N I SALL A
I went to the pet shop and I saw a

coyote N i capttitt
coyote and I kept it

NDA we SALS A SLG
and we sang a song

N I totk HeM HOM
and I took him home

N I totk he for a WLK
and I took him for a walk

I wet Bak Ho thE Palt sALP
I went back home to the pet shop

N I BT A RLSR
and I bought a rooster

N the CoyotE MAT A
and the Coyote met a

ROSRN N day R FANS
rooster and they are friends

N day we for A WALK
One day we went for a walk

N day wet to the Prk N day Liv hv L
one day we went to the park and they lived happily

E AtRN thE Coyote EN the
ever after. The Coyote and the

ROSR day PLALD ALL
Rooster they played all
day LALLG N Coyote
day long and Coyote

SAD R yoy ok
said are you ok?

Rodney, with the help of a peer, writes and sings from his own experiences. As a songwriter, Rodney uses multiple intelligences, particularly his musical and linguistic intelligences.

Historically, there have been many ways of viewing knowing. Traditionally, intelligence has been viewed as being in the head. However, Vygotsky (1978) emphasizes a "between-heads" construction of knowledge and shows how sociocultural influences play a central role in how we come to know. He is best known for the concept of the zone of proximal development, "the distance between the actual development level as determined by independent problem solving and the level of potential development as determined through problem solving under adult guidance or in collaboration with more capable peers" (86). Howard Gardner (1993) introduces the concept of multiple inteligences in his book *Frames of Mind*. He conceptualizes intelligence as "the ability to solve problems, or to create products that are valued within one or more cultural settings" (x). In this classroom opera project as in the everyday life of the children and their families, singing, reading, writing, and storytelling are valued. There are many ways to make and share meaning.

After Rodney reads and sings, his classmates applaud. He beams, feeling their acceptance and acknowledgement. Later, he audiotapes the song. A group of children gather, listen, and giggle. Later Rodney writes another song by himself. Others identify with Coyote and begin writing their own coyote songs. Viviana writes in invented Spanish spelling: "caiori esta conteto soi en mecor coiete del mundo." Mrs. Hood translates to English: "Coyote is happy. I'm the best coyote in the world." In the next scene, the children expand their communication potential even further by using their linguistic, musical, and kinesthetic intelligences as they write, sing, and dance.

FIGURE 1 *Marinita's interpretation of the Crow Dance*

Scene Seven: Producing Dances and Chants

In April 1995, at the conclusion of the opera project, Mrs. Hood gave me an audio-taped journal account of her perceptions of the experience. She says at one point: "It kept going. We wrote the words to a few of the songs by ourselves [without Dr. R's help], and at one point I wanted to get more going on. We talked about the different parts we needed, and they divided into groups. I had to assess some of the kids, and I said, "I can't help you." They came up with some incredible ideas on their own. They took the line "Old Man Crow plucked a feather from his left wing." Then they elaborated on it. "Old Man Crow told his crew to do it too." That "crew" was very powerful language. "What do you call Old Man Crow in Spanish?" They negotiated the two languages. Immediately Andrea said, 'Dueño Cuervo.' It wasn't 'Cuervo Viejo.' All of the children were singing in Spanish and singing in English."

The children also start to talk of the potential for a dance. Mrs. Hood says to me, "Could you imagine crows dancing and snakes dancing?" I tell her there was a children's social dance version of a gopher snake song that my first graders in the Hopi Nation used to sing and dance. I begin humming it, and the children ask me to teach it to them. Soon they are dancing around the room singing, "Loloqangwtu, loloqangwtu" (Gopher snake, gopher snake). Mrs. Hood later told me that when they lined up for lunch, Rodney asked, "Can we do that snake dance down to lunch?" All the way to the cafeteria they were singing, "Loloqangwtu, loloqangwtu."

Another day they are writing a chant. In my field notes I write:

All:	I hear chanting and singing. They sound like crows.
	(Robert wants to show everybody what crows do. He stands, hands down at sides, fingers widely stretched and pointed down. He lifts one foot at a time and moves forward. Dr. R plays a note each time Robert moves.)
Berto:	They start to fly. *(Gets up and holds a pose, one leg lifted behind him)*
Andrew:	I have another way. *(Slaps his hands on his thighs as the piano follows his lead)*
Robert:	Sounds like the crows are sneaking up on you.
	(Danielle stands)
Mrs. Hood:	Don't be shy. We're all your friends.
	(Danielle moves from side to side, arms flapping)
Dr. R:	*(Plays a low beat to the rhythm of her arms)*
Mrs. Hood:	I saw Luis do something.
	(Luis shakes his head)
Robert:	I think it looks like this in the picture. *(Hops on one leg, hands pointed down)*
Mrs. Hood:	What should we do?
All:	More crows! *(The class becomes a "crew of crows," all dancing to the music)*
Dr. R:	*(Plays a series of eight notes)* Let's count how many times Daniel hops on one foot and then another. I see a pattern.
All:	One, two, three, four . . . Four times! Four times!
Dr. R:	I wonder if we can all sing one, two, three, four, one, two, three, four?
Mrs. Hood:	Let's change feet at one.
All:	One, two, three, four, one, two, three, four.
Dr. R:	Watch Berto dance!

"That's what we thought the crow dance was going to be," Mrs. Hood added in her audiotape journal, "but it was a lot like the [gopher] snake dance, especially when Dr. Rinehart played it [on his keyboard]." In her journal, she recalls a story about the inventiveness of children when given the opportunity to freely explore some musical instruments and feel the beat of the music and the rhythm of the words. I go back to my field notes for details:

Robert:	(Hits the three drums that have three pitches, dat dat dat. He hits the next one, dat dat, and repeats.) Oh! that would be really good for the crow dance. It could go like dat dat dat, caw caw.
Alejandro:	I'm a crow!
Robert:	Caw caw! (Plays and says dat dat dat, caw caw)

The group likes Robert's idea. This gives another direction to the choreography of the dance as they then decide to audition for the crows roles by hopping on one leg three times, then twice on the other, in succession. In groups of four, they repeat this pattern around the room, and with the help of cross-age helpers, they all vote on who

FIGURE 2 *Marinita's interpretation of the Crow Dance (continued)*

We looked at The Shapes Of Their bodies.
We tried to do The same Thing
Wi.thour bodies. Then we danced.
Miramos a las formas de los cuerva
Formamos nuestros cuerpos como los
Cuervos, Luego bailiamos.
marinita

is best at maintaining the rhythm. At the end of their opera, they draw and write about the process. Figures 1 and 2 show Marinita's interpretation of their crow dance.

At the end of a challenging session on 6 March 1995, Dr. Rinehart takes a moment to reflect on the process. He is concerned about the degree of kindergarten participation in singing. On a VSAA documentation form, he writes this journal entry: "As a music teacher, I feel that opportunities to repeat songs will assist kids to internalize the songs. A once over, once a day doesn't always seem to help kindergarteners. Maybe if the kindergarteners took on a song and created it on their own, they might take on more ownership."

Soon after, Mrs. West invites more of the kindergarten's voice into the song writing by facilitating an imaginative song-writing session in their own classroom. As the children flap their arms and sing, "I'm flying, I'm flying, I'm flyyying," she accompanies them on her guitar. The verses reflect their love of repetition and familiar rhyme as they sing: "Crows, crows, go away, little Coyote wants to play." Later in the day on March 8, she writes in her VSAA documentation journal: "We hadn't created a song in our room until this week. Later today, at free-choice time, kids were choosing to read and sing the songs on the chart paper. Others were drawing and writing about the coyote story. [One of the children] even sang a song, 'Butterfly, butterfly come and visit me!' "

Scene Seven: Producing Costumes and Scenery

The children make very brightly colored above-the-head masks for the coyotes, crows, woodpecker, badger, and snakes. The snake headbands become an opportunity for using the mathematical sign system as the children invent colorful patterns to cut out and paste. They also use the pictorial sign system as they sponge-paint large flats to represent the mesas and desert plants.

Another session concludes with the first graders dancing out to recess. The children return to work at learning centers, where they choose from a variety of invitations to use multiple intelligences through their choices of engagements emphasizing different sign systems. Some write in their journals (linguistic); some read (linguistic); some tell stories (linguistic-oral); some make collages (constructive-pictorial); some shape coyotes and snakes out of clay (constructive); some work at a center where they are engaged in an inquiry about wolves, foxes, and coyotes (pictorial, linguistic); some are looking at nonfiction books (linguistic); some are listening to a tape of the opera as they read their scripts and sing along (linguistic-musical); others have discovered a keyboard with blank staff paper nearby. Some are writing the introductory song, "I'm a Blue Coyote," above the staff lines. One child gets a clipboard and is singing and copying the music from a song chart (musical-linguistic). They are engaged learners with emerging literacies.

Scene Eight: Sharing Transformations

"Things started happening," Mrs. Hood continues in her audio journal. She says: "The opera just kept growing and expanding through the curriculum. Kids started looking for more coyote tales. I saw a book at the bookstore called *El conejo y el coyote* (Kohen 1993), which is a Mexican folk tale where the coyote isn't the trickster. It's along the lines of a "Br'er Rabbit," where the rabbit's the trickster and the coyote is the one who's the brunt of the joke. We went into a study of wolves, foxes, and coyotes . . . reading nonfiction books to extend their knowledge base. Around this time, a very gifted boy had just rejoined the class. He was another child that needs to remember that he wasn't the only child in the classroom. He became an incredible leader. A normally quiet child was participating. Another child I thought was tuned out would stand in the back, pick up a pencil, and conduct. The kids all participated at different points. A kindergarten child receiving special education services came up with the line [that was used in a song], 'I'm flying, I'm flying, I'm flying!' Other kindergartners were creating crows on the computer and counting them. One little boy who seldom writes or draws anything recognizable drew a mesa with crows on top and a reddish squiggle. It turned out to be Coyote with his tail on fire! It was really the first piece of artwork from this child that shows an understanding of story, an understanding of a concept we are trying to build for him.

Another boy asked if he could make the crow singing. He had used stamps [in the computer program] to create in great detail Coyote getting in trouble. And all around those birds were treble clefs, and that was the music the crows were singing."

On another occasion, as I write field notes, I observe first grader Lizbeth improvising after several sessions of keyboard exploration. She seems to be inventing a melody. She has the keyboard programmed for arpeggios and the harpsichord simulator. She plays for a long time in the middle register. Another student joins her and taps lightly on a triangle. When Lizbeth stops, she looks at me and says, "I like this sound." I find a tape recorder for her, and she continues playing until it is time to clean up and then takes the tape recorder home. After that experience she appears more confident about her musical ability. Later, she shared what happened at home, "I loved it [the tape], and my sister said, 'Who made that?' and I said 'Me.' 'Who else did it?' she said, and I said, 'Bella did some,' and then my sister said, 'I wish I made a tape of music.' My sister went, 'I'm a gray coyote' (she sings), but she's not a gray coyote," Lizbeth laughed. Lizbeth even asked to be one of the lead coyote singers. Although Lizbeth hadn't auditioned for it earlier, Mrs. Hood realized that opportunities should be created for those students who unexpectedly discover themselves in the learning process, not simply during planned experiences. During the performance, Lizbeth stood poised and centered as she sang in a lead role as one of the coyotes.

"Another of the major impacts I hear," Mrs. Hood reported in her audio journal, "is that kids are just bursting with song, and the English-speaking kids are seriously attempting to use Spanish. At the same time, [a child] who in kindergarten was a monolingual Spanish speaker wrote a story recently in English. Her inventions in English were as close to convention as her percentages in Spanish [Mrs. Hood assessed the child's invented spelling in English and compared it to her conventional spellings in Spanish.] And you could read the entire story without having to have her there. I think part of this growth was due to creating in two languages for the opera."

Mrs. Hood also recorded one occasion on which the local Sunday paper invited children to write a story about a trip to a park where they had seen an animal. Her first graders liked this idea and became engaged in telling each other their stories first, then writing narratives about the coyotes or javelinas or jackrabbits they had seen. Since the stories were intended for publication, Mrs. Hood proofread them for spelling, and the children attempted to write a final draft for the first time in their school experience. One child shared a powerful story, and it was the most in the way of oral language Mrs. Hood had heard from him at any time.

Mrs. Hood added a few more comments to her journal: "The kids have taken the words home to practice and sing. The parents are singing it. Their siblings are singing it. Every child will have an opportunity to sing . . . to be up moving around on the stage . . . to be involved in a dance . . . and it just has come together that way. It continues to build."

Scene Nine: Performing and Reflecting

It's 5:00 P.M. I enter Mrs. Hood's first grade and then walk across the hall to Mrs. West's kindergarten where I am immediately put to work serving pizza. Sarah announces to me, "We are getting ready to sing our opera to grownups and kids. All we have to do is try our best to do it." She tells me she really likes the mesa song: "It's fun to sing."

After pizza and ice slushies, the children excitedly get into their costumes and share stories about the morning's matinee they performed for their peers from another school. Some say they were embarrassed at first, and many say their favorite part is the mesa song because "it is beautiful."

Lizbeth, wearing her handmade, orange-brown, tie-dyed coyote T-shirt with a "burnt" tail of yarn attached to it under the felt of her blue coyote costume, joins the group and says, "I like to sing. I know my best part. I like 'Mesa' [the song] because the mesa's brown and my favorite color is brown." Robert, dressed as a crow, joins the group. His eyes are shining as he excitedly shares his idea for a different ending to the story. Not giving up hope for Coyote, he tells me that, if Coyote had a third chance to fly and was balanced, "he really could have flied!"

Reprise: Learning That Many Ways Is the Way

The ownership, excitement, pride, and growing sense of community the children feel has been expressed in many ways during the nine weeks of writing lyrics, composing music, choreographing dances, preparing scenery, and making costumes for their own opera. Mrs. Hood hands Dr. R a stack of thank-you letters the first grade children have written to him and gives me copies (see figures 3.1-3.6). So much has happened. Throughout the opera project, the children became aware of their strengths as they developed their abilities to communicate across a number of sign systems.

The urgency of making central spaces for the arts in our public schools is reflected in the children's letters. We look at them together. Some have drawn pictures with hearts, homes, rainbows, and musical notes. Most of the letters that are written in Spanish are heartfelt expressions of thanks for helping them learn to sing and do an opera. Many say they like the music. Berto shows us how he has engaged his musical intelligence (fig. 3.1). He writes, "Thank you for helping us make our opera. I learned the drum from the opera. I want to be a drummer when I grow up. Berto." Danielle put into play her kinesthetic intelligence (fig. 3.2). She writes, "Dear Dr. Rinehart, I'm glad that we made an opera. I learned how to dance the Loloqangwtu dance. Love Danielle." Ashley developed her intrapersonal intelligence (fig. 3.3). She writes, "Dear Dr. Rinehart, Thank you for helping us with the opera. I had fun. I learned not to be shy. From, Ashley." Lizbeth drew on her musical intelligence (fig. 3.4). She writes, "Dear Dr. Rinehart, Thank you for the music and thank you for helping us. I learned to sing." Sarah engaged her interpersonal intelligence (fig. 3.5). She writes, "Dear Dr. Rinehart. Thank you for helping us with the opera. I really like it. It's great and so are you. Besides, we also find new friends." Viviana put into play her musical-linguistic intelligences (Figure 3.6). She writes (in Spanish), "One time [I heard] a coyote and he was singing coyote music for Professor Rinehart. From Viviana. My favorite song is 'Mesa'" (Figure 3a). The children's letters show us the many opportunities they had for expressing themselves in multiple ways as they uncovered the "potentials by which all humans might mean" (Leland and Harste 1994, 339).

FIGURE 3.1 *Berto's letter*

Dear Dr. Reinhardt
Thank You fou helping
us make our opera,
I learned the drum from
the opera. I want to
be a drummer when I grow
Jp. Berto

FIGURE 3.2 *Danielle's letter*

Dear Dr. Van Hrat
ImGald thet We Made
a opra I Lrid HOW to Dace The
Lo Lo Come to Dace
Love Danielle.

FIGURE 3.3 *Ashley's letter*

DeaR Dr. Rinehart
ThACO You
for HELPING
US With The Opea
I Had fnd
I lead Not To be
Seí-
fonm AShley

FIGURE 3.4 *Lizbeth's letter*

Der Dr. Rinehart Thacoy
fro The Mos Ng aNd Thacoy Fro
hapeg us I LRD Seg from
Lizbeth

FIGURE 3.5 *Sarah's letter*

DeaR D.R RiNe HarT,
THANK You FOR HaLPING US WHaTH
THE opra I raLe Likeit IT's Grat
ArD So are You BesoDS We also
FiND New FiRiNS.

FrOM SaRaH.

FIGURE 3.6 *Viviana's letter*

UNa Ves, uN
Copote i Va
Cantana Ir Mavlu
capote Para PrP
Rinehart de Viviana eSor
Cras Pa Por eL ha
opera. Mi Favorita
Cansion es MeSa.
de Viviana

The children also make a class book for their parents that describes the opera process they have just experienced. It is written in Spanish and English. The book ends with the question, "Why do an opera? ¿Por qué deben hacer una ópera?" There are four photographs of the children outside on the playground, dressed in their costumes. Voice bubbles are in the space around the margins of the pictures. This time, most of the children say something in English at varying levels of proficiency. They say:

> So we can learn better to do stuff we don't know how. It helps kids learn to be brave and proud. People might buy kids the book! The opera is important. You need to learn about it. Kids like doing it. Singing is fun! Going on the stage is fun! Es divertido. It's fun. Teachers will want their kindergartners to learn what they can do in first grade. We thought we would never do it and we found that we could. So the parents can learn how to do an opera. Kindergartners can learn about opera to go next year to first grade to show others. First graders can learn about opera to go next year to second grade to show others. It's a fun thing to learn. Para cantar mejor. To sing better. It's good to learn to do the opera so when you grow up you can be in an opera. We learned how to read. It helps you be a better student. When we were practicing, we had the words. ¡Cuando hicimos la ópera trabajamos muchos para enseñar a los papás y los niños lo que aprendimos! When we made the opera we worked a lot to teach the parents and the children what we learned! To show our moms and dads how much we learn. So we could be cooler singers! So kids could learn by having fun. To learn what an opera is. They learn to dance. Kids like the opera. It makes our families happy.

In this opera project, we learned that all children, members of the larger human family, have many ways of knowing, communicating, and being literate. In contexts that support their inquiries and imaginations, children will apply their strengths, engage in transactions that interest them, sense their interconnectedness with others, and construct deeper understandings of their possible worlds.

In this increasingly complex and globally oriented world at the point of entering a new millennium, we are learning to value the ability to think critically and imaginatively with an appreciation of the whole. Children need to learn to perceive beyond the known while learning to work collaboratively as a community of learners. They need to think creatively and express their ideas in a diversity of forms. Curricular opportunities such as the opera project create spaces for unity and equity across our diversity.

Still, educative experiences like young children's opera will not, by themselves, support the language and literacy of culturally, linguistically, and developmentally diverse young children until the dominance of existing verbocentric curricular practices and its attendant testing and exclusive funding in the schools is challenged. The arts need to be funded and made central in the public schools. To better support all children in the development of multiple literacies such as the composition and production of verbal and visual texts, songs, dances, and performances, opportunities for partnerships need to be developed among the schools, community arts organizations, local independent artists, and universities with opportunities to share experiences and ideas among nations. In this shared experience, there may be opportunities for harmony and growth within and across our linguistic, cultural, and physical differences. How do we begin? Many ways is the way.

References

Dewey, J. 1934. *Art as experience.* New York: Minton, Balch and Co.

Edelsky, C., B. Altwerger, and B. Flores. 1991. *Whole language: What's the difference?* Portsmouth, NH: Heinemann.

Eisner, E. 1994. *Cognition and curriculum revisited.* New York: Teachers College Press.

Flores, B., P.T. Cousin, and E. Díaz. 1991. Transforming deficit myths about learning, language, and culture. *Language Arts* 68:369-78.

Freeman, Y., and D. Freeman. (1988) 1994. Whole language learning and teaching for second language learners. In *Reading process and practice: From sociolinguistics to whole language.* 2d ed. Edited by C. Weaver, 558-629. Portsmouth, NH: Heinemann.

Fueyo, J. 1991. Reading literate sensibilities: Resisting a verbocentric writing classroom. *Language Arts* 68:641-48.

Gardner, H. 1983/1993. *Frames of mind: The theory of multiple intelligences.* New York: Basic Books.

Goodman, K. 1986. *What's whole in whole language?* Portsmouth, NH: Heinemann.

_____. 1994. *Phonics phacts.* Portsmouth, NH: Heinemann.

Goodman, K., L. Bird, and Y. Goodman. 1990. *The whole language catalogue.* Santa Rosa, CA: American School Publishers.

Harste, J., K. Short, and C. Burke. 1988. *Creating classrooms for authors: The reading and writing connection.* Portsmouth, NH: Heinemann.

Harste, J., V. Woodward, and C. Burke. 1984. *Language stories and literacy lessons.* Portsmouth, NH: Heinemann.

Kasten, W. 1992. Bridging the horizon: American Indian beliefs and whole language learning. *Anthropology and Education Quarterly* 23:108-19.

Kohen, C. 1993. *El conejo y el coyote.* Beverly Hills, CA: Laredo Publishing Co.

Langer, S. 1942/1957. *Philosophy in a new key.* Cambridge, MA: Harvard University

Leland, C., and J. Harste. 1994. Multiple ways of knowing: Curriculum in a new key. *Language Arts* 71:337-44.

McCarty, T. L., S. Wallace, R. H. Lynch, and A. Benally. 1991. Classroom inquiry and Navajo learning styles: A call for reassessment. *Anthropology and Education Quarterly* 22:42-59.

McDermott, G. 1994. *Coyote: A trickster tale from the American Southwest.* New York: Harcourt Brace and Co.

Merriam, S. 1988. *Case study research in education: A qualitative approach.* San Francisco: Bass Publishers

Poplin, M. S. 1988a. The reductionist fallacy in learning disabilities: Replicating the past by reducing the present. *Journal of Learning Disabilities* 21:389-400.

_____. 1988b. Holistic/constructivist principles of the teaching learning process: Implications for the field of learning disabilities. *Journal of Learning Disabilities* 21:401-15.

Purrington, S., C. Rinehart, and W. Wilcox. 1990. *Music! Words! Opera!* Saint Louis, MO: Opera America and MMB Music, Inc.

Rosenblatt, L. 1938/1976. *Literature as exploration.* New York: The Modern Language Association of America.

Rossi, P. J. 1997a. Having an experience: Multiple literacies through young children's opera. Ph.D. diss., University of Arizona.

_____. 1997b. Having an experience in five acts: Multiple literacies through young children's opera. *Language Arts* 74:352-67.

Ruiz, N., and R. Figueroa. 1995. Learning-handicapped classrooms with Latino students: The optimal learning environment (OLE) project. *Education and Urban Society* 27:463-83.

Short, K. 1989. Using sign systems to communicate effectively in a complex world. Unpublished manuscript.

Short, K., and J. Armstrong. 1993. Moving toward inquiry: Integrating literature into the science curriculum. *The New Advocate* 6:183-200.

Short, K., J. Harste, and C. Burke. 1996. *Creating classrooms for authors and inquirers.* Portsmouth, NH: Heinemann.

Spradley, J. 1980. *Participant observation.* New York: Holt, Rinehart, and Winston.

Vygotsky, L. 1978. *Mind in society.* Cambridge, MA: Harvard University Press.

14

Native American Culture and Language

Considerations in Service Delivery

Sherry R. Allison and Christine Begay Vining

Introduction

Fifty-three years ago a Navajo child was born on the Navajo Nation. One of six children, Ben was the third child born into a family with strong ties to the Navajo way of life, culturally and linguistically. At the age of three, Ben became blind. This unfortunate accident forever changed Ben's life.

"I was away from home nine months out of the year to attend school from first through twelfth grade. When I returned home to my family after the first year, I had lost command of the Navajo language! I couldn't communicate with my mother without my older brother interpreting for us." This comment comes from an individual who was taken at a very young age from all that he was familiar with, including his family, home, native language, and culture, to receive "appropriate" services. Ben has come full circle to share his story. This chapter will highlight Ben's experiences to depict the tragedy that can occur when culture and language are not taken into consideration. Sadly, due to limited resources, on and near reservation communities, disabled Native American individuals of all ages continue to be placed in off-reservation programs to receive services.

This chapter will discuss issues concerning culture and language of Native Americans and Alaska natives, and their considerations of service delivery for native children with special educational needs. However, to deliver services, one must first understand the Native people as a whole and the diversities within each community. This chapter will therefore provide a portrait of the Native American people. As Native people, we are often reminded that to know where we are going we must first know who we are and where we have come from. Our past is our future.

Ben's Story

"I became blind, as near as I can guess, at about the age of three. There is some confusion as to the cause of my visual impairment. Because of my young age, I too am not certain as to how things happened. There are two versions: mine and my family's.

"Family version: I was standing with my aunt on an earthen dike looking over a pond of water. I waded into the pond and pulled out some items. Later that afternoon, I went back to our hogan and went to sleep. That evening, someone tried to wake me up, but I didn't want to get up. I was crying and my mom said that 'maybe his legs are aching—he was walking in the rainwater. Let him sleep.' The next morning when I woke up my eyelids were completely caked over with sleep covering the entire socket and I couldn't open my eyes! My mom washed my face of all the sleep, but I had no sight! Because this had happened the day after it had rained and I had walked in the pond of rainwater which may have been from hail, the belief was that I needed some Navajo ceremonies to be performed by my grandfather who was a medicine man. I have no idea of the numbers and types of ceremonies performed on me, but I know that the Lightning Way and Wind Way ceremonies were done many times—even into my late teen years.

"On the other hand, my personal recollection and belief of the cause of my blindness seems to be more plausible, at least to me. On a trip into Gallup, my mom had picked up a can while passing by the city's refuse yard. On this particular day, I remember standing by my mom's side, clinging to her skirt as she tried to build a fire. She was pouring some fluid from the can that she had picked up. She made several attempts to start the fire, each time dousing the pile of wood chips with more fluid from the can, with the last attempt causing the flames to leap into the can, which then exploded! From what I remember, I felt something spray my face, and I ran out and said something to my sister about washing my face; and she said nothing had happened to me, but my mother's hair and skirt were on fire! I can't determine how long it was between the time of the explosion and the time I lost my sight.

"Likewise, I have no idea of the time frame between losing my sight and being admitted into the Crownpoint Indian Health Service (IHS) hospital for my vision problem. Being in the hospital was probably my first time away from home, and I stayed there for about three months. I don't know the details of my treatment, but I just remember being blindfolded with medicated gauze pads over each eye. I started getting some sight back and after three months I was discharged.

"Again, I have no idea as to how long it was before I was sent off to the New Mexico School for the Visually Handicapped (NMSVH). I also don't know the process my mother encountered in sending me away. I only remember being very young, very scared and on a bus, asleep on a seat, and waking up as some lady gave me a cookie. I arrived at NMSVH and remember going to supper where a tossed green salad was served—which was my first time to ever eat a salad! I sometimes wonder how I ate—did I know how to use a fork? As I finished, I pushed my plate away, and to show off my proficiency of the English language I said 'No gotty!' which was the extent of my English at the time.

"I was away from home nine months out of the year to attend school from first through twelfth grade. When I returned home to my family after that first year, I had lost my command of the Navajo language! I couldn't communicate with my mother without my older brother interpreting for us. I only knew how to say cat and cow! But that same summer, I relearned Navajo and never forgot it again.

"By the time I graduated from high school, I had spent slightly over 50% of my life away from home. I believe this to have been a primary factor in the alienation I felt from my relatives, particularly my brothers. They seemed to be out doing their thing, especially in activities away from the family; consequently, I spent most of my time with my mom and a younger sister. Upon leaving high school, I had a poor self-image as a Native American; I felt strongly that my own people were ashamed of and embarrassed by me; and the Bilaganas (Anglos) were the only ones who understood my limitation and were accepting of me. I didn't feel comfortable at home. Being away also deprived me of many cultural activities, particularly those reserved for the winter months.

"It wasn't until I was 27 years old that I came back to live on the reservation and it was only because I felt that I had no other choice. I had received computer training and had attempted unsuccessfully to get a job in Salt Lake City. About three weeks after submitting an application for employment with the Navajo Nation, I received a call asking when I could start work. That seemed to be the last thing I wanted to hear! First, I didn't think my own people would want me around, much less hire me! Second, I was scared stiff of moving back to the "rez"; I didn't think I would have any friends or any social life! I planned to get at least two years of work experience, then go back to the city. These two years have now stretched into 26 years. I now realize and understand that acceptance is a two-way street of communication: my fear of others was due to my not knowing them; their avoidance of me was due to their not knowing about me!

"As I reflect back on my early years, I still get a queasy feeling in the pit of my stomach when someone mentions that there is a government vehicle coming up the road. It brings back memories of the BIA personnel, who were there to take me away from my family and who seemed to have no mercy or feelings. Their treatment of me as a blind individual was to ignore me as if I weren't around, to act as if I had something contagious, or to yell at me as if I was hard of hearing. I hated those days! I also recall relatives talking about me as if I weren't there, or as if I couldn't hear. One relative thought I would easily get a job in Window Rock sitting behind a desk in an office! I hated these types of discussions because their opinions were always based on my blindness, and I resented that. The truth is that those of us with disabilities have to work harder to prove ourselves equal and worthy."

Tribal Demographics

As recognized by federal law and policy, Indian nations are sovereign. Through treaties, statues, and court decisions, tribes have a unique historic and legal relationship with the U.S. government. In exchange for land, the government agreed to provide tribes with education, health care and public safety, thus establishing legal obligations.

The Native American population has increased significantly over the past three decades and is now nearly 1% of the total U.S. population. As the only race of people who must legally prove ethnicity, there are 1.9 million individuals who have identified themselves as Native Americans in the United States (U.S. Census 1990). There has been a 38% increase in the population since 1980 as compared to a 9.8% increase of the total U.S. population (U.S. Census 1990).

There are 332 federally recognized tribes and 227 Alaska Native entities (Bureau of Indian Affairs 1996), with approximately 200 languages spoken (Leap 1981). No two tribes are exactly alike; each tribe differs in culture, language, history, beliefs, and land base. No other subgroup of the U.S. population manifests such comparable diversity. In a recent report by the Institute for Educational Leadership, Inc./Center for Demographic Policy (Hodgkinson, et al. 1990), the Native American population is described as "one percent of the people; 50% of the diversity."

It is reported that 66% of Native American people reside off Indian lands, with more than half of the Native population living in the following six states: Oklahoma (252,000), California (242,000), Arizona (204,000), New Mexico (134,000), Alaska (86,000), and Washington (81,000). The Navajo reservation, which extends into the states of Arizona, New Mexico, and Utah, has the largest on-reservation population of 159,481 (U.S. Census 1990).

The average age of the Native American people is quite young, relative to the other racial groups, with the largest being between the ages of birth to nine years. Almost 40% of the population is under 24.2 years of ages, and the median age is seven years younger than the national average (U.S. Bureau of Census 1995).

With a young and growing population, there are approximately 450,000 Native American and Alaska Native school-age children. Approximately 87% of these children attend public schools located on or near reservations and in urban areas, while an estimated 10% attend schools funded by the BIA.

Native American students have experienced less educational success in American schools when compared to non-Indian students, especially when measured in terms of standardized achievement test scores, frequency of drop-outs, graduation rates, and levels of educational attainment (Pavel, Culin, and Whitener 1997). The Indian Nations At Risk Task Force (1991) noted that schools serving Indian students ". . . have failed to nurture the intellectual development and academic performance of many Native children."

As a group, Native Americans are disadvantaged and have high rates of poverty, unemployment, and low educational achievement (O'Brien 1992). According to the 1990 U.S. Census, the national rate of high school graduates for the general population is 65% and 16% for college graduates, as compared to Native Americans, with 55.8% for high school graduates and 7.7% for college graduates. With respect to high school graduates, statistics vary for each tribe, i.e., 65.1% for Creeks and 39.9% for Navajos. The school dropout rate is higher among Native Americans than for any other ethnic minority group.

"Native Americans—particularly on tribal lands—experience some of the highest rates of chronic disease and disability in the U.S. compared to the general population. Yet they receive a proportionately smaller share of resources" (Seekins 1997).

Accurate incidence figures for all Native American and Alaska Native children with special needs are difficult to obtain because of the distinct systems involved—federal, state, county, and the Native American tribal systems. However, a 1990 National Assessment of Educational Progress (NAEP) survey, which gathered data related to race/ethnicity and disability, revealed that "Native Americans may comprise a somewhat disproportionate percentage of the special education population." Another study on the prevalence of disability among Native American children (O'Connell 1987) reported that the population of Native American school children who receive special education services is one and a half times greater at 16.8% versus 11% for the general population.

For school year 1997–98 the BIA reported that 9,785 students (19.42%) received special education services with Specific Learning Disability (4,649) and Speech or Language Impairments (3,438) as the largest categories. A 1993 survey by the Office of Civil Rights (1993) identified 10.76% of the Elementary and Secondary Special Education population as Native American, again with the leading disabilities identified as Learning Disabilities and Speech Impairments.

As the population grows so will the demand for services. American Indian infants are born with a disabling condition at three times the rate of all other babies born in the United States. According to Healthy People 2000 (1991), the baseline for incidence of Fetal Alcohol Syndrome (FAS) in the Native American/Alaska Native population is four cases per 1,000 births, as compared to 0.22 per 1,000 for the Anglo population. Visual impairments occur three times more frequently among Native Americans, while hearing losses occur four times more frequently compared to the general population. Ironically, research indicates that nearly 85% of all disabilities among the Native American people are preventable (Native American Research and Training Center 1995).

Understanding and Honoring Culture and Language

Service providers, in order to be effective in their delivery of educational as well as medical intervention, must recognize the values, beliefs, and attitudes that are influenced by culture. Culture can be defined as how people interact with one another as well as their values and beliefs. Westby (1993) states, "Culture is how and why we behave in certain ways, how we perceive reality, what we believe to be true, what we build and create, and what we accept as good and desirable" (p. 9). Hall (1976) describes culture this way: "it is not innate, but learned, the various facets of culture are interrelated—you touch a culture in one place and everything is affected; it is shared and in effect defines the boundaries of different groups" (p.16). Virtually every aspect of Native American life and the Native American worldview is influenced by culture and language. A person's values and beliefs have both a deep and subtle impact on thought, behavior, decision making, expression (including show of emotion), time, and interpretation of events.

Native American tribes, because of their unique cultures and languages, have significantly different perceptions of child rearing, change and intervention, medicine, and healing. Changes in language, kin structure, religion, land, and health behavior impact family culture and effect their perceptions, beliefs and practices about prevention, and cause and treatment of illness and disability.

Perceptions of Disability

Some families identify with a "traditional" way of life, particularly when interpreting the cause of illness and disability and making decisions about the course of treatment or intervention. Other families reject "traditional" tribal beliefs and practices and may resort to other forms of spiritual and personal support such as the Native American Church and the various denominations of Judeo-Christian churches. More and more Native American families, however, are relying on an eclectic form of support by seeking information, guidance, and healing from several different sources.

Although distinct differences in values and beliefs exist with regard to perceptions of disability, it is important to emphasize the similarities that cross cultural and linguistic boundaries. Dufort and Reed (1995) explained and highlighted some of these similarities in beliefs and practices:

- Many Native American people incorporate parts of the mainstream American system and their own culture's traditional belief systems into their understanding of handicapping conditions. This makes it possible for family members to understand the biological basis of an illness, and to have a traditional cultural explanation for why the illness occurred in their particular family.
- A fundamental theme in the Native American perspective on the cause of disabilities is that words, thoughts, and actions have the power to bring about serious illness, disability, and other kinds of misfortune. Out of this basic belief comes the assumption that parents and family members have a clear and ever-present responsibility for causing and preventing serious illness and disability in their children.
- In Native American communities, as in all societies, a diversity of beliefs regarding health, illness, and treatment exist. Some families who have children with disabilities will believe and practice according to culturally traditional ways, while others who consider themselves "modern" or "Christian" will not practice according to traditional ways at all, and still other families will define themselves as "taking the middle ground." (p.4)

Although there are similarities within Native American cultures, a diversity of beliefs exist even within families. The case story of Ben clearly illustrates a duality in perception of his illness and disability. Ben's mother viewed the disability from a "traditional" Navajo perspective, as being caused by a violation of a taboo. Ben, on the other hand, viewed his disability as being caused by a medical condition that was not immediately treated. Disabling conditions need to be understood from the western as well the cultural perspective in order to provide appropriate support systems and intervention.

Change and Intervention

Within the mainstream culture, families have great concern about how a disorder will impact their child's performance currently as well as in the future. Parents inquire about the resources available to them, how their child's impairment can be treated, and how they can help. Parents are encouraged to speak out, to become advocates for their children, and to work with professionals during assessment and intervention activities. Families are guided by the philosophy that in special education, more is better, earlier is better, and more structured is better. However, this philosophy and practice of self-advocacy, with its early, intensive, and structured intervention, creates a dilemma for Native American families who do not feel that they should "fix" their children's difficulties. Native American families view intervention very differently, and the mismatch between the values and beliefs of Native American families and professionals serving their children often creates conflicts and barriers. Families who focus more on accepting and dealing with disability may be perceived as uninterested and even uncaring about their child's educational performance and progress. The lack of parental involvement, voiced as a concern by professionals in Native American communities, is rooted in the failure on the part of the professional community to recognize and respect differences in perception, interpretation, and treatment of disabilities in Native American cultures.

Barriers to Service Delivery

In addition to cultural and linguistic differences, other obstacles contribute to the lack of resources and effective provision of educational and medical services. Jurisdictional/bureaucratic issues and recruitment and retention of professional personnel are examples of service delivery barriers faced by Native American students with disabilities and their families (Harris 1986). McMann (1994) reported several issues identified by advocates, consumers, Indian parents, and tribal leaders; these included:

- Lack of services in public and Bureau of Indian Affairs (BIA) schools;
- Children transported great distances to receive therapy services compromise the least restrictive environment;
- Long waiting lists for evaluation and identification;
- Serious lack of psychological services for Native American children with behavior disorders;
- Parents are inadequately or inappropriately informed, and therefore are not fully participating in their children's IEP;
- Children are being pigeonholed into existing programs due to a lack of specialists in occupational, physical, and speech therapy.

Educational Issues and Concerns: Assessment Issues

Native American students and children have frequently been inappropriately placed in special education classes; treatment approaches often violate client and family values; and disabilities related to learning, speech-language, and social-emotional difficulties in particular, remain mis- or unidentified. Three major issues need to be addressed to improve special education assessment and intervention services to Native American children and students. These include the use of translated instruments for screening and evaluations, the use of untrained interpreters, particularly with monolingual native-speaking families, and the lack of culturally and linguistically appropriate materials and activities.

Test Translation

Current assessment tools do not adequately assess Native American children and students, which places them at an unfair disadvantage regarding school success. Undoubtedly, there is a need for the development of culturally and linguistically appropriately procedures that will better identify the learning and language needs of Native American children and, thus reduce cultural assessment bias, which are inherent in standardized instruments. In an effort to evaluate bilingual, bicultural Native American students and children, service providers have attempted to translate various assessment tools. Parts of speech-language tests, for example, have been translated from English to Navajo to evaluate students' verbal processing, syntactic, and semantic abilities. Assessors and translators need to be aware that vocabulary words are not necessarily equivalent. Syntactic and phonological differences make the use of translated tests inappropriate and invalid in the diagnosis of impairments. Furthermore, there are differences in the complexity of the language as well as differences in the experiences students bring to the context of the assessment. The use of translated tests or segments of tools only adds to the confusion and does not address the goal or distinguishing language learning disorders from linguistic and cultural differences and second language learning difficulties.

It is also important to note that a student's poor performance could be attributed to reasons other than cognitive and linguistic deficits. According to Mattes and Omark (1984), these reasons could include (a) use of inappropriate instruments, (b) inappropriate adaptations, (c) poor testing conditions, (d) lack of test taking skills, (e) lack of rapport, and (f) differences in cultural roles and interactions.

Use of Untrained Interpreters

Potential problems also exist when using untrained individuals to interpret from English to the Native language and vice versa. Nelkin and Malach (1996) reported several problems related to the use of interpreters:

- Most providers have not been trained to work with interpreters
- Interpreters may know a particular language, but may not be accepted and respected within the family, community, or culture
- Using family members as interpreters can cause problems
- Many concepts and words, especially medical jargon, are not easily interpreted or translated into other languages.

It is essential for interpreters to receive training in confidentiality, medical terminology and concepts, cultural beliefs and practices with respect to disability, and culturally appropriate ways to explain sensitive information.

Lack of Culturally and Linguistically Appropriate Materials

The lack of culturally and linguistically appropriate materials for screening, evaluation, and intervention continues to be a prevalent issue that must be first addressed by grass-roots efforts in Native American communities. With training and the availability of literature on the topic of culturally appropriate assessment and intervention with Native American students, the use of inappropriate materials and practices that violate cultural beliefs and values appears to be declining. However, it also takes professionals who are willing to listen and learn to respect the cultural beliefs of students and families from culturally and linguistically diverse backgrounds. For example, within the Navajo culture it is widely known that certain animals are considered taboo such as the owl, snake, and bear, yet students are exposed to materials and experiences featuring these animals. DeSalvo (1995) shared her experience involving a clash of cultures:

> One interesting story involving Anglo ignorance and Navajo tradition deals with the study of animals. When visiting the local zoo, the teacher called the children's attention to a grizzly bear. However, the next day, many Navajo grandparents came to the school, upset because the bear had looked at the children. In one version, the grandparents were concerned that the bear may have taken the children's minds. They would be required to perform a ceremony for each child; often the ceremony would cost over $1,000. (p. 3)

This experience conveys the need to ensure that the materials and activities used with Native American students are culturally appropriate. Currently, materials and intervention activities for Native American students in special education, whether for evaluation or intervention, are intended for English-speaking students and primarily represent experiences in mainstream society. There is a great need for materials that reflect tribal life, experiences that are culturally relevant, and bilingual materials that are intended for native-speaking students.

Current Trends and Strategies

Several speech-language assessment instruments have been developed locally for Native Americans living on reservation lands (Bayles and Harris 1982; Uzdawinnis 1982 and Miles 1982). Currently, however, no research exists that specifically addresses the language development status of English-speaking Native American children nor appropriate language assessment instruments for English-speaking Native American children. In recent years, research has been conducted with one of the largest tribes in Oklahoma, the Cherokee, in an effort to identify language screening and assessment tools suitable for this population. Studies on non-reservation English-speaking Cherokee Indian children have indicated that standardized test are questionable for use with this population (Long 1998). It would seem reasonable that Indian children who live, socialize, and are educated among Caucasians would evidence the same type of language skills as the Caucasian children. However, Long and Christensen (1997) found there was a significant difference in the linguistic and social communication language skills between these two groups. When compared to Caucasian children (ages three, four, and five), the Cherokee Indian children performed less well on linguistic and social communication skills at age three. Another study was conducted by Long (1998) investigating the social communication language skills of five-year-old English-speaking Cherokee Indian children. This study comparing the performance of Native American children and Caucasian Head Start children on a test assessing pragmatic skills revealed significantly lower scores for

Native American children. Although research has shown that the use of standardized language instruments is questionable even with English-speaking Native American children, the practice of diagnosing speech-language disorders using standardized instruments continues to be the cornerstone of assessments and evaluations.

Promising Practices

Research indicates that appropriate assessment of culturally and linguistically diverse students requires the use of dynamic assessment procedures, which yields information on the process of how students learn. Several researcher have documented using dynamic assessment procedures to evaluate language skills of culturally and linguistically diverse students in preschool and early elementary school (Lidz and Peña 1996; Peña 1996; Peña, Quinn, and Iglesias 1992). The test-teach-retest methodology used in dynamic assessment rules out the lack of experience with test stimuli and tasks. Results suggest that dynamic assessment procedures differentiate learning differences from learning disorders. Thus, dynamic assessment procedures appear to be a promising approach which should be further explored with Native American students.

Appropriate assessment of Native American students requires the use of alternative forms of assessment. A teaming approach is encouraged to evaluate a student's academic, educational and language abilities, and to determine appropriate interventions so that the educational relevancy of a student's disability can be documented. Informal procedures such as observations in the classroom, teacher and parent reports, and informal tasks in the native language are necessary assessment procedures for bilingual Native American students. Efforts are being made to utilize home language questionnaires in addition to informal tasks, i.e., using picture cards that depict experiences with which students are familiar, to assess language proficiency and language dominance for bilingual students. In addition, language samples in both English and native language, inventories/criterion-referenced testing, and work samples (i.e., portfolios) are excellent ways to evaluate cognitive and linguistic abilities as well as to identify linguistic, cultural, and environmental influences that may impact learning. Alternative forms of assessment procedures yield information from multiple sources and contexts, thereby reducing the cultural and linguistic bias in testing.

Family and Community Systems

Among all the Native American tribes in the United States, the structure and system of families is similar. However, it is imperative to recognize the diversity among tribal group, including tribal language, customs, values, food, history, behaviors, expectations, and religious beliefs and practices. However, as tribes are in transition, so are Native families and cultures. Increasingly, many Native Americans move between two worlds, both the Indian world and the Anglo world. Today, Native American families may identify themselves as either traditional, bicultural, or assimilated, which is largely based upon location of the household residence, language spoken at home, and the participation in religious events.

The structure and functioning of Native American families are entirely interwoven with their family culture, values, and beliefs. It is important to note that cultural values impact how one views solutions to problems and the way one participates in service programs (Clark and Kelly 1992; Oppelt 1989; Heinrich, Corbine, and Thomas 1990; Fisher 1991).

Whether families live in urban or reservation settings, most Native American families are extended and often include mothers, fathers, grandparents, aunts (who are often referred to as the child's mother), uncles (often referred to as the child's father), and cousins (often referred to as brothers and sisters). It is not uncommon to have adopted relatives in the household and all living in very close proximity to one another. It is also not uncommon for relatives to share the responsibility of child care and child rearing. Uncles and aunts will often assume parental duties which are usually performed by the biological parents in others cultures.

As families relocate to urban settings, traditional forms of Native American culture are difficult to sustain because they are built around spirituality, socialization, and language. There is continuing conflict between individual and family efforts to maintain a traditional way of life while being exposed to the persuasive social and material parts of modern American society with its competing values and norms.

Equally important to the family environment is the community. An individual is part of a family and the family is part of a community. Disabilities and education cannot be separated from culture, communities, and families. When an individual acquires a disability, many families use both traditional and western service delivery systems to address the disabling condition, with traditional healing striving for harmony and balance of mind, body, and spirit. Consequently, community services are often viewed as opportunities to enhance progress and development. With respect and acceptance of the providers, both modalities can be complementary and advantageous to the families, with accepting behaviors by the providers being the key element.

Tribal communities are often small, clustered and close knit with strong interpersonal relationships. To perpetuate a sense of belonging, and because Native American individuals rarely grow independent of their family, Indian children with disabilities living in tribal communities must be given the opportunity to participate in everyday community activities. Because roles of family and tribal members are well defined, it is imperative that children (disabled or not) are provided with the guidance to fulfill their expected role in Indian society. Active participation is the best modality of teaching. However, it is important to note that each tribe views individuals with disabilities in different ways, either as a result of a violation of a taboo or a gift from the creator. Indian societies are in the state of transition, with the influence of modern culture. With public awareness and education, Indian people with disabilities are increasingly accepted into the norm of community living.

Communities often include schools. As the U.S. Congress recognizes the rights of tribes to govern themselves, an increasing number of schools have been contracted through the Indian Self Determination Act of 1975 (P.L. 93-638). To date, at least 90 tribes have Tribal Departments of Education to administer their own educational programs. Until passage of the Indian Self Determination Act, tribes participated minimally in the planning, administration, and monitoring of educational programs. With the passage of this law, maximum participation in the education of Indian people by Indians was legislated. This Act supported the right of Indian tribes to control the education of their people.

With this move to self-governance, tribal governments and communities are now expected to address the special needs of individuals with disabilities. Progress can be measured by the increase of community-based programs and the establishment of tribal policies.

Closing the Gap

Special education is no longer the exclusive province of special educators, but is now a shared responsibility among parents, administrators, and regular and special educators. During the last two decades an extensive amount of attention as been given by Congress to the education of individuals with disabilities. Court decisions and legislative actions have accelerated the movement of services which have impacted public acceptance, research, family involvement, educational reform, practices and policy development. Despite these improvements, progress has been slow to reach Indian Country.

The prevailing issues that Native American families with children with disabilities face are the very same issues that other families with children with disabilities also face: costly treatment, too few providers, lack of education, and the high expectations for involvement. Indian families, however, must also contend with jurisdictional issues and the language and cultural barriers.

Because resolutions to the issues are not expected in the very near future, service providers must learn lessons from the many stories similar to Ben's. If Ben's story is read, studied and taken to heart, one cannot overlook the mistakes of the education process. Indeed, Ben's educational process succeeded in teaching him quite well academically. However, by today's standards, Ben did not receive an appropriate education. Ben's education removed him from his family and failed to prepare him for life on the reservation and life among his people. Ben's educational process was a near catastrophe, almost taking from him his self-esteem, tribal identity, and language. However, it was successful in alienating him from his cultural practices and his family. Although today children are guaranteed a free and appropriate public education as mandated by the Individuals with Disabilities Education Act (IDEA), the culture and language of the student are rarely considered.

The spirit of the IDEA is commendable; however, to accomplish the charges as mandated is monumental. The sharing of knowledge is the cornerstone to successful implementation. The intent to involve families is a slow and arduous process, especially for the Native American population who have historically been conditioned to leave decision making to the "experts." Native American parents must be encouraged and "given permission" to participate as the "expert" of their child. Professionals must learn to take less of the lead; however, there first must be a transfer of knowledge from providers to parents and family members. The transfer of knowledge must occur through "appropriate" and innovative education to include lessons on participation, policy making, advocacy, and to some extent therapy—how they can help their own child in their everyday family routine.

Planning for Native American students must take into consideration the needs and wishes of parents and other family members. For children with more involved disabilities, older siblings may take a more active role as they may eventually take over as the primary caretaker. In planning for the Native American student, it may be more advantageous to take into consideration the community and family environments, as more than likely the student will remain (or return) to his/her native community. Rarely does a Native American individual become independent of his family. The educational programming should be meaningful and take into account what families feel is important.

As we strive to implement not only the spirit of IDEA, but also the intent, the key to accomplishing these mandates calls for a shift in paradigm—a shift in the way we believe and practice. As partners in education, parents, educators, and administrators must "get out of our boxes" and revisit, review, and revise our personal and professional cultures.

References

Altman, B. M. 1991. *Disability among American Indian and Alaskan Native children* (Draft Report). Rockville, MD: Agency for Health Care Policy and Research.

Bayles, K. A., and G. A. Harris. 1982. Evaluating speech-language skills in Papago Indian children. *Journal of American Indian Education* 21, 2.

Clark, S., and D. M. Kelly. 1992. Traditional Native American values: Conflicts or concordance in rehabilitation? *Journal of Rehabilitation* 58 (2): 23–28.

DeSalvo, A. (March 1995). *Preschool Press.* Vol. 3, no. 1:3–4. Albuquerque: Los Niños-New Mexico Model Preschool Consortium. Training and Technical Assistance Unit, NM University Affiliated Program, University of New Mexico.

Dufort, M., and L. Reed, eds. 1995. *Learning the way: A guide for the home visitor working with families on the Navajo reservation.* Watertown, MA: Hilton/Perkins Project of Perkins School for the Blind and Arizona Schools for the Deaf and Blind.

Hall, E. T. 1976. *Beyond culture.* Garden City, NY: Anchor.

Harris, G. 1986. Barriers to the delivery of speech, language and hearing services to Native Americans. In *Nature of communication disorders in culturally and linguistically diverse populations,* ed. O. Taylor. San Diego, CA: College-Hill Press.

Hodgkinson, H. L., J. H. Outtz, and A. M. Obarakpor. 1990. *The demographics of American Indians: One percent of the people; fifty percent of the diversity.* Washington, DC: Institute for Educational Leadership, Inc.

Indian Nations at Risk Task Force. 1991. *Indian Nations at risk report.* Washington, DC: US Department of Education.

Leap, William L. 1981. American Indian languages. In *Language in the U.S.A.,* ed. Charles A. Fergeson and Shirley Brice Heath. Cambridge: Cambridge University Press, 116–44.

Lidz, C. S., and E. D. Peña. 1996. Dynamic assessment: The model, its relevance as a nonbiased approach and its application to Latino American children. *Language, Speech, and Hearing Services in Schools.*

Long, E. E. 1998. Native American children's performance on the Preschool Language Scale-3. *Journal of Children's Communication Development* 19, no. 2:43–47.

Long, E. E., and J. M. Christensen. 1997. *Indirect language assessment tool for English-speaking Native American children.* Boston, MA: Poster presentation at the American Speech-Language-Hearing Association convention.

Mattes, L. J., and D. R. Omark. 1984. *Speech and language assessment for the bilingual handicapped.* San Diego: College-Hill Press.

McMann, D. 1994. Judith E. Heumann tours Indian country in the southwest. In *The epics messenger,* ed. D. McMann. Bernalillo, NM: Southwest Communication Resources.

National Center for Educational Statistics. 1993. *National assessment of education progress.* Washington, DC: US Department of Education.

Native American Research and Training Center. 1995. *Some alarming facts.* Tucson, AZ: University of Arizona.

Nelkin, V. S., and R. S. Malach. 1996. Achieving healthy outcomes for children and families of diverse cultural backgrounds. In *A monograph for health and human service providers.* Bernalillo, NM: Southwest Communication Resources.

O'Brien, E. M. 1992. *American Indians in higher education.* Research Briefs. 3 (3). Washington, DC: American Council on Education, Division of Policy Analysis and Research.

O'Connell, J. C., ed. 1987. *A study of the special problems and needs of American Indians with handicaps both on and off the reservation.* Vol. 1. Flagstaff, AZ: Northern Arizona University, Native American Research and Training Center; Tucson, AZ: University of Arizona, Native American Research and Training Center.

Office of Civil Rights. 1993. *The fall 1990 elementary and secondary school civil rights survey.* Washington, DC: US Department of Education.

Pavel, M. D., C. R. Thomas, and S. D. Whitener. 1997. *Characteristics of American Indian and Alaska Native education.* Washington, DC: National Center for Education Statistics, US Department of Education, p.1.

Pena, E. 1996. Dynamic assessment: Its model and its language applications. In *Assessment of communication and language.* Ed. K. N. Cole, P. S. Dale, and D. J. Thal. Baltimore: Paul H. Brookes.

Pena, E., R. Quinn, and A. Iglesias. 1992. The application of dynamic methods for language assessment: A nonbiased procedure. *The Journal of Special Education* 26: 269–80.

Red Horse, J. 1988. Cultural evolution of American Indian families. *In Ethnicity and race: Critical concepts in social work,* ed. C. Jacobs and D. D. Bowles, 86-102. Silver Springs, MD: National Association of Social Work.

Seekins, T. 1997. Native Americans and the ADA. In *The rural exchange,* 10: 1. Missoula, MT: Montana University Affiliated Rural Institute on Disabilities, University of Montana.

US Bureau of Census. 1990, 1995. *Characteristics of American Indians by Tribes in Selected Areas.* Washington, DC: US Department of Commerce.

US Department of Health and Human Services. 1991. *Healthy people 2000: National health promotion and disease prevention objectives.* Washington, DC: Public Health Service. DHHS Publication No. (PHS) 91-50212.

Uzdawinis, D. C. 1983. *Let's talk: Screening instruments for Native American children.* Albuquerque, NM: All Indian Pueblo Council, Inc.

Westby, C. 1993. Developing cultural competence: Working with culturally/linguistically diverse families. In *Teams in early intervention introductory module.* Albuquerque, NM: Training and Technical Assistance Unit. New Mexico University Affiliated Program University of New Mexico School of Medicine.

15

Collaborative Endeavors

On Behalf of Children with Disabilities and Their Families in the United States and Mexico

Todd V. Fletcher, Candace S. Bos, and Lorri Johnson

This book is the result of a series of cooperative binational symposiums, conferences, and workshops designed to improve the lives of individuals with disabilities and their families in Mexico and the United States. These collaborative efforts, carried out in the spirit of the U.S./Mexico Memorandum of Understanding signed in 1990 and in the context of international educational reform, have increased our understanding of educational practices and policies in the United States and Mexico and other countries throughout the Western Hemisphere. The intent of the 1990 agreement was to enhance cooperation and collaboration between our two countries and improve the quality of education for all students. The accomplishments achieved to date are noteworthy, and this book is one of many that have resulted from these *encuentros*.

In addition to regional efforts of collaboration between countries, global educational reform initiatives have established a growing commitment to provide education for all. The world conference held in Jomptien, Thailand, in 1990, which was organized by various international educational agencies, emphasized the need to ensure access and equity for all children in developing countries. More recently, the Salamanca Statement and Framework for Action on Special Needs Education, signed in 1994, was directed at restructuring educational systems throughout the world to promote the integration and full participation of individuals with disabilities throughout their respective societies while combating exclusion. The Salamanca statement declares that "inclusion and participation are essential to human dignity and the enjoyment and exercise of human rights. Within the field of education, this is reflected in the development of strategies that seek to bring about a genuine equalization of opportunity."

These regional and international initiatives aimed at educational reform are the context in which the recent activities between Mexico and the United States took place and in which this book is written. Critical to the success of any long-term collaboration with the goal of promoting better lives for their peoples is the education of children and youth in the two countries. This volume brings together educators and policy makers from both countries who voice their support of the education of infants, children, and youths with disabilities and their families. The authors review and broaden our perspectives on current practice and newly implemented legislation and policy in the area of disabilities in Mexico and the United States. From the multiple perspectives presented in this book, three common themes emerge that warrant further discussion of the issues and implications for policy and practice. The first theme voiced throughout this book is the important role that cultural and linguistic diversity plays in the education of all students, particularly of those who are challenged with disabilities. The second theme running throughout this volume is the critical need for continued development of policy and practices that support children with disabilities and their families. The third theme that comes up repeatedly in this volume is the importance of collaboration in solving the issues and meeting the challenges within and across our two countries as we continue to work toward the goal of creating better educational and employment outcomes and an enhanced quality of life for persons with disabilities and their families.

Cultural and Linguistic Diversity

If we are to achieve success for individuals with disabilities and their families, then our efforts must be guided by an understanding of the richness of cultural and linguistic diversity of our respective countries. Furthermore, we must view this diversity as a resource that contributes richness to our societies and respective educational systems, challenging us to accommodate for diversity by providing greater flexibility in our education programs. Garé Fábila de Zaldo sets the stage for this issue. In chapter 1, she describes the scope of the issue, noting that by the year 2000 there will be 600 million individuals with disabilities in the world and that it will directly affect 2.4 billion people. She urges that our efforts should work toward developing strategies to prevent certain types of disabilities and minimize discriminatory conditions, abuses, social injustices, and the marginalization suffered by individuals with disabilities. If our common goals are to achieve educational, social, and economic integration of individuals with disabilities into the community, then understanding and being responsive to the specific sociocultural variables of that particular community is critical to ensuring success.

This premise is most strongly voiced by the authors who provide insights into the cultures of Native Americans, Alaska Natives, and the indigenous people of Mexico. In chapter 6, Cruz Begay and her colleagues give us an important insight into how the indigenous and informal systems of support within the Navajo community intertwine and sometimes conflict with formal systems of support. Based on the premise that families and family involvement are the most important factors in supporting children with disabilities, the authors argue that we must understand and sustain the benefits of indigenous systems that provide support and relief to families even as we seek to engage families in the use of supports offered by private and public agencies. For example, they found in their ethnographic study of twenty-nine Navajo children with disabilities or delays and their families that many Navajo families felt that spiritual services helped their children improve, provided support in terms of gathering resources for the family, and relieved their misgivings and therefore increased their acceptance of more formalized systems of support. Martha Gorospe in chapter 7 entitled "Overcoming Obstacles and Improving Outcomes for American Indian Children with Special Needs" also highlights the importance of cultural diversity and suggests that a critical component for the education of service providers is learning about the children and their families' cultures. She notes that mutual respect and understanding between the service provider and the family is the foundation for effective programs. Becoming culturally responsive is a lifelong process.

If we define culture as a set of cultural norms that determine beliefs, attitudes, behaviors, values, roles, perceptions, and what is valued as good and desirable, then, as suggested by Martha Gorospe, over time it will become easier to accept that there are no right or wrong ways of doing things, just different approaches. Sherry Allison and Christine Begay Vining in chapter 14 on Native American culture and language suggest that the prevailing issues that Native American families with children with disabilities face are the same issues as those of other families who have children with disabilities, that is, costly treatment, too few providers, lack of education, and family involvement in their child's education and development. However, Native American families must also contend with jurisdictional issues and cultural and linguistic diversity.

The importance of dealing with linguistic diversity was voiced by many of the authors. The limited access to assessments in the children's first language and the need for programs that support the development of the children's first language and culture in conjunction with other languages and cultures were cited as examples of the need to attend to linguistic and cultural diversity. Richard Figueroa in his discussion of what is wrong with special education for Latino students in the United States (chap. 11) cautions us against using an additive model, in which special-education programs are simply added to bilingual education/English as a Second Language programs without careful thought of the children's linguistic and cultural diversity. Nadeen Ruiz encourages educators and policy makers to situate learning so that it builds on the students' linguistic and cultural roots (chap. 12). Pamela Rossi, in chapter 13, provides an excellent example of how this can be accomplished within the context of visual, dramatic, and language arts in her description of an opera project. Similarly, Henriette Langdon in her discussion of strategies for supporting preschool children from Mexican backgrounds gives suggestions for intervention that tie the two languages and cultures and integrate themes that are being used in the home and preschool/day care (chap. 5). These strategies also incorporate the parents and family as key players in supporting the child's language development.

Development of Policy and Practice to Support Children with Disabilities and Their Families

During the last twenty-five years several major international and regional educational reform initiatives have advanced educational practices and policy to support children with disabilities and their families. Beginning with chapter 1, Garé Fábila de Zaldo provides a history of the social integration of individuals with disabilities from a global perspective as she traces the human rights work of the United Nations and key world agreements. She notes that historically we have begun the transition from social isolation and persecution to social, educational, and economic recognition and integration into the community. Garé Fábila de Zaldo makes strong recommendations that can assist us in developing a more positive, respectful community for individuals with disabilities and their families. These include technical cooperation among countries to learn from each other's experiences, always keeping in mind sociocultural and economic differences; the inclusion of children with disabilities in general-education programs, coupled with extensive professional training for teachers and administrators; and educational programs designed to raise awareness and teach society about the rights and worth of individuals with disabilities.

While Elba Reyes (chap. 4) and Richard Figueroa (chap. 11) trace the legislative and political developments of the Individuals with Disabilities Education Act and bilingual special education in the United States, Berta Watkins (chap. 2), Sofíaleticia Morales (chap. 8), Eliseo Guajardo Ramos and Todd Fletcher (chap. 9), and Georgina Reich-Erdmann (chap. 10) focus on the development of recent education reform issues in Mexico for infants, children, and adults with disabilities. We learn that Mexico, much like the United States, has legislated support for preschool and school-age children with disabilities to be integrated into general education in the New General Law of Education. Based on the 1992 National Agreement for the Modernization of Basic Education, a sweeping educational reform was begun, and there has been a massive decentralization of education, returning sovereignty to the states and allowing them to operate basic educational services according to the diverse conditions that exist in their particular population. Based on this new legislation, service delivery models known as Units of Support Services for Regular Education are being established to assist general-education teachers and support professionals so that students with mild to moderate disabilities have access to the core curriculum. These teams provide support to a cohort of schools and their teachers by modifying and adapting methodological approaches, objectives, content, assignments, and materials. The other model of service delivery in Mexico, Multiple Attention Centers, is replacing institutions that previously served students with severe disabilities. The goal of these centers is to provide the core curriculum and quality education to students with disabilities who are unable to be successfully integrated into public schools. For infants and preschool children, Centers for Infant Development serve children in more populous areas, and community-based programs serve rural and indigenous populations and urban populations with low socioeconomic status (see Watkins, chap. 2).

New legislation has brought about widespread change both in the United States and Mexico. Sofíaleticia Morales notes that new legislation in Mexico that favors the inclusion of children with disabilities into general education is a great educational challenge but does not reduce the controversy imbedded in the decision. Georgina Reich-Erdmann (chap. 10) highlights four issues related to this new Mexican legislation that parallel issues in the United States (see chap. 4): (a) a greater demand for education in relation to nationwide availability, (b) the uneven quality of education among the different regions in Mexico, (c) the number of children who fail to learn appropriately and who are retained, and (d) the number of children who drop out of school before finishing their education. In Mexico, this frequently occurs in the elementary school, frequently by the third grade. Parallels can be drawn between Mexico and the United States. For example, both countries give students with disabilities the right to an appropriate education, namely, Mexico's New General Education Law and the United States' Individuals with Disabilities Education Act, in least restrictive environments.

Collaboration and Dialogue: Keys to Success

Throughout this book the educators, policy makers, and parents who voice their views make collaboration the foundation for the successful education and well-being of children with disabilities and their families. This collaboration exists on every level. Those authors who focus on early intervention (see Watkins, Jackson-Maldonado, Reyes, Langdon, and Begay, Roberts, Weisner, and Matheson) stress the importance of collaborating with the family and making the family a key element in the development of the child. They speak of the need for educators and service providers to work closely with families to deal with stresses on the family that are created when a child with a disability is brought into the family. Likewise, at the center of the inclusion movement in both countries is the development of collaborative networks that integrate and support students in the least restrictive environments and provide access to the general-education curriculum. With the decentralization of the educational system in Mexico, there are many opportunities for increased collaboration among general and special-education professionals, the students, and their families. With the focus on quality education, these networks are crucial pathways for the success of the children and their families. Finally, an ongoing dialogue between countries is critical in educational reform and the development of policy. This affords us opportunities to learn from each other's research, policies, and practices. As Judith Heumann and Sofíaleticia Morales (the leading officials for special education in the United States and Mexico, respectively) suggest, it is through sharing our unique approaches to overcoming barriers to equal education that we renew each other's commitment to progress for children with disabilities and their families.

As we move into the third millennium, the possibilities for greater collaboration and dialogue between our two countries in advancing the issues of access and equity for individuals with disabilities are numerous. However, great care must be taken to ensure that models and practices developed in one country or region within a country not be transplanted to another area without consideration of the specific context variables and unique characteristics of each community. The exchanges that have taken place over the past few years have provided us with innumerable examples of our similarities and differences and, most importantly, have generated a profound respect for the uniqueness of our respective societies and educational systems.

These activities were guided by a common conceptual framework designed to improve the human condition of individuals with disabilities. Based on the goals and expected outcomes, key issues and ideas were identified and formulated by putting four questions: first, how can we begin to develop collaborative working relationships and educational networks between the United States and Mexico to create greater opportunities for the education of individuals with disabilities; second, how can we create avenues to share resources; third, how can resources that already exist be utilized more effectively to solve problems and meet the needs of individuals with disabilities; and fourth, how can we use the North American Free Trade Agreement (NAFTA) as a tool for creating greater educational opportunities for persons with disabilities.

This book is only one outcome of this shared agenda of collaboration. What we can accomplish in the future is limited only by our imagination, hard work, and perseverance. Paraphrasing the words of one Mexican educator, the blending of two cultures engaged in a common purpose to change government agendas is a revolution. Our task is to continue to discover, adapt, and implement efficient educational approaches and policies by means of collaboration and dialogue in the social, economical, and political contexts of our two countries.

Acronyms

AEC Association for the Promotion of Community Education

AIM for the BEST Assessment and Intervention Model for the Bilingual Exceptional Student

APEINAC Asociación Científica de Profesionales del Estudio Integral del Niño A.C.

ATI Aptitude Treatment Interaction

BIA Bureau of Indian Affairs

BINL Basic Inventory of Natural Language

BOLT Bahia Oral Language Test

BSM Bilingual Syntax Measure

CAM Centers for Multiple Attention

CAP California Assessment Program

CDI Communicative Development Inventory

CENDI Centers for Infant Development

CONAFE Confederación Mexicana en Favor de las Personas con Discapacidad Intelectual

CREDE Center for Research on Education, Diversity, and Excellence

DHHS Department of Health and Human Services

DIF Programa Nacional para el Bienestar y la Incorporación al Desarollo de las Personas con Discapacidad (National System for the Integral Development of the Family)

EDUSAT Satellite Education

EOWPVT Expressive One-Word Picture Vocabulary Test

EPICS Education for Parents of Indian Children with Special Needs

EWNU Educational Workers National Union

FAPE Free and Public Education

FAS Fetal Alcohol Syndrome

GED General Equivalency Exam

GEL General Education Law

HUD Housing and Urban Development
IDEA *or* IDEA-97 Individuals with Disabilities Education Act of (1997)
IDHC Inventario del Desarrollo de Habilidades Comunicativas
IEP Individualized Education Program
IHS Indian Health Service
IFSP Individualized Family Service Plan
INECI Instituto Nacional de Estadística Geográfica e Informática (National Census)
K-ABC Kaufman Assessment Battery for Children
LAB Language Assessment Battery
LAS Language Assessment Scales
LAUSD Los Angeles Unified School District
MLU mean length of utterances
MUMS Mothers United for Moral Support
NAC Native American Church
NAEP National Assessment of Educational Progress
NAFTA North American Free Trade Agreement
NASDE National Association of State Directors of Special Education
NMSVH New Mexico School for the Visually Handicapped
NPND National Parent Network on Disabilities
OLE Optimal Learning Environments
OSERS Office of Special Education and Rehabilitative Services
PARC Pennsylvania Association for Retarded Children
PES Public Education Secretariat
PLS Preschool Language Scale
PLS-3 Preschool Language Scale-3
RSP Resource Specialist Program
SARRC South Atlantic Regional Resource Center
SEN National Education System
SEP Secretaría de Educación Pública (Department of Public Education)
SEP/DEE Secretaría de Educación Pública/Departamento de Educación Especial
SES socioeconomic status
SICD Sequenced Inventory of Communication Development
SOMPA System of Multicultural Pluralistic Assessment
SPELT Structured Photographic Elicitation Language Test
TLC Tratado de Libre Comercio (free trade agreement)
TVIP Test de Vocaulario en Imágenes Peabody
USAER Units of Support Services to Regular Education
VSAA Very Special Arts Arizona
WIC Women, Infants, and Children
WISC-R Wechsler Intelligence Scale for Children-Revised
WRRC Western Regional Resource Center